## About the Cover

The illustration on the cover is a detail from the mural, *MaestraPeace*, which adorns the Women's Building, a multiethnic, multicultural, multiservice center in San Francisco whose mission is to provide women and girls with the tools and resources they need to achieve full and equal participation in society.

This spectacular mural is a culmination of a multicultural, multigeneration collaboration of seven women artists, and is a colorful work of art that sings to our community. The mural was painted in 1994 by Juana Alicia, Miranda Bergman, Edythe Boone, Susan Kelk Cervantes, Meera Desai, Yvonne Littleton, Irene Perez, and many helpers.

Covering two exterior walls, *MaestraPeace* is as educational as it is inspirational and serves as a visual testament to the courageous contributions of women through time and around the world.

# GENDER IDENTITY, EQUITY, AND VIOLENCE

# GENDER IDENTITY,

# EQUITY, AND VIOLENCE

### Multidisciplinary Perspectives
### Through Service Learning

*Edited by*

*Geraldine B. Stahly*

Foreword by Robert A. Corrigan

STERLING, VIRGINIA

Sty/us

COPYRIGHT © 2007 BY STYLUS PUBLISHING, LLC

Published by Stylus Publishing, LLC
22883 Quicksilver Drive
Sterling, Virginia 20166-2102

**Library of Congress Cataloging-in-Publication Data**
Gender identity, equity, and violence : multidisciplinary
perspectives through service learning / edited by Geraldine
B. Stahly.—1st ed.
     p.   cm.—(Service learning for civic engagement)
     Includes bibliographical references and index.
ISBN 1-57922-217-X (cloth : alk. paper)—
ISBN 1-57922-218-8 (pbk. : alk. paper)
1. Women—Social conditions—21st
century.  2. Women—Education.  3. Student
service.  4. Social justice—Study and
teaching.  5. Feminist theory.  I. Stahly, Geraldine B.,
1944–
HQ1155.G44   2007
305.43'3718090511—dc22
2006033686

ISBN: 978-1-57922-217-8 (cloth)
ISBN: 978-1-57922-218-5 (paper)

Printed in the United States of America

All first editions printed on acid free paper
that meets the American National Standards Institute
Z39-48 Standard.

Bulk Purchases

Quantity discounts are available for use in workshops
and for staff development.
Call 1-800-232-0223

First Edition, 2007

10   9   8   7   6   5   4   3   2   1

# CONTENTS

## SECTION THREE: FEMINIST PEDAGOGY AND SERVICE LEARNING

## SECTION FOUR: WOMEN AND VIOLENCE

## SECTION FIVE: SERVICE LEARNING AND RESEARCH

# ACKNOWLEDGMENTS

W e would like to give special thanks to colleagues both within and external to the California State University who serve on the advisory board for the monograph series. Debra David, Barbara Holland, Kathy O'Byrne, Seth Pollack, and Maureen Rubin continue to provide invaluable advice on the development of the current volumes and the dimensions the series will explore in the future.

Thanks to Eileen Andrae, Lauren Baughman, Bryan Forward, and Kraig Brustad, for granting permission to use material from their letters in Chapter 13, "DNA as a Tool for Social Justice: Service Learning and Paternity Testing in Tanzania, Africa" by Ruth Ballard.

Thanks to Juana Alicia, Miranda Bergman, Edythe Boone, Susan Kelk Cervantes, Meera Desai, Yvonne Littleton, and Irene Perez for permission to use a detail from the mural *MaestraPeace* on the cover.

This material is based upon work supported by the Corporation for National and Community Service under Learn and Serve America Grant No. 03LHHCA003. Opinions or points of view expressed in this document are those of the authors and do not necessarily reflect the official position of the Corporation or the Learn and Serve America Program.

# FOREWORD

erhaps once in a generation a movement comes along to redefine—
even transform—higher education. I can point to the GI Bill of 1944,
which opened the gates to a much broader population than had ever
before enjoyed the opportunity to receive higher education. The civil rights
struggle and the later antiwar movement galvanized students and faculty
across the nation. Many of us participated directly in these movements;
many more worked then, and in the years that followed, to overhaul what
we perceived as an outmoded university curriculum as we struggled to open
up the university to new ideas, new teaching strategies, and most of all, to
underrepresented populations.

To this list, I would now add community service learning. I consider this
movement in higher education as exciting as anything I have experienced as
an educator. Service learning, and its central role in our goals of campuswide
civic engagement and ethical education, may be the most significant development on our campuses since the curricular reforms of the 1960s. In fact, I
believe that it will prove to be *the* higher education legacy of the early 21st
century, and that it will have a lifelong impact on our students.

Since service learning began to take formal hold throughout the nation
in the early 1990s, it has come to be seen as much more than community
volunteerism linked with academic study. It is a vehicle for character and
citizenship development—in short, for all that we most value in a liberal
education. Through thoughtfully structured service-learning experiences,
students can test and apply the values of a healthy democracy to some of the
most complex and challenging issues of our time.

In recent years, higher education has begun more deliberately to pursue
a historic mission: what I might call moral education—our responsibility
both to our students and society. The Association of American Colleges and
Universities terms this "core commitments," and calls on us to educate our
students "for personal and social responsibility." This is the highest aim of
liberal education. It is the culmination of our mission to service, to preparing
our students with the skills and desire to contribute positively to our

*xi*

democratic society and to the greater world, to fostering a campus climate where speech is open, but where we can disagree—even passionately—without venom or hatred, and to ensuring that our students find in the classroom a safe and receptive environment in which to express, test, and challenge varying views.

A true liberal education encompasses far more than the breadth of knowledge and exposure to fields other than one's major that typically shape general education programs. That is certainly necessary, but liberal education transcends subject matter. Liberal education addresses both mind and heart. It is a set of experiences that give our students the tools they will need to think about complex issues and to deal with them as informed, ethical citizens. Liberal education helps our students deal with ambiguity and contradictions, helps them evaluate competing arguments and perspectives so that they will not have to fall back on the comfort—and distortion—of a binary, good/bad, worldview.

Complexity characterizes our key social missions, as we seek to foster in our students respect and understanding of other cultures and viewpoints together with the skills they will need to move positively and effectively in a diverse and global society. I am most emphatically not talking about indoctrinating our students—presenting our values and asking them to take them as their own. Rather, I am talking about teaching our students *why* and *how* to think and reason about ethical and moral issues—not presenting them with answers, but developing their skills in finding their own way.

Liberal education prepares our students to act—and to do so in the context of values that take in the needs and concerns of others. Viewed in this context, the value of civically focused service learning is clear. It places our students in the arenas where ethics and efficacy need to join, where disciplinary boundaries are often irrelevant and integrative learning occurs naturally, and where students can gain a profound experience of their capacity—and responsibility—to effect positive change. As an antidote to cynicism and passivity, it is hard to top service learning.

Looking at the society into which they are graduating, our students might be excused for being cynical. From the front page to the business page to the sports section, headlines repeatedly reflect the ethical lapses of our society. This profound lack of integrity—the failure of a moral value system—is not restricted to one political party, to one religious group, to one ethnic group, or one gender group. It cuts across our society. In giving a final message to graduating students, I have asked them to seek one goal: to say no—say no to greed, say no to opportunism, say no to dishonesty, and decide that integrity—their own moral compasses—is what really matters.

If we accept that aim—and I believe we do—then service learning deserves a proud and prominent place in our curriculum. This series provides less a road map than a spur to creative course development for all faculty and administrators eager to adapt a powerful educational tool to a particular institution's nature, community, and student population.

Robert A. Corrigan
President, San Francisco State University
October 6, 2006

ABOUT THIS SERIES

Many service-learning practitioners are familiar with the comprehensive series of monographs on *Service-Learning in the Disciplines* produced and published by the American Association of Higher Education (AAHE) between 1997 and 2005 (The series is now published by Stylus Publishing, LLC). Each volume of the series focused on a specific discipline—accounting, biology, composition, and so on—and provided a rich collection of exemplary practices in service learning as constituted around a disciplinary theme. Edward Zlotkowski (1997–2002), then senior associate at AAHE and series editor for the monographs, wrote that in "winning faculty support for this [service-learning] work" it was important to recognize that faculty "define themselves largely in terms of [their] academic disciplines," and so it was logical to design a series around disciplinary themes. The AAHE series became a primary reference for faculty who were considering adopting service-learning pedagogy, and the community of service-learning practitioners have much for which to thank the editors and contributors to those volumes. Other resources that were discipline specific—such as collections of syllabi—also helped to promote service learning to the level of the widespread acceptance it enjoys today on both the national and international stages.

Over the past few years, as the civic engagement movement has gained momentum, as educators have taken on the challenge of producing graduates who are engaged civically and politically in their communities, there has been a growing reexamination of service learning as the means for producing "civic learning" outcomes, that is, the combination of knowledge, skills, and disposition to make a difference in the civic life of our communities. The ubiquitous three-element Venn diagram—three interlocking circles representing enhanced academic learning, meaningful community service, and civic learning—that defines the field of service learning at its intersection (Howard, 2001), continues to do so, but there has been a marked redirection of emphasis from academic learning to civic. Nonetheless, as John Saltmarsh points out in his 2004 white paper for Campus Compact, *The Civic Purpose of Higher Education: A Focus on Civic Learning,* service learning is "the most potent method for achieving civic learning if civic learning outcomes are a part of curricular goals" (p. 7).

In parallel to this shift in emphasis, a second, related movement within higher education, *integrative learning,* has begun to take hold. As characterized by the American Association of Colleges and Universities (AACU) in partnership with the Carnegie Foundation for the Advancement of Teaching (Huber & Hutchings, 2004), integrative learning encompasses practices such as thematic first-year experiences, learning circles, interdisciplinary studies, capstone experiences, and other initiatives to foster students' ability to integrate concepts "across courses, over time, and between campus and community life" (p. 13). These two educational reform movements—civic engagement and integrative learning—provide the motivation for the creation of the current series, *Service Learning for Civic Engagement.* Each volume of the series will focus on a specific social issue—gender and power, race and immigration, community health, and so forth—and then solicit contributions from faculty *across* disciplines who can provide insight into how they have motivated their students to engage in learning that extends beyond the boundaries of disciplinary goals. In some cases chapter contributors will be faculty within the "obvious" discipline relevant to a particular issue (e.g., women's studies faculty utilize service learning in the pursuit of knowledge on gender issues), but each volume will include multiple chapters from other disciplines as well. As each volume illustrates, when faculty step outside the normal confines of disciplinary learning, they can provide profound, transformational experiences for their students. Thus, the volume on gender issues includes examples from philosophy, psychology, ethnic studies, and more, and the volume on social justice includes contributions from communications, engineering, nutrition science, and so on.

It is also our intention to design each book as a collective whole. Each volume illustrates an array of approaches to examining a community issue, and we hope that, by exploring examples across the disciplines, faculty will be inspired to develop their own concepts for courses that combine academic and civic learning.

Over the past 10 years, service learning has enjoyed tremendous support throughout the California State University (CSU), from which most of our contributors have been recruited. The 23 campuses of the CSU form the largest university system in the country, with 405,000 students enrolled each year. Through strategic efforts and targeted funding, the CSU has created a systemwide network of service-learning offices with a center on each campus, a coordinating office at the chancellor's office, statewide conferences and initiatives, and a wide variety of service-learning courses and community-based research. In 2005 alone more than 1,800 service-learning courses provided opportunities for 65,000 students to participate. California, now one of four states designated minority-majority (i.e., a state in which a majority of the population differs from the national majority) by the U.S. Census Bureau, is rich in ethnic diversity and is home to great cities as well as vast rural areas. Virtually every societal issue challenges Californians, and our universities have pledged to use our resources to develop innovative ways to address them. It is this mixture of diversity and innovation that has created an environment for the success of service learning in the CSU represented in this series.

Gerald S. Eisman
CSU Service-Learning Faculty Scholar
July 19, 2006

## References

Howard, J. (2001). *Service learning course design workbook.* Ann Arbor, MI: OCSL Press.

Huber, M. T., & Hutchings, P. (2004). *Integrative learning: Mapping the terrain.* The Academy in Transition. Washington, DC: Association of American Colleges and Universities.

Saltmarsh, J. (2004). *The civic purpose of higher education: A focus on civic learning.* Unpublished white paper for Campus Compact.

Zlotkowski, E. (1997–2002). (Ed.). *AAHE series on service-learning in the disciplines.* Sterling, VA: Stylus.

**Gender Identity, Equity, and Violence
Activity/Methodology Table**

| Chapter | Discipline | Service Activity | Methodology | Applications | Type of Partner | Size of Class |
|---|---|---|---|---|---|---|
| Chapter 1: Bettcher | Philosophy | Outreach<br><br>Support group assistance<br><br>Event planning<br><br>Internet and community-based research | Conceptual analysis<br><br>Critical reflection<br><br>Moral reasoning<br><br>Feminist theory | Social sciences | Various NPOs (domestic violence, HIV prevention) | 50 students |
| Chapter 2: Tintiangco-Cubales | Asian American studies | Political fashion show | Epistemological pedagogy<br><br>Critical performance pedagogy<br><br>Visual arts/media literacy | Ethnic studies and women's studies<br><br>Social science<br><br>Fashion/art | Community | 30–40 students small teams |

*(continues)*

**Gender Identity, Equity, and Violence**
**Activity/Methodology Table**
**Continued**

| Chapter | Discipline | Service Activity | Methodology | Applications | Type of Partner | Size of Class |
|---|---|---|---|---|---|---|
| Chapter 3 Ulasewicz | Apparel design and merchandising | Internships Community experience | Socio semiotics | Women's studies Design Sociology Communications | Clothing bank | 90 + broken into groups |
| Chapter 4: Carinci | Education | Class observation Curriculum evaluation | Observation Content analysis Pre/Postcritical reflection | Education Preservice teacher programs Sociology Ed. foundation | School districts K–12 classrooms University classrooms | 25 students |
| Chapter 5: Kouri | Sociology and women's studies | Tutoring and supervising elementary school children Assisting elementary school teachers | Qualitative research methods | Sociology Psychology Women's studies Elementary ed. | Local elementary school | 42–48 students |

| Chapter | Discipline | Service Activity | Methodology | Applications | Type of Partner | Size of Class |
|---|---|---|---|---|---|---|
| Chapter 6: Ward | Women's studies/recreation (women and leisure) | Improvement of community services for women (resource development/program delivery) | Problem-based learning<br>Field research<br>Critical feminist pedagogy<br>Reflection (written and oral, group and individual) | Campus and community settings | Campus and community service agencies<br>Senior centers | 10 students |
| Chapter 7: Cayleff and LaGrotteria | Women's studies | Provide leadership to a multicultural high school club exploring gender, race, global, and social class issues | Multicultural principles and feminist pedagogy | Africana and Chicana/o studies<br>Education<br>Liberal studies | Inner-city international multicultural high school setting | 15–45 high school students<br>12–14 undergraduates<br>1 master's student |
| Chapter 8: Ituarte | Criminal justice | Community event planning | Consciousness-raising—public display and performance | Prejudice reduction classes<br>Sociology<br>Ethnic studies<br>First-year seminar | Campus community | Small teams |

(continues)

**Gender Identity, Equity, and Violence**
**Activity/Methodology Table**
**Continued**

| Chapter | Discipline | Service Activity | Methodology | Applications | Type of Partner | Size of Class |
|---|---|---|---|---|---|---|
| Chapter 9: Ahrens and Rozee | Psychology | Addressing sexual assault on Campus | Problem-based learning | Women's studies<br>Sociology<br>Social work<br>Public health | University | Five small groups (5–8 students each) |
| Chapter 10: Klaw and Ampuero | Psychology | Intimate violence prevention | Peer education | Education<br>Peer counseling<br>Peer leadership | Local K–12 schools<br>Community centers<br>Religious organizations<br>Programs for at-risk youth<br>Domestic violence shelters | 15–35 students |
| Chapter 11: Cowan | Psychology and women's studies | Administrative assistance, fund raising, volunteer training at crisis centers | Public education | Rape crisis<br>Domestic violence<br>Violence against women | Sexual assault centers<br>Shelters for battered women | 10–20 students |

| Chapter | Discipline | Service Activity | Methodology | Applications | Type of Partner | Size of Class |
|---|---|---|---|---|---|---|
| Chapter 12: Laganà | Psychology/gerontology | Needs assessment<br>Educational workshops<br>Educational or clinical interventions | Participatory research<br>Interviewing and assessment | Psychiatry<br>Social work<br>Counseling<br>Women's issues | Residential facilities for seniors<br>Hospitals<br>Day centers for seniors<br>Shelters for abused women | 25–75 students |
| Chapter 13: Ballard | Genetics | Bringing affordable and accessible DNA-based paternity testing to single mothers in Tanzania, Africa | Problem-based learning<br>Service-based scientific research<br>Consciousness-raising | Gender power and financial inequity<br>Poverty in women and children<br>Third world issues<br>Population genetics<br>DNA forensics | University and government | 4–6 students |

# CONTRIBUTORS

**Courtney E. Ahrens** (chapter 9) is assistant professor of psychology at California State University, Long Beach. (cahrens@csulb.edu)

**Marilyn C. Ampuero** (chapter 10) is a senior with a double major in psychology and behavioral science at San Jose State University. (Marilyn_ Ampuero@yahoo.com)

**Ruth Ballard** (chapter 13) is associate professor of biological sciences at California State University, Sacramento. (ballard@csus.edu)

**Talia Bettcher** (chapter 1) is assistant professor of philosophy at California State University, Los Angeles. (tbettch@calstatela.edu)

**Susan E. Cayleff** (chapter 7) is professor of women's studies at San Diego State University. (cayleff@mail.sdsu.edu)

**Sherrie Carinci** (chapter 4) is associate professor of teacher education at California State University, Sacramento. (carincis@csus.edu)

**Robert A. Corrigan** (Foreword) is president of San Francisco State University. (president@sfsu.edu)

**Gloria Cowan** (chapter 11) is professor emeritus at California State University, San Bernardino. (gcowan@csusb.edu)

**Gerald S. Eisman** (series editor) is the Service-Learning Faculty Scholar at the California State University Office of the Chancellor. (geisman@ calstate.edu)

**Silvina Ituarte** (chapter 8) is associate professor of criminal justice administration at California State University, East Bay. (silvina.ituarte@ csueastbay.edu)

**Elena Klaw** (chapter 10) is assistant professor of psychology at San Jose State University. (eklaw@email.sjsu.edu )

**Kristyan M. Kouri** (chapter 5) is a lecturer in the departments of sociology and women's studies at California State University, Northridge. (kristyan.m.kouri@csun.edu)

**Luciana Laganà** (chapter 12) is associate professor of clinical psychology at California State University, Northridge. (luciana.lagana@csun.edu)

**Angela J. LaGrotteria** (chapter 7) is a doctoral student in women's studies at Emory University in Atlanta, Georgia. (alagrot@emory.edu)

**Patricia D. Rozee** (chapter 9) is professor of psychology and women's studies at California State University, Long Beach. (prozee@csulb.edu)

**Geraldine B. Stahly** (volume editor) is professor of psychology at California State University, San Bernardino. (gstahly@csusb.edu)

**Allyson Tintiangco-Cubales** (chapter 2) is assistant professor of Asian American studies at San Francisco State University. (pinayism@sfsu.edu)

**Connie Ulasewicz** (chapter 3) is assistant professor of consumer family studies/dietetics at San Francisco State University. (cbu@sfsu.edu)

**Veda E. Ward** (chapter 6) is professor of leisure studies and recreation at California State University, Northridge. (veda.ward@csun.edu)

# INTRODUCTION

*Geraldine B. Stahly*

The Chinese say "women hold up half the sky," and it is generally acknowledged that across cultures no single element determines human experience—from the moment of birth or even before—more than the fact of one's sex. Nevertheless, the scholarly study of gender in the academy is too often relegated to the women's studies department and a few additional humanities and social sciences courses taught by "token" feminist scholars and attended mostly by interested women students.

It need not be so. The topic of gender touches every discipline, and the approach to teaching and learning embodied in feminist pedagogy is as applicable to the effective learning experience of men as women. Indeed, Schacht (2000) described using this approach as a "white, male, heterosexual" professor teaching the Sociology of Sports to a class of mostly male athletes. He opined, "Using a feminist pedagogical approach not only involves inclusively centering the social categories of gender, class, race and sexual orientation in all classroom discussions, but also recognizes all class participants' experiences and perspectives to be equally necessary in the creation of knowledge. . . . In sum, I have found that using a feminist pedagogy is beneficial for both female and male course participants" (p. 1).

The authors of the 13 chapters in this volume bring excitement and innovations to teaching about gender from a wide range of theoretical and discipline perspectives. They exhibit the inclusiveness that is central to feminist pedagogy—a perspective that centers the educational enterprise in the analysis of the interconnectedness of social categories that have traditionally divided and given root to inequality and oppression and aims for no less than social transformation. Empowerment is a core value in gender education, and the experiential approach nurtures that goal. This volume provides many examples of the power of learning through experience as the authors demonstrate that "the authority of the feminist teacher as intellectual and theorist finds expression in the goal of making students themselves theorists of their own lives by interrogating and analyzing their own experience" (Weiler, 1991, p. 462).

"Feminism recognizes education both as a site for struggle and as a tool for change making" (Briskin & Coulter, 1992, p. 249). Civic learning is the natural extension of feminist pedagogy since both seek to blend knowledge, skills, and values in the service of social change. Likewise, the feminist perspective enhances civic learning by keeping a social justice focus and teaching students to think critically about institutionalized oppression as they engage in their service-learning activities. Through concrete examples of both service learning and experiential approaches, this monograph describes the adventure of moving beyond the walls of the university, to make the community the classroom and students the agents of social change. Many chapters incorporate the students' own voices in describing how the core concepts of their classes came alive through their community experiences. There are illustrations of the students' engagement in a wide variety of social issues and descriptions of teaching strategies that stimulated students to think critically and in new ways.

This volume provides instructors with fresh approaches by incorporating service learning in addressing the social issues related to gender from multiple discipline perspectives. The monograph invites instructors to "take the leap" and join the adventure of teaching through community engagement by sharing a wealth of ideas that work—problem solving, hands-on examples both in the chapter contents and the extensive appendices that follow each chapter. Appendices include sample syllabi, experiential exercises, evaluation strategies, service-learning guidelines, and a wealth of material that can be adapted to a wide range of teaching situations.

The volume is divided into five sections exploring gender issues. Section one, Gender and Identity, tackles the issue of identity, a foundational issue in gender studies, from a surprising and engaging variety of perspectives.

In chapter 1, "Gender, Identity, Theory, and Action," the author, Talia Bettcher, introduces herself as a philosopher and a transgendered woman—qualities that uniquely equip her to inspire and guide students in the use of philosophical principles to critically exam "identity-centered beliefs." The theoretical perspective of "world-traveling" introduces students to the notion that people move through different social realities (worlds) that impose on and change identity—an individual may express a "different self" in a "different world." The service-learning experiences in the class introduce students to wider worlds of possibility—including the choice to become involved in social activism with grassroots groups addressing gendered and transgendered oppression—that are designed to challenge students to a deeper examination of the themes of the class.

In chapter 2, "Final Project Runway: In the "*I*'s" of Asian American Women," Allyson Tintiangco-Cubales invites students in an interdisciplinary ethnic studies course to explore their own gendered identity through the "lens of race." The experiences of Asian American women are summed up in what the instructor calls the *I*'s (Immigration, Imperialism, Industries, Interdependence, etc.). Performance art is used for creative consciousness-raising. In an interesting twist, the gendered oppression of "fashion" is "reclaimed" as fashion becomes the medium for students to tell their own stories and illustrate the *I*'s. The service-learning project, and culminating experience of the class, is the Final Project Runway—a fashion show in which the students model their creations as highly personalized fashion statements of their gendered and ethnic identity, presented to the community as an educational, cultural, and consciousness-raising experience.

In chapter 3, "The Gendered Meaning of Dress," Connie Ulasewicz introduces students in fashion and apparel classes to "socio semiotics"—Gottdiener's (1995) concept of the adornment of the body as a cultural communication—as a methodological lens to explore how the act of dressing "communicates" a gendered identity, as well as reflects a myriad of other aspects, such as age, ethnicity, social class, and economic status. Experiential activities in the class include critical analysis using the "lens of socio semiotics" to examine textbooks, magazines, newspapers, Web sites, and personal photos. Students' service-learning projects include working with incarcerated girls to develop nightshirts that incorporate their original artwork—often expressing their gendered identity.

Section two, The Social Construction of Gender in an Educational Setting, is core to the monograph since education is both the genesis of much gender learning and the ultimate focus of our enterprise to understand and teach gender. The chapters also present a common progression—the first is a class that makes extensive and effective use of experiential learning but does not yet include service learning with explicit benefits to a community agency, followed by an example in the second chapter of experiential learning blossoming into service-learning pedagogy with the full civic engagement of students.

In chapter 4, "Examining Gender and Classroom Teaching Practices," Sherrie Carinci inspires future teachers to become gender literate through exercises and direct community classroom observation that provide examples of the kind of experiential framework that is often the first step an instructor takes toward developing a service-learning class. Students explore the unstated lessons in gender inequality as they examine the "classroom as curriculum," learn about gender-fair approaches, and use a "gender lens" to critique current methodology, such as "cooperative learning" that may actually reinforce stereotypes of boys as "leaders" and girls as "followers." The presentation of the rich research base for gender-fair approaches, such as the practice of the "connected classroom," allows students to bring together knowledge of gender, race, and culture

In chapter 5, "Feminism, Public Sociology, and Service Learning: Issues of Gender in the Primary School Classroom," Kristyan M. Kouri presents fully developed service-learning classes that introduce students in Introductory Sociology and Women's Studies to the discipline of public sociology and participant-observer research methodology. She illustrates how the use of service-learning pedagogy allows students to better understand classic and recent sociological theories by direct experience. Concepts such as "hegemonic male behavior" and "borderwork" come alive for the undergraduate students as they observe the playground activities of the grade school children they are tutoring.

Section three, Feminist Pedagogy and Service Learning, explores the richness of feminist theory's deep connection to social justice and community activism and the natural fit between feminist and service-learning pedagogy.

In chapter 6, "Women as Social Warriors: A Framework for Community Service Learning Combining Amazonian Feminist Thinking and Social Justice Education Theories," Veda E. Ward brings the unique perspective of Amazonian Feminism—a celebration of women's physical and spiritual strength—to her upper-division women's studies courses to inspire her students to social activism and civic engagement. The course explores the powerful images of the woman warrior throughout history—from Brunhild to

Wonder Woman. This iconic vision, used within a social justice framework, becomes the "powerful conceptual 'cement' to energize social consciousness through relevant community service-learning assignments." Ward demonstrates that students are able to reframe their community experiences of "volunteering" into a more coherent feminist concept of women wielding a "sword of justice" to end oppression and facilitate social change.

In chapter 7, "Placing Gender and Multicultural Competence at the Center: The Young Women's Studies Club," Susan E. Cayleff and Angela J. LaGrotteria describe a 12-year collaboration between their university and the Young Women's Studies Club of a local high school. Undergraduate students in a two-semester American Women's History class compete (only half are chosen) for the opportunity to mentor a racially diverse, low-income group of inner-city high school women. The college women learn and then transmit to their protégés the core values of an experiential approach to teaching that incorporates feminist theories, highlighting the multicultural and nondominant principles of Paulo Freire's (1970) "pedagogy of the oppressed."

In chapter 8, "Learning About Prejudice, Oppression and Hate: Reversing the Silence," Silvina Ituarte explores the inner connections of hate crimes with gender bias and male privilege, using Harro's (2000) "Cycles of Socialization," and expands this theoretical model to embrace a wide range of oppressed groups. Student discussions of their experiences of "male privilege" (sexism) leads to their understanding of the more difficult concepts such as "skin privilege" (racism). The culminating event is the Day of Silence—an all-day activity planned and executed by the students. The chapter includes a wealth of ideas for experiential teaching, from having students' use their favorite magazines to explore the gendered nature of the "cycle of socialization," to developing students' empathy for disabled individuals by the surprising difficulty they experience in attempting to complete children's puzzles by looking only in a mirror.

Section four, Women and Violence, gives a substantive overview of research and practice in prevalence, causes, and intervention and describes creative and effective service-learning projects that address gendered violence.

In chapter 9, "Using an Ecological Perspective to Understand and Address Sexual Assault on Campus," Courtney E. Ahrens and Patricia D. Rozee present an ecological model that systematically analyzes violence against women in ascending order of complexity from the individual level through the group, organizational, community, and societal level. By highlighting the dynamic interplay between the individual and the environment, students learn to contextualize gendered violence in a way that directs them away from simplistic "blame the victim" formulations and toward understanding and social activism. The chapter provides a substantive review of research findings on rape—legal definitions, prevalence, causes, consequences and prevention strategies—and suggests service-learning projects for social action at each level of the ecological model.

Chapter 10, "From 'No Means No' to Community Change: The Impact of University-Based Service Learning Related to Intimate Violence Prevention," Elena Klaw and Marilyn C. Ampuero describe Love, Sex, and Power, a capstone senior psychology majors' seminar. Students increase their understanding of gendered violence and hone their skills in analyzing and synthesizing empirical research as they present research papers and posters on relationship violence at campus community dialogue sessions and at a research poster fair. As a culminating class event, students as peer educators present scripted community workshops that focus on prevention through dispelling antiwoman myths. The authors of this chapter include an enlightening discussion of the challenges and rewards of introducing innovative, multidisciplinary service-learning pedagogy in a "traditional" academic department.

In chapter 11, "Service Learning in a Psychology Course: Women and Violence," Gloria Cowan describes the transformation of a psychology class, Violence Against Women, from a standard format that "brings the community to the students" with lectures and guest speakers, to a more dynamic service-learning structure in which all of the students "go to the community"—each completing at least 40 hours of volunteer training in either a rape crisis center or a shelter for battered women. The insightful discussion of the obstacles and challenges of converting a traditional class to service learning—and the rewards the instructor and students reap from the richer learning experience—provides ample testimony to the value of civic engagement that allows the students to be, as one student reported in her journal, "actually part of the solution."

Section five, Service Learning and Research, concludes the volume with two chapters that explore the role of service-learning projects in socially conscious research.

In chapter 12, "Empowering Older Women Through Service-Learning

Research," Luciana Laganà provides a rich overview of the literature of service learning in research settings and provides examples of how students can learn both core theory and research methodology in hands-on research endeavors. The chapter adopts a phenomenological approach and is full of examples that meet the author's goal to empower older women by including them both as consults in the design of projects and as beneficiaries of the resulting service-learning activities and research.

In the last chapter, "DNA as Tool for Social Justice: Service Learning and Paternity Testing in Tanzania, Africa," Ruth Ballard provides an example of international and cross-cultural research in the discipline of biology. In an innovative and exciting service-learning project, biology students field-test the effectiveness of a DNA sampling kit under the challenging conditions of rural Africa. The DNA tests the students perform are used to assist abandoned women and children in supporting their legal claims of financial support from the biological fathers who have relocated to urban areas during a period of social upheaval. The chapter provides an intriguing model for cross-cultural and multidisciplinary civic engagement as the students learn about both biological science methodology as well as the role science can play in addressing gender inequality in a society in turmoil.

September 12, 2006

## References

Briskin, L., & Coulter, R. (1992). Feminist pedagogy: Challenging the normative. *Canadian Journal of Education, 17*(3), 247–263.

Freire, P. (1970). The adult literacy process as cultural action for freedom. *Harvard Educational Review, 40*, 205–225.

Harro, B. (2000). Cycle of socialization. In M. Adams, W. J. Blumenfeld, R. Castaneda, H. W. Hackman, M. L. Peters, & X. Zuniga (Eds.), *Readings for diversity and social justice: An anthology on racism, anti-Semitism, sexism, heterosexism, ableism, and classism* (pp. 15–20). New York: Routledge.

Schacht, S. P. (2000). Using a feminist pedagogy as a male teacher: The possibilities of a partial and situated perspective. *Radical Teacher* 2:2 (http://radicalpedagogy.icaap.org/content/issue2_2/schacht.html)

Weiler, K. (1991). Freier and a feminist pedagogy of difference. *Harvard Educational Review, 61*(4), 449–474.

# SECTION ONE

---

# GENDER AND IDENTITY

# I

# GENDER, IDENTITY, THEORY, AND ACTION

*Talia Bettcher*

As a philosopher, I am acutely aware of the stereotype of philosophy as utterly disconnected from the everyday world. Therefore, when I introduce philosophy to students for the first time, I am concerned to show its relevance to daily life. Central to my approach in teaching philosophy of gender is the concept of "identity" (or "sense of self").[1] I see individuals as possessing a sense of who and what they are (how they "fit into the world"). Such a sense of self involves a "map" of the world that is largely value laden and action guiding. Our identities are built upon beliefs about the world: about gender, sexuality, race, and religion, which may not always be true or well grounded. Philosophy can help us examine such identity-central beliefs with a critical eye. Just as Socrates asked questions about the nature of piety, justice, and the like, we can also ask questions such as "What is a woman?" and "What is a man?"

## Identity in Theory

Using this approach, I encourage students to think reflectively about their identity-founding beliefs and the ways in which these beliefs guide their behavior. Here it is important to stress that our sense of who and what we are and how we fit into the world generally involves norms, which can govern our behavior. For example, often women may find themselves evaluated according to prevailing cultural aesthetic norms, which are supposed to connect in deep ways to the overall sense of self as valuable. Again, men may find themselves evaluated according to prevailing norms about excellence in various sorts of achievements. The point is that such norms can have a taken-for-granted status; they can guide our actions in ways that go largely unquestioned. To the extent that philosophy as a discipline takes seriously reasoning about moral, aesthetic, and other norms, it is the ideal discipline for examining the grounding (or lack thereof) of such gender-regulated behavior.

## Identity in Practice

As a transsexual woman, I am aware of how unreflective views about the nature of gender and sexuality can have an impact on the day-to-day lives of real people; I have also seen how theories about gender have failed to capture my own experience of gender, or else reduced transsexuality to an abstract object of investigation.[2] Indeed, there is a long history of research and scholarship that regards transsexuals and other transgender people as exotic and problematic objects of investigation.[3] Contemporary trans studies have involved, among other things, a departure from the historical objectification of trans people in theory and research, such that trans people themselves have emerged as subjects/authors instead of just as objects. In this way, some of the extreme transphobic aspects of theory and research have been removed (or at least thinned out), and trans studies have taken on a kind of political liberatory dimension.[4]

The now-dominant model of trans theory and politics is itself fairly specific and open to dispute. It evolved simultaneously with (and in relation to) the queer theory and politics of the early nineties. While the relationship between queer theory and transgender theory and politics has certainly witnessed tensions, current transgender theory and politics borrows many of the key themes of queer theory/politics, not the least of which is an attack on gender/sex binaries, and the view that all gender/sex is socially constructed.[5] As an interdisciplinary field, trans studies draws on history, psychology, sociology, anthropology, philosophy, and biology (to name a few).

Central to my approach in introducing students to trans studies is the notion that theory is political, and that the very course itself is inevitably bound with political considerations. For example, I make it clear at the outset that a starting point of the course is that the lives of trans people are valid and legitimate. In this day and age, however, such an assumption is inherently problematic and controversial. Likewise, the decision to teach a course problematizing the validity of trans lives is a political decision. In general, one important theme of the course is the relationship of theory to politics. How does it actually relate to the lives of the people it is designed to examine? Who is developing the theory and for what purposes? Can the theory help guide or promote resistance? For whom?

## Intersectionality

A concept that is essential to both courses involves the recognition that various forms of oppressions are deeply bound together, and that as a consequence, any discussion of gender or sexuality must be embedded within a broader sociocultural discussion of race, class, religion, and the like. The gender norms, which govern identity, are surely deeply bound with racial and class-based stereotypes as well as very specifically located cultural norms. For example, it is pretty hard to talk about a beauty ideal that (young) women are supposed to attain in our culture without noticing that this ideal tends to be *White*. Similarly, racist stereotypes of Black men and women tend to involve masculinization and hypersexualization.[6] In this way, gender and racial oppression are deeply blended. What this means is that attempts to investigate issues of gender and sexuality, abstracted from considerations such as race, are in danger of coming from a place that takes race, for example, as ultimately unimportant and detachable from issues of gender. In effect, it is to come from a privileged *White* place in which race appears to be no problem.

These issues and concerns are central in the course Philosophy, Gender, and Culture, weaving throughout it as a major theme. They are also quite relevant in the course Introduction to Transgender Studies. One of my concerns with current trans studies is the fact that it emerges from a fairly specific cultural location (White, academic, American, Anglo). While there has been some critique of the biases inherent in the prevailing framework, there remains a dearth of writing from people who do not come from that location, and the discussions of transgender issues for the most part appear to be abstracted from related issues such as race.[7]

## "World"-Traveling

The notion of "world"-traveling is also important in both of these courses— indeed it informs my approach to service learning and civic/social engagement more broadly. This concept, introduced by philosopher María Lugones (1987), involves the view that people may move within very different social realities or "worlds."[8] Integral to this "world"-traveling is the fact that one has a different self (or is a different person) in different worlds. Indeed, a change in "world" is basically defined through a change in self. The insight derives from the experience of being bi- or multicultural: moving between different cultures and sometimes occupying several at once. One of the important features of this view is the recognition that sometimes who and what we are can be to some degree determined by others. Sometimes conceptions of who we are may be imposed upon us from without, and sometimes we may be blind to how we appear to others. Thus, our own sense of self (self-conception) may blind us to some of our actions, to their meanings, to their effects upon others. This is especially important because insofar as our own identities involve a larger picture of the world and how we fit into it, they also include a conception of other people and our relations to them. Because of this, there is a danger that we view others only in terms of ourselves—a danger that is only augmented if our map places other people in categories that are racist, sexist, or in other ways harmful to them. One of Lugones's points is that in order to be open to see others as they see themselves—and to be able to identify with them—it is important that one be open to seeing oneself differently, open to the fact that one may be viewed by others in a way that does not necessarily accord with one's own self-conception. In a word, one must "world"-travel.

## Service Learning

In both courses I offer students the option of service learning. This is one strategy among many that I use to help promote course objectives. In the course Philosophy, Gender, and Culture we focus specifically on topics such as domestic violence, sexual assault, homophobia, and regulations of intersexual and transgender bodies. One of my goals is to argue that much of these forms of violence flow in part from harmful gendered conceptions of self. Some of the agencies that we work with include ones addressing domestic violence and sexual assault (such as the East Los Angeles Women's Center, Prototypes), and ones that have specific programs for lesbian/gay/bi/transgender/queer (LGBTQ) people (such as the Los Angeles Gay and Lesbian Center, Asian Pacific AIDS Intervention Team, Bienestar Human Services). For the most part, students perform various activities that are needed by the agencies at the time they are placed. They have worked in the planning of domestic violence vigils, been involved in outreach activities, provided assistance during support groups, helped organize events, and provided child care and assistance in compiling and distributing resource materials. Through service learning, students are not only given the opportunity to experience the connections between the issues discussed in class and the real world, they are also hopefully led to challenge beliefs that ground their own sense of the world and their place within it not only through reflecting upon what they have learned, but by effectively "world"-traveling.

When I teach Introduction to Transgender Studies, most of the students who take it are not themselves transgender, and many have not had any real interaction with transgender people and do not know very much about them. As a consequence, the course is inevitably a kind of introduction to trans realities and what it is to be trans. Naturally, this raises the difficulty that transgender people are often exoticized and marginalized. Obviously classroom assignments and a transgender instructor are themselves insufficient to undermine this tendency. So, it is for this reason that I think service learning is an important way of encouraging "world"-travel on the part of the students.

Additionally, beyond introducing students to trans theory and the history of trans studies, it is important to illuminate the connection between such theory and the real-world politics in trans communities. Because of that, I think that it is important for students to have an experience being involved in trans community organizing at the grassroots level. By doing this, students are not only enabled to go beyond the theory to real flesh-and-blood people, they are able to see the limits, advantages, and disadvantages of transgender theorizing and the political nature of theorizing about trans people. For example, it is a sad fact that much of transgender theory fails to adequately centralize issues of race and class. As a consequence, it ends up using problematic assumptions that go largely unquestioned. By having students work with agencies and organizations that provide services for transgender people in Los Angeles, they are thereby enabled to see the limitations of a culturally situated theory.

In this course, the agencies we worked with included members of the Los Angeles Transgender Youth Consortium (TYC). The TYC addresses the impact of HIV on young transgender people (ages 13–29) and comprises several organizations including Asian Pacific AIDS Intervention Team, Bienestar Human Services, Children's Hospital Los Angeles, Minority AIDS Project, and Van Ness Recovery House (Prevention Division). Additionally, we worked with FTM-LA Alliance, a Los Angeles–based community-building organization for FTM-identified individuals.[9]

In this course, students who chose the service-learning option helped conduct outreach, provided backup supportive services for support groups, conducted various forms of information gathering/resource building (concerning trans-friendly resources, trans-friendly surgeons, relevant funding opportunities), and also developed brochures with some of the information they had researched. Prior to their service, all students were required to participate in an HIV 101 training session led by representatives from the TYC. Additionally, students had received basic transgender 101 training by the time they started working in their placements. What students seemed to get out of the service experience was not only what they learned through the specific services they provided for their agencies, but also the fact they had basically entered an unfamiliar world. In entering this world they had the chance to interact with trans people as real people in real communities, working to improve their lives.

Because I offer the service learning as an optional component in both classes, it is especially imperative that additional work be done to integrate student community work with what is happening in the classroom. In both classes, I offer panel presentations and guest speaker presentations on most of the topics that we cover. For example, in Gender, Philosophy, and Culture, we have a guest speaker from the East Los Angeles Women's Center present on issues of domestic violence and sexual assault. I have found this essential in breaking down the model of professor as chief information source. By drawing on expertise from the community (particularly agencies that we are working with in service learning) a kind of knowledge is brought into the classroom that cannot come from books. Clearly, the point is not merely for students to learn about the realties of sexual violence. How do they address them in their daily lives? What sorts of forces and situations do they contend with in reality? By having experts who address these issues by leading conversation in the classroom, an important gap between theory and actual student life can be breached. Indeed, we have had occasions when students in the classroom came to confront personal issues of domestic violence or abuse. Because there were experts present, these situations could be handled effectively and professionally.

This has proven even more important in Introduction to Transgender Studies. By inviting transgender leaders involved in grassroots community activism in Los Angeles, an important counterpoint can be offered to the nature of the theory that grounds most of trans studies. Some of the topics that were covered included an introduction to trans issues (Trans 101); the medical/psychiatric model of transsexuality; Camp Trans and the Michigan Womyn's Music Festival; and transphobic violence. Additionally, in Introduction to Trans Studies, I required that students who did not choose the service-learning option attend at least one community-based event and write about it. While I understand that for some students a full service-learning commitment is not a reasonable option, it seemed essential to me that students be required to at least physically travel at least once during the course to a world that was not necessarily their own. While I do not have a similar requirement in the Philosophy, Gender, and Culture course, I do require that students attend specific cultural events that are being held on campus during that quarter. For example, one year our class attended the campus National Coming Out Day. It turned out that I was one of the speakers, so I used this opportunity to come out to my students as transgender.

To be sure, one of the major reasons that work with community partners has been so successful, and facilitated a tighter integration of course content and community service, is that I have had independent relationships with and commitments to many of the agencies. For example, I have had a long relationship with the East Los Angeles Women's Center, serving on its board of directors for over five years. I am also an active member of the Los Angeles transgender community and have played a role in grassroots organizing and community work. Because I have a community vantage point on some of the issues as well as that of an academician, I think that I am better enabled to guide the students. I also think that it is important that the instructor demonstrate a commitment to civic/social engagement. Short of this model, it is hard to see how an instructor can authentically promote this in her or his students. Additionally, I think that it goes some considerable distance in undermining tendencies of marginalizing or objectifying the community. I found this especially important in Introduction to Transgender Studies, where objectification is always already a pressing danger. Indeed, the fact that

I had already engaged in many projects with our partners, and had formed meaningful friendships, helped move the entire class from something located on the UCLA campus, to a kind of genuine trans community intervention. In this way, a possible two-sidedness on the part of the instructor can be important in helping to open doors for student "world"-travel.

## Reflections

Because I have taught Philosophy, Gender, and Culture over the course of several years, it has changed and evolved, and I have had the opportunity to explore several different types of reflection activities. Perhaps the most effective is the weekly journal, which I have used in the past to guide students in reflecting on the connection between specific concepts discussed in class and their service experience. As class size increased, however, it became more realistic to assign short response papers. I also have students complete a set of reflection questions at the beginning of the course and the end of the course. I have also worked in collaboration with our mostly student-staffed volunteer placement organization on campus (Educational Participation in Communities) conducting group reflection sessions for our service-learning students. These exercises led by student facilitators involve, among other things, having students select objects (from their backpacks, etc.) to represent who they are in relationship to their service (which they then share in groups), as well as putting together collages from magazines about their service experiences. One reflection activity that I have found successful in service learning is when students answer the question "Who am I?" By focusing on a few aspects of their identity (such as "What does it mean for me to be a man?" etc.) and then relating this to what they have learned in their service experience, students are enabled to connect concepts and experience directly to the notion of identity. Students can then work together in groups to stage presentations, which end up being dialogues between the different identities.

In Introduction to Transgender Studies, I have students complete a term paper that integrates many of the different features described above. Some of the general questions they are expected to answer included the following:

- In which agency have you been placed? In which program?
- Whom does the agency serve?
- What is the mission of the agency?

- What do you think some of the major issues are that confront the clientele? The agency itself?
- What are some of the strategies that the agency uses to address these issues?
- Describe some of the activities that you did for the agency. What was the point of the activities? How did they fit into the agency's mission?
- Describe some of the interactions that you had with clients and with coordinators.
- What sorts of things have you learned about "trans issues" that you did not know before?
- How has this experience challenged you personally (if at all)?
- Are there any particular experiences that were especially meaningful to you? Discuss.

Students are then asked to reflect upon some of the issues presented and discussed in class in lectures and in readings. In particular they are asked to reflect upon the following questions in their paper: Does the theory illuminate the actual experience? Does the actual experience challenge a rethinking of the theory? What does this have to say about "trans issues" and the relationship between those issues and academia? And what does this reveal about you and your own relationship to gender?

The paper assignment involves three stages. First, the student met with me in person to discuss his or her service-learning experience and to talk about the overall direction of the paper. Then, the students wrote rough drafts. This enabled me to give fairly detailed comments on their work, encouraging them to explore issues that they may not have paid enough attention to. Finally, they submitted their final drafts. Because the assignment also had specific questions requiring students to gain certain information about the agency they were working with, this also seemed to encourage some focused, meaningful dialogue with their supervisor.

## Engagement

In the case of civic/social engagement, my objectives are limited to the following: First, I intend for students to come away with an increased sense of social/cultural responsibility. Second, I intend for students to be more capable of moving beyond their own perspective, being sensitive to the perspective of others, and being capable of critiquing their own subject position. Third, I intend for students to develop a deepened, more nuanced knowledge of the play of gender (sexual, racial, class) politics in everyday reality—including in the classroom and in the very deployments of theory.

The last of these is the easiest to determine, and I have certainly found that in general the students who have engaged in service learning have been able to make certain observations and critiques that they would not have been able to do in the classroom alone. For example, a student in my Philosophy, Gender, and Culture course who was doing outreach for the transgender program at Asian Pacific AIDS Intervention Team saw firsthand racial division and fragmentation among trans women, and the ways this gets played out even in the occupation of space (e.g., at dance clubs). He had been under the impression that the category "trans" was more homogenous and unified. While I can try to explain in class how the issues of race and class intersect transgender issues, I can also only go so far as a White, Anglo trans woman. A reality, which goes well beyond the classroom, is required.

The second of these, in my experience, is the hardest for students to actually achieve. Students—well, all of us, I suppose—are generally reluctant to engage in a kind of self-assessment or to see themselves from the perspective of another. Yet I continue to believe that this is an indispensable exercise (for all of us). Indeed, it is the key to successful world traveling. I have found that very good service-learning students can move in this direction. For example, a student in Introduction to Transgender Studies wrote in her paper:

> Before this class, I never questioned the fact that I was female or what being a female entails, yet that has changed. After some self-contemplation, I realized that I held both masculine and feminine traits yet in the same vein, questioned whether or not labeling the traits as such even mattered. Whether the attribute was masculine or feminine it did not change the fact that I had it. . . . This re-evaluation of my own relationship to gender allowed me to become even more accepting of different types of people and value the incredible diversity of human beings.

Students are often enabled to move beyond an easy objectification (especially in the case of transgender people) to the recognition that they are in the presence of genuine, flesh-and-blood human beings. Thus, one of the students working with Bienestar in Introduction to Transgender Studies writes: "What I did at Bienestar was converse with the transgender women and come to realize that transgender women are like everybody else. I did not have a note-pad . . . it was actual conversation that took place."

Finally, we genuinely want our students to become more motivated to engage in social/political issues. Yet, to be sure, short of serious long-term follow-up, this is not easy to measure. One measure is that many students continue volunteering well after their service-learning experience. Indeed, some of my students have been recognized at volunteer recognition events and even found employment at some of their placement agencies. However, I think one of the most powerful example of this sort of impact came from a student who worked with Bienestar Human Service during the Introduction to Transgender Studies course. At the end of the quarter, we discovered that the transgender program was not going to receive funding, and as a consequence the program would have to close. The transwomen who worked at Bienestar organized a staged response to this. This student showed up at this event to speak from his own firsthand experience and to point out the valuable work that he saw performed in this program. His presentation was informed by the realities he had experienced and the empathy and the friendships he had developed with the women he had worked with. This young man—whose ambition was to become a lawyer and advocate for those sometimes forgotten—seemed to have already learned something important and to have already taken a stand. It was a sharp example of informed reflective social/civic engagement in a truly deplorable situation. It was an example of somebody who had clarified who he was and why that was important.

## Evaluation

Community partners evaluate student participation and their success in community service through attendance sheets, evaluation forms (often coordinated through Educational Participation in Communities) and discussions with me. My general principle is that students are awarded an A for this component of the course and their grade is lowered only in case they fail to perform their tasks responsibly and in good faith. Through the reflection activities, I evaluate student success in achieving learning outcomes (including the civic outcomes mentioned above). I have found that students tend to be reluctant to engage in deep reflection and so it is important that the reflection activities be rather explicit and directive in order to encourage this type of inquiry. For example, a very simple way of measuring journal entries is to assign three points: one point for a discussion of in-class concepts, one point for discussing community-based experience and learning, and one point for reflecting upon the connections and disconnections between them (half and quarter points are used). Student paper topics include (as part of the assignment) specific sections, which require reflection on connections between theory and practice and on the overall sociocultural context. I take this sort of reflection as a necessary requirement of completing an assignment satisfactorily, I am not as demanding in my expectation that students demonstrate the capacity of challenging their own subject position. Rather, this I take this as a hallmark of a strong paper (B plus and above).

## Conclusion

This coming year I will have the opportunity to teach Philosophy, Gender, and Culture again for the first time in a couple of years. I am looking forward to it, and I also eagerly await the next opportunity to teach Introduction to Transgender Studies. In the future, my intention is to clarify more distinctly the relationship between identity, "world"-travel, reflection, and social/civic engagement outcomes. I suspect that by fine-tuning these connections, I will be better enabled to guide students in examining themselves in ways that may not always be comfortable. I also hope to work even more closely with community partners in creating a truly integrated course. Greater attention to these features will help both courses become true vehicles of identity reassessments, "world"-travel, and social engagement. What I have learned, at any rate, is that by being both an instructor and a community activist, I am in a better position to help students increase their capacity for social engagement through thinking about identity, by partaking in "world"-travel, and by recognizing that even theorizing itself can be deeply political.

## Notes

   1. For a brief discussion of the notion of *identity* I have in mind and its relation to gender, sexuality, and homophobia, see Hopkins (1996). In my understanding of it, *identity* involves the following features: (a) reflexivity (i.e., it is a conception of oneself); (b) implication of others (i.e., a picture of the world that includes more than oneself; (c) temporality (i.e., an interpretation of the past and expectations and

plans directed toward the future); and (d) agency (i.e., the view of oneself as a moral subject).

2. *Transgender* is often used as an umbrella term, which brings together different kinds of individuals who have gender identities and/or expressions and performances that are taken to differ from "the norm." For example, transsexuals, cross-dressers, drag kings and queens, and some butch lesbians may be viewed as "transgender." Sometimes the prefix *trans* (as in *trans people*) is used as a way of avoiding the sometimes contested assimilation of transsexuals under the term *transgender*. MTF is often used to refer to male-to-female trans people and FTM is often used to refer to female-to-male trans people. All of this terminology is subject to political contestations and I do not intend to use it to attribute self-identities.

3. For an introduction to the notion of "trans studies" see Prosser (1997).

4. The move in this direction is best captured by Hale (1997).

5. For one of the most influential popular formulations of these ideas see Bornstein (1994).

6. For a discussion of such issues see hooks (1992, pp. 145–156).

7. For critiques see Namaste (2005, 2000) and Roen (2001).

8. See Lugones (2003). For a discussion of the relevance of "world"-traveling in the context of trans studies, see Hale (1998).

9. For an explanation of FTM see note 2.

I would like to thank my former students Alice Bui and Derek Murray for their kind permission to cite passages from their work. I would also like to thank Marie Auyong, Miguel Martinez, Alva Moreno, Alexis Rivera, Sonia Rivera, Bamby Salcedo, Kimberly Scott, Lauren Steely, Terri Tinsley, and Alexander Yoo for the various ways in which they helped bring many of the service-learning projects or in-class discussions to life. I give special thanks to Susan Forrest for her continued support and her invaluable comments and criticism.

## References

Bornstein, K. (1994). *Gender outlaw: On men and women and the rest of us.* New York: Routledge.

Hale, C. (1997). Suggested rules for non-transsexuals writing about transsexuals, transsexuality, transsexualism, or trans. Retrieved from http://sandystone.com/hale.rules.html

Hale, C. (1998). Tracing a ghostly memory in my throat: Reflections on FTM feminist voice and agency. In T. Digby (Ed.), *Men doing feminism* (pp. 99–128). New York: Routledge.

Hopkins, P. (1996). Gender treachery: Homophobia, masculinity, and threatened identities. In L. May, R. Strikwerda, & P. Hopkins (Eds.), *Rethinking masculinity:*

*Philosophical explorations in light of feminism* (2nd ed.) (pp. 95–115). New York: Rowman & Littlefield.

hooks, b.(1992). *Black looks: Race and representation.* Boston: South End Press.

Lugones, M. (2003). Playfulness,"world"-traveling, and loving perception. *Hypatia,* 2(2), 3–19. Reprinted and updated in M. Lugones (2003), *Pilgrimages/peregrinajes: Theorizing coalition against multiple oppressions* (pp. 77–100). New York: Rowman & Littlefield.

Namaste, V. (2000). *Invisible lives: The erasure of transsexual and transgender people.* Chicago: University of Chicago Press.

Namaste, V. (2005). *Sex change, social change: Reflections on identity, institutions, and imperialism.* Toronto, Ontario, Canada: Women's Press.

Prosser, J. (1997). Transgender. In A. Medhurst & S. R. Munt (Eds.), *Lesbian and gay studies: A critical introduction* (pp. 309–326). London: Cassell.

Roen, K. (2001). Transgender theory and embodiment: The risk of racial marginalization. *Journal of Gender Studies, 10*(3), 253–263.

# 2

# FINAL PROJECT RUNWAY

## In the *I*'s of Asian American Women

*Allyson Tintiangco-Cubales*

She stepped onto the stage as the finale of the show. With great confidence, a Filipina superheroine emerged draped in a red cape and wrapped in black spandex from head to toe. With a hip-hop strut, she performed a proud catwalk across the runway. An omniscient female voice in the background narrated the superheroine's adventures fighting against global, local, and personal oppression. Photos of her "enemies"—White female comic-book icons—flashed behind her. The narrator, a classmate, ends the Asian American Women's fashion show with the words: "Your revolution will not happen between these thighs." The Filipina superheroine embodied the lesson plans, dialogue, and the purpose of our Asian American Women's course.

At San Francisco State University (SFSU), I teach Asian American Studies 603: Asian American Women as part of my regular charge as a tenure-track professor. In this course, I aim for students to learn the stories of sacrifice, struggle, and survival of Asian American women. Domestic violence, negative media portrayals, body mutilation, exploitative labor practices, sexism, heterosexism, and sex trafficking are only some of the major issues that are covered in this course. Despite the intensity of these issues, I try to make sure that I do not portray Asian American women as powerless victims, especially since most of the students who usually take the course are Asian American women and men. Students are encouraged to personalize the issues learned in the course in hopes that they will find ways to address them in their daily lives. Through interactive lesson plans and creative projects, including a culminating fashion show, I aim to provide students with ways to educate each other as well as their communities about the global, local, and personal issues of Asian American women.

At the end of the semester, the students in this course produce a fashion show representing the *I*'s of Asian American women. The *I*'s covered in the course are: Intersectionality, Immigration, Imperialism, Industries, Interdependence, Identities, Issues, Ideologies, Images, and Involvement. Fashion plays a dominant role in the oppression of women and their bodies. For Asian American women in particular, cultural/ethnic fashion has been co-opted, essentialized, distorted, and commoditized by American industries. This "Final Project Runway" was designed as a symbolic "reclaiming" and "reimagining" of fashion as a site of self-determination, political education, and community organizing.

In the Asian American Women's course, I draw the curriculum and pedagogy from the disciplines of history, sociology, anthropology, psychology, literature, and art. In this chapter, I have divided the description of the course into looking at how I teach the *I*'s of Asian American Women, how the students share what they learn about the *I*'s in the community off campus, and how the students and I reflect on the *I*'s.

## Ethnic Studies and Service Learning

At SFSU, home of the Third World Liberation Front and Movement, we have the only College of Ethnic Studies in the nation. The college consists of American Indian studies, Raza studies, Africana studies, and the largest department, Asian American studies. SFSU has a unique population of students. Out of the total 23,074 undergraduates enrolled in the fall of 2005, Asian Pacific American (APA) students (including Filipinos and Pacific Islanders) made up 36.7% of the entire population, surpassing White non-Latino students who made up 33.6%.[1] APA students were the largest ethnoracial group on campus, and about 58% are women. Embedded in the very foundation of ethnic studies is service learning and "learning service." As an interdisciplinary field, ethnic studies has the flexibility to include various methods of service. It is in this context that I teach the Asian American Women's course.

At some universities, courses like the Asian American Women's course enroll non-Asian students who want to learn about Asian American women.

This course is not only an upper-division course on the history and contemporary issues of Asian American women, it also becomes a location in which APA students can study their own personal history, or "herstory," and contemporary issues, along with the stories of Asian American women in their families. This course, which is an elective for the Asian American studies major and fulfills a general education requirement, usually has 30 students enrolled. Since more than 90% of the students who have taken the course are APA, with about 60% APA women, the identities and epistemologies of the students became central to the course curriculum.

I have made a concerted effort to develop creative ways to integrate the students' voices in the classroom. Constructing projects that allow the student's personal experiences to be connected directly to the issues of APA women both in the United States and globally has been somewhat organic but not without challenge. In ethnic studies, and in the course on Asian American Women that is the focus of this chapter, there are no rigid borders between those receiving and those providing in our service-learning projects. The service-learning projects that we create in ethnic studies may not necessarily aim to serve "other" communities; more often than not, the students are members of the communities they are serving. Projects that I name "learning service" are those that provide students a space to be critical of their own identities, an ownership in the realm of service, and the encouragement to give back to their "own" communities.

## Introducing the Course and the *I*'s of Asian American Women

In this course the students and I take a journey into the *I*'s of Asian American women: Intersectionality, Identities, Imperialism, Immigration, Industries, Interdependence, Ideologies, Involvement, Issues, and Images. We examine the social, political, cultural, and economic experiences of women of Asian descent in America from the 19th century to the present. We explore, analyze, and compare the experiences of immigrants and American-born Filipina, Chinese, Japanese, Korean, South Asian, Southeast Asian, Pacific Islander, and mixed-race women, paying close attention to the intersections of gender, race, class, sexuality, and nationality in their lives. Topics include immigration and migration, labor, families, relationships, activism, art, culture, identity, feminism, sexuality, war, globalization, representations, community, youth, and love. Course materials include primary and secondary research, books, articles, oral histories, poetry, short stories, films, and videos. Each class session includes a lecture, discussion, and a creative activity.

I borrow from Trinh T. Minh-ha's (1990) theories about identity and difference and her analysis of the pronoun *I* as holding the power to exclude others who are different than "I." According to Minh-ha, " 'I' is based on subjectivity and culture that has 'never been monolithic.' " (p. 375). I play on her usage of *I* and instead of seeing *I* as an exclusive identity, I explore *I*'s in this course that connect the experiences of all Asian American women. To creatively present the ideas in the course, I have created a mnemonic device focused on the *I*'s of Asian American women. I play with the letter *I* and its play on the "eyes" of Asian American women, which are often exoticized, and also the reference to eyes as a metaphor for perspective.

The following brief descriptions are accessible ways to understand the *I*'s of Asian American women:

### Intersectionalities and Identities

These *I*'s refer to the intersections between the epistemologies and identities of Asian American women. Some view this as an intersection between the sociohistorical constructions of race, ethnicity, class, gender, sexuality, and citizenship. The intersectionality of identities can also be affected by nativity, diasporic migration, labor, culture, age, feminism, war, globalization, and all the following *I*'s.

### Imperialism

This refers to the policy and practice of forming and maintaining an "empire" by seeking to control raw materials (land, resources, bodies, labor) and the world markets by the "conquest" of other countries and the establishment of colonies. This includes the policy and practice of seeking to dominate the economic and/or political affairs of underdeveloped or "weaker" countries. This *I* also brings in the use of colonialism and war for the maintenance of imperialism. Ultimately this discussion includes the effects of imperialism in the lives of Asian American women on the global, local, and personal levels. Imperialism is also a starting point for the discussion on the immigration of many Asian American women.

## Immigration

This concept includes the diversity of immigration policies and patterns of the Asian American women who first came to the United States as early as the 1800s to those who are immigrating today. The discussion around immigration not only focuses on those who are leaving Asia but on those who were also left behind in the earlier waves of migration, especially the women. The discourse on immigration in this course takes into account the "homeland" push factors including poverty and political persecution, and for some Asian women, the patriarchal, patrilineal, and patrilocal societies where girls were reared to serve men and to procreate. Along with these push factors, the U.S. pull factors, including the possibilities of economic prosperity, family reunification, liberation, and policies, create the contexts in which Asian women come to the United States.

## Industries

Industry includes the places Asian American women work and the types of conditions in which they work. In the course we ask how Asian American women's experiences vary from the work of merchant's wives and prostitutes, farmworkers and *pensionadas*,[2] and more currently, between professionals and working-class women. This then leads to a discussion on labor and class. This *I* should also try to explain the context in which these women find particular types of work in specific jobs. The focus on industries begins the dialogue about productive labor for wages and reproductive labor.

## Images

Images encompass media images, images of Asian American women in society, and how Asian American women view their own images. There is a relationship between how particular images that are based on stereotypes, along with American and Asian American standards of beauty, affect the ideas that women have about their own body image. This leads to the topic of how Asian American women "alter" their bodies to fit society's images of them, and the relationship between negative media portrayals and body mutilation.

## Issues and Involvement

Along with the issues of body image, the main issues discussed in this *I* include domestic violence, exploitative labor practices, sexism, heterosexism,

mail-order brides, and sex trafficking. This not only includes the type of issues Asian American women endure but also the ways in which they address
these issues. Students are exposed to Asian American women's involvement
in organizations or movements.

## Ideologies

This *I* is a discussion on what types of ideologies Asian American women
may subscribe to, including hegemonic and counterhegemonic paradigms.
We ask about what these women believe. What do "we" believe and why,
since many of the students in the class are Asian American women and men.
The focus on ideology is always coupled with a discussion on culture, both
as a static belief that often becomes an excuse for our ideological tendencies
and culture as a dynamic notion that can be shaped by critical thought
and production. In this course, I also focus on the three main waves of
feminism—third world feminism, womanism, and Pinayism (*Pinay* is a col-
loquial term for *Filipina*)—and the possibilities of an Asian American wom-
en's feminism.

## Interdependence

This *I* focuses on the role of Asian American women in the family and community. This *I* revisits the discussion on reproductive labor. I focus on Elizabeth Uy Eviota's (1992) definition of work being of two general types:
productive work for exchange and reproductive work for use and satisfaction
of immediate needs. Reproductive work refers to the production of people.
Reproductive labor includes the bearing and caring of children regardless if
one is paid or not paid for this type of work. Nurses and home care and
daycare providers are examples of those who might get paid for this type of
work. Stay-at-home moms, working moms, parents, guardians, and grand-
parents often participate in reproductive labor that is often unpaid. This reproductive labor is part of the interdependence in the family and the
community that provides the ideological maintenance of the human being
and enables individuals to fit into the social structure of society (Eviota,
1992). With interdependence, Asian American women's participation in the
family and community is sometimes exploited, underestimated, and undervalued in its importance to the survival and maintenance of Asian America.

These *I*'s are the pillars of content in the Asian American Women's
course. They are a means toward a social justice education that draws from

the political to the personal and encourages learning service and community engagement. To illustrate the ways in which the *I*'s are discussed in the course, the remainder of this chapter will be divided into the following sections: (a) teaching of the *I*'s, which will focus on the interactive lesson plans and creative projects of the course; (b) learning of the *I*'s, which will focus on the Final Project Runway and serves as the culminating assignment where the students share with the community their learning of the *I*'s; and (c) reflecting on the *I*'s, which will share the words of the students regarding their experiences in the course.

## Teaching the *I*'s

For each of the *I*'s, I develop interactive lesson plans and/or creative projects to encourage the students in the course to critically analyze and develop ways to address the issues of Asian American women. I try to provide ways for students to transform the classroom into a "community" in which they serve each other. This is a way to integrate the notion that learning from each other can lead to community responsibility similar to that of civic responsibility. In this course I aim to provide a social justice education, which Adams, Bell, and Griffin (1997) describe as the inclusion of "an interdisciplinary subject matter that analyzes multiple forms of oppression (such as racism and sexism), and a set of critical, interactive, experiential pedagogical principles that help students understand the meaning of social difference and oppression in their personal lives and the social system" (p. xv).

Within this social justice education, I borrow from critical pedagogy, which "is concerned with the elimination of oppression, the resurgence of hope and possibility—in short, with the making of a better world in which to live. A better world for all" (Shaw, 2006). Building on these fundamental ideas of social justice education and critical pedagogy, I draw from experiential education, feminist pedagogies, and ethnic studies to practice four main types of pedagogies: epistemological pedagogy, performance pedagogy, media literacy, and visual art pedagogy. Using these elements of a social justice education provides opportunities to encourage students to pursue civic and community responsibility—in essence learning service. The following sections illustrate a few examples of how these pedagogies are interwoven in the course.

## Epistemological Pedagogy

In essence, ethnic studies is based on the study of experiences, and with the overwhelming majority of students being Asian American, I try to encourage the students to learn through an epistemological pedagogy, that is, an exploration of how we know what we know. This type of pedagogy allows students to develop a critical discussion on how the larger social constructs of culture, race, class, and gender play out in their personal experiences. The course combines theoretical approaches (through texts and lectures) and experiential approaches (through story collection, personal recollection, and performance) brought together by personal and group reflection. Through the following activities and assignments, students uncover their ways of knowing by studying their own experiences and the experiences of Asian American women in their families/lives (see Appendix).

### Intersecting Life

Through this exercise students discuss their life stories according to race, class, and gender with one other person in the class. In a larger group discussion we draw out the connections between these sociohistorical constructed lenses. The students not only get to know each other, they also begin to see the ways in which we tackle the issues in the course through the lens of intersecting identities.

### Immigration and Imperialism Timelines/Matrix

In this assignment, the students research the Asian American women's herstories. They are put into random groups, and each group is assigned one or two ethnic groups of Asian American women to conduct research on their homeland context (e.g., immigration policies and patterns) and their U.S. context (e.g., pull factors, industries, labor, and class). They share their findings with the class. Through this project, the students get to explore what is available with regard to information on Asian American women. This is also where the Asian Americans in the class begin to see how their own stories fit into the larger historical context of the Asian American women's experience.

### Never-Ending Reproductive and Productive Labor

The main focus of this exercise is on the "industries" in which Asian American women work and their roles in the family and in their communities through "interdependence." The exercise involves a calculation and comparison of the number of work hours (both reproductive and productive) performed each week by men and women.

### Oral Herstory Project

Oral stories are an important tradition in many cultures, and collecting stories is often used as a research method. As one of the last projects that the students complete in this course, it brings all the *I*'s together. Students individually interview an Asian American woman 40 years or older. As a group, students can choose to write a group paper, put together a magazine, put together a video, or write a series of children's books/stories to share the stories of the interviewees.

## Performance Pedagogy

As epistemological pedagogy has been practiced since the beginning of ethnic studies, art and performance have been a part of its methodology. Often there is an intersection between epistemological and performance pedagogy. For example, the poetry workshop is based on students' experiences, and it also involves a performance activity. Performance pedagogy not only keeps the students on their toes, it also prepares them for their culminating project, the fashion show. Through performance pedagogy the lesson plans come alive.

### Performance Poetry

To create opportunities for students to make connections between the *I*'s, particularly Industries and Interdependence, I conduct a poetry workshop based on women's birthing stories and their work in their own families. Each student chooses a woman in his or her own family to write about. I conduct an in-class poetry-writing workshop. The students also have the opportunity to complete their poems outside of class. The following week they share their poems in a poetry reading. The students' poems are very personal, and having a safe space to share them is key. Each semester, this is one of my favorite activities, because it brings the students in the class together. Poetry reading is a process of humanization, one of the main goals of critical pedagogy.

### Performing Scenarios

In the discussion on Ideologies, Issues, and Involvement of Asian American women, I give the students scenarios to act out in front of the class. They develop a five-minute performance (skit, poetry, dance, music, mime) based on the scenarios I assign them. The scenarios include issues of sex workers, mail-order brides, overseas contract workers, unplanned pregnancies, suicide, issues between being a feminist and being an Asian American woman, conflict between Asian American women, and class issues.

## Media Literacy and Visual Art Pedagogy

Media literacy and visual art pedagogy are key ways to engage students to be more critical of how the media portrays Asian American women, and the students also get to use media and art to pursue alternative ways to present the images of Asian American women. The following are key lesson plans that prepare the students for their fashion show.

### Dragon Ladies, Suzy Wongs, and Lucy Lius

In the Images Unit, which occurs toward the middle of the semester, I have the students form groups to work with for the whole semester. The first group assignment is the media literacy assignment where each group is required to view outside of class a set of films, TV shows, or media images that depict Asian American women. Each group must select a one-minute clip of its assigned media to share with the class and describe what these images represent. The description must involve at least two $I$'s.

### Voodoo Doll Assignment

Following the media assignment, each group is instructed to make a voodoo doll representing an Asian American women's body image alteration/issue. This a great visual arts assignment that prepares them for the fashion show. The dolls are even used as part of an altar at the fashion show. The assignment gets the students really thinking about the products and media used to socialize Asian American women to create particular ideas about their body image. The students are encouraged to use products, media images, articles, or stories that portray their assigned Asian American women's body image alteration/issue.

## Learning the $I$'s

At the end of the semester, the students in this course are required to put together the Final Project Runway, a fashion show representing the $I$'s of

Asian American women. They are to share this fashion show with the off-campus communities. They aim to bring in people from their communities, targeting those who may not know a great deal about the issues Asian American women face.

This project shows how the students have learned the *I*'s, and it pulls together the epistemological, performance, media literacy, and visual arts pedagogies used in the lesson plans and creative projects. There is a direct relationship between what students have learned in the classroom and what students present in the fashion show. Final Project Runway takes the *I*'s learned in the Asian American Women's course and shares them with the off-campus communities. It is usually held in the evening at a nightclub, and many Asian Americans attend. Creating the designs and organizing the fashion show gives students a deeper understanding of the *I*'s, while also providing them an opportunity to use performance and art as a means toward social justice.

### *The Spring 2005 Final Project Runway Show*

The following is a description in the program for the Spring 2005 Final Project Runway Fashion Show:

> Because Asian American women are not centered in a traditional fashion
> Because we are objects of fashion
> Because our fashion has been stolen and commodified
> And because fashion confines us
> We decided to take fashion back and
> Become the subjects of our own designs!

Photos of all the voodoo doll designs were on the front cover of the program. There were nine designs produced by the students in the course, and all the *I*'s were represented. The first design to take the stage was titled *From Kimono to Apron*, and it focused on interdependence. This design opened the show with a Chinese male dressed in an oversized kimono; when it opened she/he was wearing an apron with various items representing the type of work Asian American women are expected to do for the family and for the community. The next design, *Your Empowerment = My Disempowerment*, also dealt with an issue in the family and the community. The main issue presented was that in the Asian American community, domestic violence is often accompanied by silence in the family. Both of these designs focused on the family and drew from some of the personal stories that students shared in class.

Along with issues in the family, students created designs that brought out the global and local issues of Asian American women, the industries they work in, and the connection to immigration. *Priceless* was a design that was presented as a detailed skit about an Asian American woman who was working in a sweatshop, undergoing unsafe working conditions, and being abused by her boss. Interestingly, a mother of a student in that group worked in a factory, and he was able to draw from his mother's own experiences. Another design, *Trafficked*, was presented through a moving melancholy song sung in Tagalog and accompanied by an acoustic guitar. This design emphasized the issues of women's bodies being trafficked and exploited. They were also able to make connections to the effects of imperialism on poverty in the Philippines.

One of the thematic threads that was revisited in many of the designs was that of multiple identities and intersectionalities. Like the kimono design, *Layers*, *Breadwinner*, *Versatile*, and *Closer to My I*'s all dealt with the intersections of Asian American women's epistemologies and how they are often playing many roles in the communities they live in. These designs also challenged the notion that Asian American women are passive and submissive. The show came to end with the superheroine design *Your Revolution Will Not Happen Between These Thighs*, pulling together all the *I*'s and expressing the possibility of creating a radical understanding of the Asian American woman's ownership of her destiny.

After the show, the students were excited, but drained. The students felt so compelled to do more to share their stories that they decided to create a class zine, or self-published magazine, to commemorate the experiences of Asian American women. They included their poetry, artwork, and excerpts from the oral herstory papers.

## Reflecting on the *I*'s

It was not until this first fashion show was over that I fully understood its true purpose and possibilities. The Final Project Runway was more than a show to the students, and for some it was more than a service-learning experience; many felt it was an expression of their experiences, their epistemologies, and their engagement in their community. The student outcomes were based on their own words in their reflection papers and their discussions after the show. Through their reflections students expressed the impact of the Final Project Runway, the course, and their learning of the *I*'s. One Filipina student in the class stated the following:

> I think the final Runway Project really brought to life the various situations that women experience. It's another form of learning. Taking the class out of the classroom and creating a project that students can call their own, is important and should be part of the curriculum, in other classes. Often times, teachers are the ones presenting. However, through the Runway Project, the students were the ones who were given the chance to present what they learned throughout the semester. It gives the students ownership of the class. It also gives them a chance to pay tribute to the sacrifices and triumphs of Asian American women.

The students in the class took great ownership of the fashion show, and they were affected not only by what they learned but also by how they learned it. Many students, in their responses to the fashion show, pointed out the empowering nature of the final project. One Asian American male student captured the sentiment of many in the class when he wrote, "It was great seeing Asian women in our class claim negative images and smash them! The imagery presented at the runway showed Asian American women as strong, non-subservient, powerful icons who shape their own history." Not only was the show empowering, it also allowed the students, especially the Asian American women in the course, to "shape their own herstory."

## Appendix

### *Epistemological Pedagogy: Lesson Plans*

*Intersecting Life*

On the first day of class, students are asked to find a partner. One partner is designated as person A and the other is person B. A is instructed to tell B his or her entire life story according to *race* in one minute. Students usually get confused and demand further instructions, but I tell them to "just do it" to simulate the conditions in which they are forced to identify themselves. After person A is finished, B gets a turn, and after both have finished, the class discusses the issues and details that arose. Once a significant list has formed, I then have the students repeat the same exercise beginning with person B. This time they are to tell their story according to the concept of *class*, and these steps are then repeated from the perspective of *gender*. Once all lists have been developed, I add another column called *intersectionality*, and as a class we discuss how the lists of race, class, and gender intersect. Through this exercise, they not only get to know each other, they also begin to see the ways in which we are about to tackle the issues in the course through the lens of intersecting identities.[3]

*Immigration and Imperialism Timelines/Matrix*

In this assignment, students research Asian American women's herstories. Students are placed into random groups, and each group is assigned one or two ethnic groups of Asian American women. They are then given two weeks to collect visual images that represent their assigned group and to prepare a 10-minute creative presentation comparing and contrasting the experiences of the assigned groups that covers the following main themes:

- Homeland Context: Push Factors—What was the status of women prior and as a result of imperialism, colonialism, and war?
- Immigration Policies and Patterns—List the main dates and policies that affected the immigration of the assigned group.
- U.S. Context: Pull Factors—Why did they come to the United States? How does the United States benefit from their immigration?
- Industries, Labor, and Class—What types of work did they participate in? What were their working and living conditions?
- Resources—This is a list of resources about the assigned women's ethnic group. They should include at least one book, one academic article, one magazine or news article, and one Web site. The students must also reference readings from the course.

*Never-Ending Reproductive and Productive Labor*

The main focus of this exercise is the industries Asian American women work in and their roles in the family and in their communities through interdependence.

Students complete a worksheet that looks like the one on p. 39:

**Labor and Family Worksheet**
**When you were 10 years old, who was doing "work" in your household?**

|  | *Women* | *Men* |
|---|---|---|
| **Productive labor for wages** | Type of employment: | Type of employment: |
|  | Hours per week: | Hours per week: |
| **Reproductive labor No wages** | Hours per week: | Hours per week: |
| Cooking |  |  |
| Cleaning |  |  |
| Laundry |  |  |
| Shopping |  |  |
| Disciplining |  |  |
| Emotional support |  |  |
| Helping with homework |  |  |
| Gardening |  |  |
| Paying the bills |  |  |
| Planning for the future |  |  |
| Communicating with extended family |  |  |
| Picking up children from school |  |  |
|  | Total hours of reproductive labor: | Total hours of reproductive labor: |

This is only a partial list of reproductive labor. After the students finish their worksheets, we calculate the total and compare the possible disparity between the work performed by women and men. This exercise also brings out a discussion regarding the notion of work when wages are included and when they are not, along with how we view the value of one's work dependent on wages.

*Birthing Stories*

After they complete the calculations of the work in their own households, I have the students write their birth stories. To prepare, they read the short stories in *Yell-Oh Girls*, edited by Vickie Nam, to give them ideas on how to present the stories of these experiences. I have students interview their mothers or someone who may know the story of their birth. This is an amazing exercise that connects them to their roots and the value of giving birth and motherhood. The students who are comfortable doing so share their stories.

## Performance Pedagogy: Lesson Plans

*Performance Poetry*

To begin this assignment, students are asked to divide a piece of paper into three columns. Each student chooses a woman in his or her own family to write about. They are then instructed to list 5 to 10 words that describe that person in the middle column. They then label the first column as "work," and they list 5 to 10 words that represent the work the woman does both in terms of productive and reproductive labor. After the first two columns are completed, they are asked to label the third column "our relationship." They are then instructed to write 5 to 10 words that describe their relationship with that woman. Here is an example of how the three columns might look:

| Work | Ester | Our relationship |
|---|---|---|
| Cooking | Immigrant | My Mom |
| Cleaning | Strong | Supportive |
| Disciplining | Beautiful | Conflict during teens |

After the columns are completed, they are asked to write a poem based on the three columns. They are often asked to start the poem in class and finish it before the next class.

*Performing Scenarios*

In the discussion on ideologies, issues, and involvement of Asian American women, I give the students scenarios to act out in front of the class. They are to develop a five-minute performance (skit, poetry, dance, music, mime) based on the scenarios I assign them. They are instructed to do the following:

1. Show the *conflict* through a performative art form.
2. Describe the *context* by using three words from the Feminism, Womanism, Pinayism glossary that I hand out.
3. *Connect* the global, local, and personal elements of the scenario.
4. *Create* and *collectivize* alternatives and responses.

The scenarios include issues of sex workers, mail-order brides, overseas contract workers, unplanned pregnancies, suicide, issues between being a feminist and being an Asian American woman, conflict between Asian American women, and class issues.

## *Media Literacy and Visual Art Pedagogy: Lesson Plans*

### *Dragon Ladies, Suzy Wongs, and Lucy Lius*

Each group is assigned movies or images to view outside of class and prepare an analysis of the images of Asian American women using two *I*'s. They then prepare responses to the following questions:

- Explore how an audience of non–Asian Americans may view the image. How do these images play out in real-life situations?

- Explore how an audience of Asian American men may view the image. How do these images play out in real-life situations?

- Explore how an audience of Asian American women may view the image. How do Asian American women internalize media images?

These are a few examples of media I assign to the class:

- *Flower Drum Song: The World of Suzy Wong*, and/or *South Pacific*
- *The Thief of Baghdad, Shanghai Express, Dragon Seed*, and/or *The Good Earth*
- *Heaven and Earth* and *Farewell My Concubine*
- *The Joy Luck Club* and *Mississippi Masala*
- *Wayne's World, Romeo Must Die, Next Friday*
- *Charlie's Angels* (movie) and/or *Shanghai Knights*
- TV shows and other media: MTV, *Music Stars, Grey's Anatomy*, and so on.
- News anchor women and Internet images of Asian American women

*Voodoo Doll Assignment*

Each group is assigned to make a voodoo doll representing an Asian American woman's body image alteration/issue. The students are encouraged to use products, media images, articles, or stories that portray their assigned Asian American woman's body image alteration/issue. Each group has about five minutes to present their doll to the class. The presentation of the doll should give a critical history of the assigned Asian American woman's body image issue. As an example, one group took an Eskinol bottle of skin-lightening potion and used the bottle to construct the doll. They used a magazine photo of a light-skinned Filipina as the head, cotton balls as the legs, and eye makeup applicators as the arms. We had a fruitful discussion on how the idea of "lighter skin" became a standard of beauty in the Philippines because of colonialism and how it continues to be sought after by Filipinos here in the United States.

Students are asked to consider the following in analyzing body alteration/issues:

- History of Asian Women and the Body: Foot binding, covering/clothing of the body, veils/hijabs. How are Asian women's bodies treated in Asia? How has war and imperialism affected how these women's bodies are viewed and treated? How do these practices or treatment continue or change when they are in the United States?
- Size, Weight, and Height: What is acceptable to society? Who is the correct size, weight, and height? Is it different for Asian American women? What is desirable? Why?
- Eating Disorders: Anorexia and bulimia. Bring stats on Asian American women. Why do we do this to our bodies? Is there something specific that forces Asian American women in particular to become anorexic or bulimic?
- Altering Breast Size: Silicone implants, reduction, the history of the bra. What do we desire and why? When did breasts become taboo to show? Why can men show off their chests and women must hide? How is the issue of breast size different for Asian American women?
- Sexuality, Exoticism, and Sensuality: What is the relationship between the Asian American woman's body and her sexuality? How are they exotified? What is the history of orientalism, and how does this relate to how the Asian woman's body is viewed around the world?

- Eye Surgery: "Eye"liner, "eye"lid, "eye"brow. Why? Is it cultural? Is it colonialism? To what lengths do Asian American women go just to pursue beauty? Whose beauty standard affects the pursuit of these surgeries?
- Body Type: Muscular versus feminine: What type of body is most desirable? Are we obsessed with body type? Do we define Asian American women by how their bodies are shaped? Does this affect Asian American women's participation or lack of participation in particular sports?
- Skin Color/Skin-Lightening/Makeup: Phenotype and the beauty myth. Colonialism or culture? What is the beauty myth? Do particular Asian American women view lighter skin as better than darker? Where do these ideas come from?

## Notes

1. Chicano and Latino students combined make up 16.4% of the population, African American students are about 7.1%, and Native Americans make up 1.0%.

2. Pensionadas were Filipinas who came to the United States as colonial government-sponsored scholars. They came to pursue a college education or graduate-level work. The Pensionado Act of 1903 allowed Filipino students to further their education in the United States. The pensionados, both men and women, were from middle-class or wealthy backgrounds.

3. This lesson plan is based on a workshop conducted by Maria Padilla, who at the time was the director of the Academic Advancement Program at UC Berkeley.

## References

Adams, M., Bell, L., & P. Griffin. (Eds.). (1997). *Teaching for diversity and social justice: A sourcebook*. New York: Routledge.

Asian Women United of California. (1989). *Making waves: An anthology of writings by and about Asian American women*. Boston: Beacon Press.

Chang, G. (1997). The global trade in Filipina workers. In S. Shah (Ed.), *Dragon ladies: Asian American feminists breathe fire* (pp. 132–152). Boston: South End Press.

Chow, C. S. (1998). *Leaving deep water: Asian American women at the crossroads of two cultures*. New York: Dutton.

Chow, E. N. (1994). Asian American women at work. In M. B. Zinn & B. T. Dill

(Eds.), *Women of color in U.S. society* (pp. 203–228). Philadelphia: Temple University Press.

deJesus, M. (2005). *Pinay power.* New York: Routledge.

Eviota, E. U. (1992). *The political economy of gender: Women and the sexual division of labour in the Philippines.* London: Zed Books.

Foo, L. J. (2002). *Asian American women: Issues, concerns, and responsive human and civil rights advocacy.* New York: Ford Foundation.

hooks, b. (2000). Rethinking the nature of work. In M. Marable (Ed.), *Feminist theory* (pp. 96–107). Cambridge, MA: South End Press.

Hune, S., & Nomura, G. M. (2003). *Asian/Pacific Islander American women: A historical anthology.* New York: New York University Press.

Matsumoto, V. (1993). *Farming the home place: A Japanese American community in California.* Ithaca, NY: Cornell University Press.

Minh-ha, T. (1990). Not you/like you: Post-colonial women and the interlocking questions of identity and difference. In G. Anzaldúa (Ed.), *Making face, making soul: Haciendo Caras* (pp. 371–375). San Francisco: Aunt Lute Books.

Nair, A. T., & Nakiboglu, H. (2004). Back to the basics: Service learning and the Asian American community. *Journal of Civic Commitment,* (3). Retrieved from http://www.mc.maricopa.edu/other/engagement/Journal/Issue3/Nair.pdf

Nam, V. (2001). *YELL-Oh girls! Emerging voices explore culture, identity, and growing up Asian American.* New York: Quill.

Okihiro, G. (1994). Recentering women. In *Margins and mainstreams: Asians in American history and culture.* Seattle: University of Washington Press.

Parennas, R. (2000). *Servants of globalization.* Stanford, CA: Stanford University Press.

Shah, S. (1997). *Dragon ladies: Asian American feminists breathe fire.* Boston: South End Press.

Shaw, A. (2006). *Possibilities: The critical pedagogy Web site.* Unpublished dissertation, University of Texas, Austin. Retrieved from http://www.21stcenturyschools .com/Possibilities.htm

Takagi, D. (1993). Maiden voyage: Excursion into sexuality and identity politics in Asian America. *Amerasia Journal, 20*(1), 1–17.

Tung, C. (2004). The cost of caring. In L. T. Võ, M. Sciachitano, S. H. Armitage, P. Hart, & K. Weathermon (Eds.), *Asian American women: The frontiers reader* (pp. 178–200). Lincoln: University of Nebraska Press.

Võ, L. T., Sciachitano, M., Armitage, S. H., Hart, P., & Weathermon, K. (2004). *Asian American women: The frontiers reader.* Lincoln: University of Nebraska Press.

# 3

# THE GENDERED MEANING OF DRESS

*Connie Ulasewicz*

The core of my discipline, often described as fashion, clothing, or apparel, requires an understanding of a practice we all participate in on a daily basis, is a topic with great cross-disciplinary implications, and is relevant to many community-based programs. Defining clothing as any covering for the human body, such as a pair of pants, a shirt, or a jacket, seems straightforward and clear. However, when we partake in clothing the body or making decisions on how a body should be clothed, what fit of pants, color of shirt, or style of jacket is appropriate, proper, or necessary, we participate in the activity of dressing. The term *dressing*, or *dress*, is more inclusive than clothing. Dressing includes the total presentation of all body coverings (pants, shirts, jackets) and other accessories such as ties or belts, as well as any modifications to the actual body, such as altering the skin or hair through makeup, tattooing, scarring, cutting, or dyeing (Barnes & Eicher, 1992). Understanding the meaning of dress has relevance in fields as diverse as anthropology, drama, sociology, and business.

People of all ages, ethnicity, gender, and social class wear clothing. But the question remains, how do we engage in the act of dressing? How do we define our age, ethnicity, gender, and social class through our choice of clothing, style of hair, placement of a tattoo, or wearing of makeup? Further, are these really choices or do we feel constrained by our age, ethnicity, gender, and social class to wear a particular color, size, or style? The subject matters of clothing and dress can be taught through lecturing and class discussions, but the real learning occurs when connections are made outside the classroom, with the greater community.

Service learning may be thought of as an experiential approach to learning in that it allows for an active engagement outside the classroom and in the community (Kupiec, 1993). An experiential approach to learning allows for an understanding of a content or discipline at a visceral or even subconscious level. An experiential approach may include active participation in activities outside the traditional classroom, and/or it may also include bringing the outside community into the traditional classroom via presentations, forums, and dialogue. An experiential approach to learning necessitates activities and assessments that allow for a reflective analysis of an experience, an agreement that there will be no one correct answer, and an understanding that learning the content will occur at a pace that will be different from the even pace of a 12-, 14-, or 18-week curriculum.

For me, deliberating the integration of community service activities with educational objectives is foundational to my teaching and research. However, initially I experienced feelings of frustration at the need to classify my pedagogy as one of service learning, as there seemed to be little support for this methodology. As an appreciation for, and an understanding of, the need and benefits to students and communities of community service learning has increased, it now feels good to be a leader of this academic enterprise.

As educators and learners it is our mission not just to teach, but rather to engage students in the active process of learning a subject or a discipline. The premise of this chapter is that pushing the classroom walls outside a building and into the community, permitting assessment to be more reflective than predetermined, and engaging students in the process of learning rather than being taught will be experiential and can be termed service learning. My own bias is that the study of clothing and dress is often trivialized, but its relevance is core to the study of civilizations. This chapter will present a methodological approach for actively participating in the study of dress regardless of the discipline. The focus of this monograph is gender, and at the heart of this chapter are decisions made for and by people regarding dress, gender, and identity. Specific activities and learning guidelines will be discussed, as will student placements in the community and student responses to their experiences.

## Discipline Perspective and Methodology

Fundamental to my perspective of engaging students with service learning, and the intersection of dress and gender, is the Freireian pedagogy that endorses a "problem—posing education [which] affirms men and women as beings in the process of becoming—as unfinished, uncompleted beings in and with the likewise unfinished reality" (Freire, 1921/2000, p. 83). When students actively pursue activities and experiences that foster a reflective analysis of the practice of dressing, their realities change. Pants, a shirt, or a jacket are not studied as merely body coverings but rather as representative of the identity of the wearer who chose them or the organization that prescribed them. The representation is in the single element or combination of the colors, size, and fit of the clothing and the physicality of the person dressing in the clothing. These elements, or signs, carry powerful messages regarding the inherent values of the wearer as well as the group or the institution that prescribes them. Students are specifically asking, how does clothing make meaning, and how is gender communicated or experienced through dress?

An effective methodological lens to study how clothing communicates a gendered identity is one coined by Gottdiener (1995) as "socio-semiotics." The tradition of semiotics stems from a linguistic foundation, concerned with meaning making and representation and can be classified as a branch of the science of communication (Sebeok, 1986). The premise of socio-semiotics is that any cultural object is both an object of use in a social system with a generative history and social context, and also a component in a system of signification (Gottdiener, 1995). Through the socio-semiotic lens, how the body is adorned with particular clothing, hair, or tattoo styles would then be analyzed by defining the social system and the social context in which they are worn to determine their signification. For example, a red T-shirt has no inherent value or meaning, but if worn by a youth today on the streets of many U.S. cities, this T-shirt can signify gang wannabe or gang membership. Because of the potential for mixed messages of certain clothing styles, many middle schools and high schools have dress codes or are mandating uniforms for students. Advocates of dress codes and uniforms argue that dress can shape the behavior and thoughts of wearers and/or perceivers (Lennon, Johnson, & Schultz, 1999).

As clothing is not gendered, it is the act of wearing a particular color, size, or fit on the body within a particular culture, at a particular moment in time that sends the message regarding the gender appropriateness of the individual beneath its folds, or conversely makes the clothing a masculine or feminine style. As Judith Butler (1990) explains, "because gender is not a fact, the various acts of gender create the idea of gender, and without those acts there would be no gender at all (p. 273). The act of dressing and the choices one makes of how to adorn the body will reinforce or cause ambivalence in understanding one's gender. In the 1920s fashionable women wore their hair as short as men did, a notion that caused great ambiguity while reinforcing a new feminine identity. Because short hair was associated with men, were the women wearing short hair taking on the "manly traits" of decision maker or independent thinker?

The basis of socio-semiotics is polysemy, meaning a single sign can convey multiple meanings. The meaning or significance of wearing a red T-shirt will be different based on the age and possibly race or geographic location of the wearer. The objective for my students is to analyze clothing and its relationship to defining and contributing to a gendered identity through this semiotic lens—semiotic in that the colors, patterns, shape, and fit of individual articles of clothing and the way they are worn together are signs of, in this case, the gendered beliefs of practices of a culture.

## Courses, Learning Objectives, Exercises

The semiotic methodology can be used to interpret gendered dress practices at any point throughout the academic career in many varied disciplines. As aforementioned, I believe that as educators, our role is to create lifelong learners, and I enforce this idea by thinking of my curriculum as expanding across the students' entire college careers and lives. For majors, I will introduce the Freireian pedagogy and socio-semiotic methodology early in their academic careers with the hope that by the time they graduate they will have integrated the concepts into their ways of being. As introductory courses tend to enroll greater numbers of students, in these classes students are exposed to a variety of activities and community agencies. They learn of service-learning possibilities and how they, as students, are connected to the community. As students advance in their programs, fulfill internship requirements, and are exposed to community organizations, they are more likely to feel comfortable looking for and working within the communities to meet their hour requirements.

I also have felt tremendous gratitude from students who are exposed to presentations regarding my community-based research early in their academic careers and who, when we are together for other classes, ask me to update them on new research developments. Their requests validate my belief that as educators our research styles and practices must be integrated into our teaching practices. We become role models of civic engagement; our activities spark interest and can become the link to student involvement in the community. The following section contains exercises and activities integrated into my curriculum for a large lecture-style class and internship class.

## Lecture-Style Class Activities and Feedback

The creative activities that follow were developed for general elective courses for upper-division majors and nonmajors. They are used in our social psychology of dress class titled Fashion, Clothing, and Society that generally enrolls over 100 students each semester. As using the socio-semiotic methodology to understand dress and gender is new to many students, these foundational discussions and activities are helpful to focus on how gender is consciously and unconsciously expressed through the nonverbal communication tool of clothing and dress. The goal is to unite the abstract world of theory presented in the text or assigned readings with the unique experiences of students from a cross-section of the university.

### Learning Activity 1

This exercise (see Appendix A) is an interactive, information-gathering group activity that arouses curiosity and much lively debate on the topic of gender and dress. Sources used include readings from the class textbook, magazines, newspapers, Web sites, blogs, and personal photographs. The *objective* is for students to choose images of everyday dressed people representative of different ages, genders, cultures, or ethnicities. The conversation will move into topics of fashion, race, gender identity, and class differences, which are all terrific points of departure for further exploration and analysis. Students speak of stereotypic judgments or assumptions regarding what a particular color, fit, or style of clothing represents. It is generally during this exercise that we develop a working understanding and definition of gender as a concept that is socially created and reconstructed. Students begin to view clothing as a tool or nonverbal communicative device that assists or confuses the process of gender construction. By using the semiotic lens, the way the body is dressed can easily be broken down into visual signs (color, shape, fit, style) and analyzed. The pictures assist, as they are representative of the cultures and periods of time they illustrate. After this exercise, students' understanding of the concepts range among curiosity, intrigue, and true clarity, but all are primed for more reflective analysis.

*Learning Activity 2*

Exercise 2 (see Appendix B) was developed to allow students the opportunity to delve within and think more personally about how they create their gendered identities and to speculate where in their socialization process their gendered practices began. As the focus is on the specific visual signs or clothing tools used, often pictures are found and family or friends participate in the process. Memories surface regarding what they had to wear to participate in certain social activities. Journaling, when diligently followed, allows students to notice patterns in their participation of dressing.

Class discussion erupts the day of journal turn-in with a perfect forum for total engagement in the topic of the gendered meaning of dress. The understanding is at a much deeper level than after Exercise 1 because of the personal involvement of reflective analysis. One spring semester on this day the weather was unusually hot; the discussion focused on why none of the males in the class were wearing shorts and a majority of the females donned shorts or skirts. A consensus was reached that the males felt their calves were not in good enough shape and they were self-conscious about not appearing "manly" enough, hence pants were a body covering to conceal. After Exercises 1 and 2 students broadened their semiotic lenses with a greater appreciation for the relationship between dress and the construction of gender ideas and were ready to venture outside the classroom.

*Learning Activity 3*

Exercise 3 (see Appendix C) was developed as a platform to engage students with my community-based research. My work has been in a juvenile justice facility in San Mateo County where I am studying how the dress of the girls can be changed or altered to allow them to be perceived and to feel more like girls. I was invited to the facility to conduct informal interviews about the uniforms currently worn by the girls residing there and to determine whether they met the girls' developmental needs and whether they assisted the institution in its rehabilitative goals. The study was preliminary to a redesign of the uniform. At another level, the study was to explore how the facility's uniforms communicated the cultural reality of detainment in the juvenile justice facility to the girls and the staff the girls interacted with daily.

At the time of my initial study the girls' uniform consisted of a bright orange short-sleeved, cotton T-shirt; white sports bra and cotton underpants; royal blue cotton pants or nylon shorts with elastic waistband; a maroon cotton and polyester sweatshirt; white socks; and black sneakers fastened by hook-and-eye closures. Printed with black letters on the back of the T-shirts, sweatshirts, and underpants were the name of the institution and the size of the clothing. The T-shirts, sweatshirts, and pants were oversized, most girls wearing what was labeled large or extra large regardless of body size. The same T-shirts and sweatshirts were worn by the boys and girls, the color being their primary difference. The fit and sizing were actually based on male measurements, as with most serviceable institutional clothing. As my work evolves, presentations about it evolve to include changes made to the uniform based on current findings.

My presentation initiates an awareness of the relevance of gendered clothing practices that exist in the real world. Exercise 3 was developed as a method in a class with a large enrollment to integrate the community into the classroom, to mediate the intellectual and personal reflections of students as they try to make meaning of the community they have entered. Some students enhanced the community activity by offering to work with me on a self-esteem project currently under development in the new girl's program at the aforementioned juvenile justice facility. Students were permitted entry to assist me in the planned activity of working with the girls living in the juvenile hall, as they wrote and designed positive affirmations or sayings with pictures of animals, butterflies, or other nongang-related objects on nightshirts. The overall objective was to allow the girls on the unit (doing time in the juvenile justice facility) to wear gender-specific nightshirts, with their original artwork drawn on the front. The following reflection describes how one of the students experienced this community activity:

> One girl told me she had only been there [at the facility] for a short time and was angry because she asked the supervisors every day what was going to happen to her, how long she'd be in there, and they couldn't give her

an answer, so her sketch for the nightgown design reflected her anger, and then we talked and created a more positive outlook, she reflected on her mother and God for her nightgown in the end.

Another girl designed her nightgown with lots of slang, which I didn't see the problem with because it was of a positive language, but she was told to revise it and then I understood the reason and the purpose for the revision. Gang-related slang was not permitted. I learned so much in such a short time about the teaching and advising of young girls through designing a nightgown.

I could go on and on about each girl and their individual impact they had on me.

Those creative minds hopefully will continue to participate in artistic expression.

The following reflection from an international student clearly expresses how enriching this design activity was for her:

During the activities, I thought [the] girls were having a good time. Some of the girls were very creative and artistic; some of them were just hoping the time to go over [would go by]. Many of them were interested in Chinese or Japanese characters. They asked me to draw characters on their shirts and I was pretty happy about that. I remember when I was in high school in Oregon, my friends used to ask me [the] same things and I wrote characters for them on a paper or sometimes on their skins. In Oregon where there were no Asian people around and [the same for] girls in [the] Juvenile halls, they do not know much about other countries, especially Asian countries, so it was new and exciting for them to see different things that they have never known. One girl was really surprised at how different Japanese is compared to English, and she was so amazed that I can [could] speak [it]. I was glad that I became one of the people to tell about different cultures to open up their view of the world.

Another student reflected on a similar feeling of pleasure related to sharing cultural heritage:

Actually a table of girls I was helping happened to be Hispanic and they asked if I spoke Spanish. Once I told them I did they really felt comfortable and opened up. One girl asked if I lived on my own, what school I went to, and if I liked school. She was really impressed that I happened to be the same nationality as her and accomplish all these things.

## Internship Class Activities and Feedback

The opportunities for students to engage in the community using a socio-semiotic methodology are many, as it opens them to analyze how cultural meanings are produced and conveyed in the social realm. The focus of this section is to share representative feedback from students engaged in internships where the knowledge and understanding of dressing the body in gender-appropriate clothing were central to the student interaction.

Many communities in the United States have organizations, clothing banks, or clothing closets that provide clothing for the financially challenged or underprivileged community. One such agency is the intern site many senior students choose, rather than a traditional specialty or department store, to experience retail merchandising skills and giving back to the community. A core value of many clothing banks is to provide clothing for women and men that will make them feel better and raise their self-esteem when they go for a job interview or reenter the work force. The appropriateness of the clothing is often based on the traditional gender norms. For the male it's a solid blue, white, or tan button-down collared shirt, striped or patterned tie, double-pleated fly-front pant, and single-breasted jacket that matches or contrasts with the pants, belt, and shoes. For the female, the shirt is called a blouse that may be patterned or a bright color and generally has a round neck with no collar, may include a scarf, a pair of pants or a skirt, nylons or tights, belt or no belt, and shoes. The actual styles chosen will depend on two factors: the ideas, values, and opinions of the dresser or store associate and the individual being dressed. It is a common practice at these organizations for the individual being dressed to rely on the suggestions and encouragement of the sales associates, in this case the students.

During an experience such as that described, where students participate in activities for an extended period of time, they develop a greater appreciation for the people/clients/shoppers and themselves. After engaging in community service-learning experiences for a required 120 hours over the course of a 16-week semester, students were asked to reflect on their experiences concerning decisions regarding dress from the socio-semiotic perspective. The following responses are a representative sampling of their reflections:

> You think you are just helping the person by giving them clothing and tips on how to care for themselves, but they become more confident with your help. You are helping them get their life back together and for that they

are very grateful. We get a lot of people who call or write and let us know how they are doing and if they got the job.

Most customers feel happy from what they buy in the store, especially they feel great with spending not too much money, but they have a lot of clothing. Sometimes, customers like to hear my opinions on style, color matching. I like to help them when they have difficulty on choosing color or the length of skirt or matching accessories.

As far as [male] clients are concerned we almost always dressed them in suits or slacks, a dress shirt and always a tie. We were trying to emphasize how important it was to look clean and professional for an interview.

Often we have international students in our classes whose reflections offer an insight from a cultural perspective. For these students an internship offers them a unique university experience, for they cannot work in the United States because of their visa status. This first reflection is from a student from Japan, and the second a student from Hong Kong:

I felt a lot of social and economical class differences that the United States has. I did not feel that I was helping [the] community but helping certain customers. Some or most of the customers are [the] same all the time. I felt those customers rely on us, and they are having [a] good time shopping there. The more I [came] to know more people, they recognize[d] me as well.

Sometimes, customers like to hear my opinions on style, color matching. For instance, one of our customers came and shopped, she told us that she [had] got an interview [a] couple [of] days later, so she had to find some clothing for that interview. I asked her what kind of job that she was going to do and what kind of interview that she had to attend. I tried to get more information about her interview; [and] then we gave our suggestion[s] to her. I help[ed] her to pick her clothing. She was very happy from our opinions and suggestion[s]. We all hope that she could get the job finally. I feel really happy to help people in that way, especially the customers [that] listened [to] our suggestion and opinions.

The excitement, value, and true learning of these experiences are so evident from these reflections. Students practice the problem-posing education, endorsed by Paulo Freire (1921/2000), and the following reflections give credence to their participation in the process of being. It would not be possible to replicate these experiences in a traditional classroom:

> Working for a nonprofit organization meant interacting with a segment of the public that I had not previously worked with or knew much about. Experiencing the bigger picture is what motivated me and kept me going, I thought about it with each client that came in. I loved when you saw their excitement and their hope at starting new.

> I learned how to talk to all different kinds of people, how to convince them and how to deal with difficult questions and people. I have a positive impression [of] volunteer work, so I am willing to do more of [it].

> This experience was a great challenge in my life. I liked working with all sorts of people and helping them achieve a certain look, like if they wanted an outfit for an interview. You really do care about their well-being and hope they make it in life.

Upon my reflection, the true value of learning resounds in these students' reflections. If as Cone and Harris (2003) stated our role as educators is to help our students understand their role as interpreters of culture, why do more of us not engage fully in the community? Possibly the real fear keeping more faculty members from community-based or service-learning pedagogy is assessment.

## The Challenge of Assessment

The task of choosing the best assessment tool for a learning outcome can be daunting, yet it is one that needs to be addressed each semester with a new course or syllabus. Consideration about how best to measure changes in academic knowledge, content learning, or civic/personal skills through the process of service learning is critical. As Sherril Gelmon (2002) explains, assessment provides a valuable mechanism for communicating what the student has learned through the course work and service-learning component or activity. I find the process of assessing service-learning activities has been a pedagogical shift. It necessitates students taking an active roll in the learning process and creates openness for me to accept what can sometimes feel like a lack of control. I no longer set the pace or the specific expectations for a directed outcome. I have less success managing this feeling when the class size is large, or when there is much factual content that needs to be covered. Honestly, as a nontenured assistant professor, the core of the nervousness is the fear that the students will not learn the required curriculum in the given time to meet the course objectives. Further, without a test, how will my assessment of their learning be valued by my peers and evaluators?

As service learning gains momentum on my campus, and administrators support students exploring academic and civic learning through community involvement associated with their course work, my fear of assessing the learning from this pedagogy is diminishing. My greatest challenge is to allow others, community members and students, to actively engage in the planning of the curriculum and contribute their ideas for assessment. For example, the supervisor of the juvenile justice facility shared the following comments with me regarding the self-esteem nightgown project implemented at the facility:

> They [the nightshirts] are making a tremendous difference. Usually I hear complaints from staff regarding the girls wearing inappropriate clothing to bed or they are uncomfortable with wearing the thin, issued gowns to bed. I have heard none of these issues; the shirts and drawings clearly make a difference. When can we do this again?

These remarks are so satisfying and inspirational; clothing was the tool or platform for the learning process and gender-specific practice.

The activities and student reflections presented are intended to inspire and instill a relevancy in the learning of gendered practices. Decisions are made by and for people daily regarding how we/they dress with conscious or subconscious understanding of clothing's gendered meaning. Studying clothing and dress practices and their relationship to gender through the socio-semiotic lens provides a rich context for learning. As students become more civically engaged within the context of the university experience, their realities are changed, as are ours, and the true value of experiential learning is understood.

## Appendix A

### Learning Activity 1

*Developing the Socio-Semiotic Lens*

The purpose of this activity is to stimulate thought and discussion regarding clothing and gender through a socio-semiotic lens. Pictures from magazines, books, or your own personal photos will be analyzed to postulate if there is/are any identifiers from clothing (e.g., size, shape, or color) that signify gender.

The Objectives

- To share ideas and discuss with group members if there are gendered norms for dress in different cultures and give examples of what they might be
- To identify specific clothing identifiers or styles of clothing worn by men or women, girls or boys in different cultures, of different ages, in various activities that signify gender

The Activity

1. Bring to class 8 to 10 dressed images of people from catalogs, magazines, Web sites, or your own photographs. To make the images appear more gender neutral, remove or cover the head, hands, or feet.
2. Working in small groups, try to determine which images are representative of a male and a female. Specifically, what are the clothing signs/identifiers (e.g., size, shape, color), and what do they signify? What are the similarities and differences in different cultures and age categories? How have some of the "rules" of dress and gender changed over the past 5 to 10 years?
3. Each group will pick one spokesperson and present its findings to the class.

## Appendix B

### *Learning Activity 2*

#### Gender Expectations

The purpose of this activity is to broaden your awareness of how and when you use clothing to define your gender and to analyze on what basis you make your decisions.

The Objectives

- To reflect on the relationship between clothing and dress on a personal level

- To be able to identify gender-clothing norms that you participate in and reflect on what you feel they are based on (e.g., your race/ethnicity, culture, family, religion, friends) and to develop an appreciation for gendered norms across your life span

The Activity

1. For two weeks keep a daily journal of how you dress. Mark the entries by day (e.g., Week 1 Monday, Tuesday . . .). List the social activity (e.g., out with friends) and a full description of how you dress (e.g., washed hair, spent time making it look good, shaved, put on lotion, black Nine Inch Nails T-shirt, tight black jeans, Batman buckle, black socks, new black/brown Vans, hooded gray zip-up sweatshirt). Describe what gender significance it has (e.g., I want to look good for me because of who I am, not this guy-girl thing. But, it is the tightness of the clothes, like the pants I wear, that may be considered more feminine or Emo. But hey, we are going to listen to some friends play music and I feel good.). You may include pictures, sketches, and so on in your journal. You may hand write and paste in entries.

2. At the end of the two weeks, write a two- to three-page reflection of the activity. Read back over your entries, think about your entries and reflect on each of the following questions. Your reflective paper must be typed.

   - Are your gender dress decisions based more on your family beliefs? Religious beliefs? Race/ethnic beliefs? Cultural beliefs? Personal interests? Marketing campaigns? Friends? How have they changed throughout your life?
   - When participating in what social activities do you make the most dress decisions based on gender?

## Appendix C

### *Learning Activity 3*

*Community Activity*

The purpose of this activity is to understand how institutions in the community (e.g., banks, schools, retail stores, clothing manufacturers, business, hospitals, jails) use clothing and dress to define gender within their business practice/organization.

The Objectives

- To identify how dress is used by organizations and businesses in society
- To understand how gender-dress practices reinforce gendered norms

The Activity

1. Identify a local community organization/business and investigate (e.g., collect pictures, speak with people, research the history of the organization) and research what the expectations or dress codes are for the volunteers/employees/members.
2. Use your socio-semiotic lens and describe the specific articles of clothing or types of dress that are acceptable for men and women. Are there different requirements based on gender?
3. Speak to as many people as you can in the organization to understand from their perspective the meaning of dress in their organization.
4. Reflect on your findings. Do the gender dress practices reinforce gendered norms? Why or why not? Document your findings through a written, drawn, or verbal presentation.

## References

Barnes, R., & Eicher, J. (Eds.). (1992). *Dress and gender: Making and meaning in cultural contexts*. New York: Berg.

Butler, J. (1990). Performative act and gender constitution: An essay in phenomenology and feminist theory. In S. E. Case (Ed.), *Performing feminism: Feminist critical theory and theatre* (pp. 270–281). Baltimore: Johns Hopkins Press.

Cone, D., & Harris, S. (2003). Service learning practice: Developing a theoretical framework. In *Introduction to service learning toolkit* (pp. 27–39). Providence, RI: Campus Compact.

Freire, P. (2000). *Pedagogy of the oppressed* (M. B. Ramos, Trans.). New York: Continuum. (Original work published 1921)

Gelman, S. B. (2001). How do we know that our work makes a difference? In *Introduction to service learning toolkit* (pp. 231–240). Providence, RI: Campus Compact.

Gottdiener, M. (1995). *Postmodern semiotics.* Cambridge, NY: Blackwell.

Kupiec, T. (Ed.). (1993). *Rethinking tradition: Integrating service with academic study on campus.* Providence, RI: Campus Compact.

Lennon, S. J., Johnson, K. K., & Schultz, T. L. (1999). Forging linkages between dress and the law in the U.S. Part II: Dress codes. *Clothing and Textiles Research Journal, 17*(3), 157–167.

Sebeok, T. A. (1986). The semiotic web: A chronicle of prejudices. In J. Deely, B. Williams, & F. E. Kruse (Eds.), *Frontiers in semiotics* (pp. 35–42). Bloomington: Indiana University Press.

Ulasewicz, C. (2004). *Uni/form: Social control and acculturation in a juvenile justice facility.* Unpublished doctoral dissertation, Fielding Graduate University, Santa Barbara, CA.

# SECTION TWO

## THE SOCIAL CONSTRUCTION OF GENDER IN AN EDUCATIONAL SETTING

# EXAMINING GENDER AND CLASSROOM TEACHING PRACTICES

*Sherrie Carinci*

O ur country's future educators are being trained in classroom management techniques, developing teaching strategies, and understanding the pedagogical style that will work best in the classroom. However, it is this author's opinion that educators are not entering the classroom prepared to teach using gender-equitable teaching approaches.

Though there is minimal research on the subject of teacher preparation related to gender-equitable pedagogy, there is a long history of findings of gender inequalities in the classroom. Most of the past research has focused on the disadvantages experienced by girls. However, recent reports have indicated that males in schools are also at risk of being academically neglected and may suffer from various forms of emotional trauma within the school environment (Tyre, 2006). It is the position of this author that males' engagement in school curriculum, issues of bullying, and high dropout rates should be acknowledged. But these challenges for boys in school are not new, especially for boys of color. The "boy crisis" has been an ongoing problem for boys for decades. It is important that the attention being paid to males and education does not distract from the continuing educational challenges facing females. As this chapter will clarify, gender inequities still exist in today's classroom for females in teachers' interaction patterns with students, in the lack of females represented in school curricula, and in issues of harassment and bullying affecting girls on school campuses. The discussion of gender, both female and male, needs to be paramount when training future teachers. Though this chapter addresses the issues of females, both males and females could benefit from gender-fair teaching approaches explored here.

Current research suggests that nominal training is being offered to kindergarten through 12th grade educators on gender-equitable teaching approaches, and most teachers are not aware nor have the training on the importance of gender inclusion methodologies and their impact on the learner (Carinci, 2002; Sanders, 2002). Because of the lack of training on equitable approaches, educators are not prepared to make the needed changes in methods of assessments, curricula choices, interaction patterns, or teaching strategies that would foster a gender-equitable learning environment.

Research indicates that, when teachers are given instruction on equity issues, the material usually focuses on stereotypes, interaction patterns, and the underrepresentation of females in math and science curricula (American Association of University Women [AAUW], 1999). What is absent from teacher training are practical solutions to gender bias and methods to make the classroom more equitable (AAUW, 1999; Campbell & Sanders, 1997; Sanders, 2002). The lack of attention to or absence of gender-equity training being provided at all levels of education to faculty indicates there is a need for the topic to be addressed in the university class setting.

With the research presented in this chapter and the suggested experiential learning activities, it is hoped that students will be able to recognize and critically examine the development of the individual as an integrated physiological, psychological, and social being with regard to the gender dynamics that permeate today's classrooms. In addition, this chapter will illustrate how experiential learning pedagogy can provide insight into how an inequitable class experience can affect a student's personal life choices that can have an impact on decisions, such as choice of a college major and/or career.

Numerous courses in most universities address gender equity and/or women's studies pedagogies in various ways. The course that is the inspiration for this chapter is titled Sex-Role Stereotyping in American Education. This general education undergraduate course addresses the life-span effects of gender stereotyping, with specific attention to the gender experience of students (kindergarten to college) and how education influences future career choices. The course offers several experiential and observational opportunities to help foster the understanding and real-life consequences of gender inequities in the classroom.

The uniqueness of this course is that it examines the social construct of gender throughout our educational system and its impact on the learner. One goal of the course is to raise the consciousness of students by having them examine teaching methodology in regard to gender inclusion in course curricula. It is important that students are aware that teachers bring their own bias toward gender into their teaching and interaction patterns with students. The experiences of students in the course support the importance of the students' "seeing themselves" in curriculum areas such as curriculum content, instruction methods, and faculty–student and student–student interaction patterns in the classroom.

Sex-Role Stereotyping can serve as an instructional model for faculty who wish to offer students the opportunity to engage in a discussion, supported by research, on the impact and importance of gender inclusion of teaching practices that can help empower students to be change agents of their own learning. The model presented in this chapter outlines the factors necessary to study gender and its impact on the learner. To do so, it is necessary to incorporate the following in the class curriculum: Examine how past and present school curriculum choices may have influenced a student's individual behavior and life choices based on gender assumptions, identify gender stereotyping in the classroom and discuss the effects on the learner, critically analyze how gender affects a student's university career path and higher-learning educational choices, and identify and examine a student's own career choice based on society's beliefs of appropriate gender roles in the workplace.

In order to have a gender-equitable classroom many researchers refer to the idea of "connecting" to the curriculum, which encourages a phenomenological definition of objectivity that honors the feminine experience within the traditional male pedagogy. "Objectivity, in connected teaching, as in connected knowing, means seeing the other, the student, in the student's own terms" (Belenky, Clinchy, Goldberger, & Tarule, 1997, p. 224). This chapter examines research and educational concepts that support the constructs of the connected classroom (Noddings, 1984) and its impact on the learner. Numerous educational scholars acknowledge that many women are plagued with feelings of self-doubt, "confirming women's own sense of themselves as inadequate knowers" (Belenky et al., p. 224). It is the goal of this chapter to examine and promote a discussion pertaining to students who perceive themselves to be limited by presubscribed gender expectations that are too often supported, rather than remedied, by current university teaching methodologies.

## Gender Inclusion and the Classroom Instruction

Several primary quantitative and qualitative studies have determined that there are inequities that occur in the American classroom at all levels of education (Sadker, 1999, 2002; Sadker & Sadker, 1994; Sadker, Sadker, & Klein, 1991). Sadker, Sadker, & Long (1989) concluded that there are significant drops in self-esteem and levels of achievement motivation for the female learner once she enters middle school. The inequities for the female students are perpetuated by instruction methods, curriculum context, and classroom interaction patterns. Research by Sadker (2002) concludes that "females have fewer contacts with instructors in class. They are less likely be called on by name, are asked fewer complex and abstract questions, receive less praise or constructive feedback, and are given less direction on how to do things for themselves" (p. 238). In the same study, Sadker determined that, although women are entering college in record numbers, "women and men are following very different career paths with very different economic consequences. Although the majority of college students are female, the college culture is strongly influenced by male leaders" (p. 239).

## Gender Equity and Curriculum

### Formal Curriculum

The implementation of gender-equitable approaches is introduced through two aspects of a curriculum. The AAUW (1992) report *How Schools Shortchange Girls* stated that gender equity can be implemented through formal curriculum offered by schools and classroom curriculum (p. 60). Formal curriculum is defined by the AAUW as the content of curriculum materials offered in the academic setting. In many cases, the formal curriculum is the material that schools or districts require teachers to cover in a particular discipline. Unfortunately, sexism still exists in many schools' formal curriculum through the omission of female experiences, gender stereotyping of both sexes, and tokenism. The AAUW report (1992) summarized the impact of formal curriculum stating:

Formal curriculum is the central message-giving instrument of the school. It can strengthen or decrease student motivation for engagement, effort, growth, and development through the messages it delivers to students about themselves and the world. Curricular materials that do not reflect the diversity of students' lives and culture provide incomplete and inaccurate messages. (p. 60)

Formal curriculum includes various forms of instructional resources, such as textbooks, computer instruction, and methods of assessment. A study by the AAUW (1999), *Gender Gaps*, indicated that:

While textbooks have become more gender-conscious in recent years, many still place female characters in stereotypical roles that reinforce biases. At the same time, computer technology is a seductive classroom resource, but one that involves a gender imbalance favoring boys in experience, use, course taking, and interest. Consequently, technology may exacerbate rather than diminish inequities by gender as it becomes more integral to the curriculum. (p. 59)

## Classroom as Curriculum

As important as formal curriculum is in the academic structure of education, it is not the only means for students to enrich their learning. What students experience in the classroom can be just as important as the formal material presented to them. *How Schools Shortchange Girls* defined classroom curriculum as "meaning the ways in which materials are taught" (p. 60). Not only do faculty play a central role in exposing students to a wide variety of ideas, concepts, and beliefs that are not necessarily covered by the formal curriculum, but the manner in which faculty present material is also central to the students' learning experience. Unfortunately, many faculties are not aware of the subtle gender inequities that take place inside the classroom, both in the material presented and in the behavior of the instructors.

In considering the effect of material on gender bias, instructors are influential in curriculum efforts toward gender equity through the choices of books, course materials, and the classroom structure used in their classrooms (AAUW, 1992; Campbell, 2004; Owens, Smothers, & Love, 2003; Sadker & Sadker, 1994). Females are not seen as main characters, their names are not used in titles, their pictures are not shown in illustrations, and they are featured less often as active doers.

Historically, textbooks show females in roles that are "less exciting, less problem solving, and less involved in life than the roles for males" (Levine & Orenstein, 1994, p. 4). Male preference in school curriculum begins as soon as students enter the classroom. Male preference, though subtle, is often seen in curriculum choices of the instructor. Goss (1996) indicated that even teachers show a preference to male-centered books, stating:

> Elementary teachers who were asked to list their favorite books to read aloud to children reported more books about males than about females, only 21% of which contained a female protagonist. The ten most popular book choices by these elementary teachers included an even smaller proportion of female characters, as eight of these books had a male protagonist, and only one had a sole female protagonist. (p. 4)

Goss implied that a percentage of teachers, when choosing books, prefer books with a male-centered story line. Her study demonstrated that teachers may have an unconscious preference for male-centered books in their classroom. This unconscious preference for male-centered books results in teachers not offering equal female role models to the female students. Campbell (2004) wrote "students seem to develop self-esteem and a sense of being socially centered when they see their role models in books and in other educational material" (p. 137). Though improvements are being made in gender role images in books, studies find that school curricula offer more male role models for male students and that teachers prefer male-centered stories. The preference to males as the model student continues on into the university classroom, and in some disciplines females are barely visible in the course content and/or curriculum.

The method of instruction is also a critical issue when discussing equity in the classroom. Sadker, Sadker, and Long (1989) stated, "When researchers looked at lecture versus laboratory classes, they found that in lecture classes teachers asked males academically-related questions about 80 percent more often than they questioned females; the patterns were mixed in laboratory classes" (p. 121). This research is significant because many of today's classrooms are taught using a lecture format as the main method of instruction. The AAUW (1999) has determined, "Few classrooms foster 'connected learning,' nor are the majority of classrooms designed to encourage cooperative behaviors and collaborative efforts" (p. 72). Many high school and university classrooms, frequently accommodating a large number of students, do little to foster the collaborative classroom where some students would benefit academically from the connections with faculty and peers.

## Gender Equity Concerns in the Classroom

### Faculty Interactions Patterns With Students

Various researchers have noted that males and females do not receive the same education in schools. Sadker and Sadker (1994) have studied the problem of gender bias in schools and reported that "teachers interact with males more frequently, ask probing questions, give them more precise and helpful feedback" (p. 45). The cumulative effect of this behavior takes a measurable and destructive toll on the students, especially the female students. Other research indicates favoritism toward males when calling on students (AAUW, 1999; Owens et al., 2003). Researcher Dianne Horgan (1995) summarized the effects of instructors' failing to give feedback to females, stating:

> Teachers often fail to give direct feedback or criticism because they don't want to hurt their feelings or discourage them. But protective attitudes like this often backfire: If girls don't receive feedback in elementary school, they don't learn to respond to criticism. (p. 48)

Part of the reason for the different treatment of males and females is the notion that males need to be called on more in order to keep them engaged. This classroom management technique starts in preschool, becomes a habit of teachers that pervades kindergarten through 12th grade, and continues into the university classrooms (Block, 1984). Studies have found that teachers actually "teach" males more than they "teach" females, with males twice as likely to receive individual instruction (Horgan, 1995; Jones Evans, Byrd, & Campbell, 2000; Lips, 1989; Serbin & Connor, 1981).

In the typical classroom environment, boys receive more of the teachers' attention by being disruptive, and often when girls do receive the teachers' attention it is for being "good" (well behaved, rule following, and quiet). This behavior in females fosters what Dweck (1977) called "a learned helplessness" (p. 45) that is seen in the classroom. Researchers have also used a similar concept, the "silenced voice," when referring to females who lack confidence and have a low sense of self because of their voices not being heard in the classroom and society (Brown & Gilligan, 1992; Fine, 1993; Gilligan, 1982). A study by Duffy, Warren, and Walsh (2001) examined teacher's interaction patterns with 597 high school students. Thirty-six math and literature/language teachers were observed for their classroom interaction patterns with students. This study determined that the majority of teachers in the study initiated significantly more interactions with male students than with female students.

Because of gender socialization patterns that exist in our society, instructors have different expectations for females and males. Various classroom studies have shown that instructors are more likely to allow males to talk more and to interrupt classroom instruction than they are for females to engage in the same behaviors (AAUW, 1992; Orenstein, 1994; Sadker & Sadker, 1994). From these interruptions, more time is spent answering the males' questions than the females' questions, and, more important, students learn that the male voice and concerns take first priority in the classroom (Block, 1984; Duffy, 2002; Lips, 1989). D'Ambrosio and Hammer (1996) studied 41 Catholic elementary schools and concluded that in teacher–student interaction, male students receive more praise, acceptance, remediation, and criticism. Other studies echoed similar findings in "gender domination" and embedded discrimination based on gender in numerous classrooms (Bendixen-Noe & Hall, 1996; Lee, 1997).

### Student to Student Interaction

When studying gender issues in the classroom, it is important that educators are aware of the gender dynamics between female and male students. Research by the AAUW (1992) stated that the use of cooperative groups helps female students become more engaged in the class curriculum and discussion. Campbell (2000), in support of cooperative learning as a teaching tool, stated, "Cooperative learning helps teachers to deal with the societal problems of racism and sexism. It provides excellent strategies for directly working against different forms of prejudice" (p. 265). However, when implementing cooperative learning methods in the classroom, gender dynamics between students need to be addressed. Studies cited by the AAUW (1992) indicated that, when placed in mixed-sex groups, males will respond more often to other males; females, however, will respond equally to both sexes, not showing a preference for males or females in mixed-group interactions.

Block (1984) stated that females are also more helpful and concerned about the welfare of the group, and males are typically more concerned about competition and individual success. The California Department of Education, Office of Gender Equity (1992), stated:

> The educational implications of the play group structure for girls is to foster interpersonal skills transferable to one-on-one or small group situations only. However, boys' play group structure enforces both leadership and followership skills transferable to achievement and work domains. (p. 2)

With the lack of proper training on gender dynamics between students, the goals of an equitable classroom and a fair environment for all students to learn is weakened. Noddings (1992) suggested that, when educators employ cooperative instructional practices in the classroom, all students will feel they have an opportunity to learn. Noddings (1992) also concluded that with cooperative groups in schools students will learn to contribute to a more democratic society.

The use of cooperative learning may be incorporated in many classrooms, but little training is being given on gender dynamics once students are placed in small groups. Faculty should be aware of the role gender plays once students are placed in cooperative learning groups and should be proactive in addressing inequities. Research suggests that male students are often given the lead role or the position of power within group interactions (Edwards, 2004; Tannen, 1994). This position of power is demonstrated in who is more influential in the decision making of the group and/or represents the group's finding to the instructor or the class. Because of gender socialization patterns set in our society, male students often listen to and acknowledge the contributions of other males in the groups, frequently leaving female students as bystanders in the cooperative group interactions. Females are often given the role of secretary (note taker) of the group. Hence the gender role division affects the benefits of the cooperative-learning group experience.

Though cooperative groups can be beneficial to promoting community and inclusion in a classroom, the process in which the groups are created can also have a gender slant. Faculty must be cognizant that, once groups are assigned, the male position of power does not dominate the group activity. Faculty will often use a variety of methods to assign students to cooperative learning groups (counting off numbers, personal interest, content related). The danger arises that one student (frequently male) becomes the accommodatee and another student (frequently female) becomes the accommodator. The accommodator/accommodatee practice can be observed when students physically move to the assigned group in the classroom—the female students become the accommodators by literally moving to the location in the room of the dominant, often male, member of the group. It is more common to see female students move to the male students in cooperative learning settings.

Many factors contribute to this unconscious or perhaps conscious inter-action in the classroom. Research suggests that within our society females are socialized to be nice, follow rules, and foster harmony—behaviors that could play a role in this classroom interaction pattern (Brown & Gilligan, 1992; Campbell, 2004; 1992; Orenstein, 1994; Pipher, 1994). Gender dynamics of the cooperative group experience in the classroom are very subtle but can add to an inequitable learning environment. Even the most well-intentioned teach-ers will often miss subtle acts of inequity in the cooperative learning experi-ence. What the male student learns early on and what is often reinforced throughout years of classroom interactions is that by his sheer maleness, he has more rights and voice in the classroom, even within a cooperative-learning group setting.

## Equitable Teaching Approaches

Gender-fair teaching approaches have been supported by several sources (AAUW, 1992; Jones et al., 2000; Tracy & Lane, 1999; Wilbur, 1992). They include (a) a cooperative learning classroom structure, (b) an extended wait time for students' responses, (c) a review of the curriculum for equitable rep-resentation of females and males in the course material, and (d) offering var-ied methods of assessment of student's knowledge (AAUW, 1992; Sadker, Sadker, & Long, 1989). Weiler (1988) suggested that society needs to con-struct new ways of looking at schools' success and females' participation in schools. Her studies indicated that the teacher's own sense of self and views on equality are important factors in the implementation of gender-equitable approaches in the classroom.

Several approaches and techniques can foster equity in the classroom. Gender equity training of teachers, at all levels in the academic community, can have a significant impact on students' and faculties' understanding of gender equity issues. Research indicates that there are various ways in which faculty can promote a more gender-equitable learning environment (AAUW, 1992; Campbell, 2004; Sadker & Sadker, 1994). Some of the ways suggested by the California Department of Education, Office of Gender Equity (1992), are to help, all students see themselves in the curriculum being studied; offer alternative ways of instruction; use varied forms of assessment; review classroom design to make sure that females are represented in who is presented as role models and examples used in the classroom; ensure that females are as visible as males in videos viewed in class; and make sure that females are equitably represented in all formal and classroom curriculum efforts.

## Gender Equity and Field Experience

It is important that the experiential component take gender equity issues into account in balancing the needs of the student and the needs of the community. In this case, the community needs involve equitable representation of females in the formal curriculum and instruction patterns in schools. As students become aware of gender dynamics in today's classroom, they can take the information presented in this chapter and incorporate the ideals and concepts into their own life choices and future teaching practices. It is imperative when blending gender equity ideals into a field experience that the knowledge and the course content are closely related (Karasik, 2006). Students' reflection assignments are the critical tool in helping students find the meaning in their course work and how it relates to their field experience. "Reflection can take many forms, from in-class discussions and 'mad minute' essays, to journal, papers and portfolios" (Karasik, 2006, p. 6).

In Sex-Role Stereotyping, students are required to do two assignments that help facilitate the experiential learning for this course. The first assignment is to write pre- and postreflection papers on how influential gender inclusion was in the student's education experience. Students are asked to reflect on the following question: Did the student's gender make a difference in his or her chosen area of study (the declared major)? This reflection paper is revisited after students have studied scholarly research on gender inclusion and classroom participation and engaged in various class activities examining gender dynamics in the schools. At the end of the unit, students are asked to write a second reflection paper on the same topic. This assignment helps student's implement what they have learned in the course and apply their understanding of the subject and the educational ramifications on the student's life choices. This pre- and postreflection assignment is a helpful tool that allows students to see their growth and understanding on the subject of gender and education.

One mission of this chapter is to make the course content relevant by having students take the scholarly research on gender-equitable teaching approaches and apply this information to the school experience. The student's second assignment offers an experiential learning piece that asks students to spend time in a classroom (kindergarten through high school) observing a teacher and his or her methods of instruction used in class. Students write an analysis paper examining faculty interaction patterns in their teaching. Based on the research presented in this chapter, students are asked to incorporate and cite research on gender roles and bias in classroom teaching practices. Also included in the students' papers is a review of the course curriculum of the class they are observing (textbooks, class assignments, and videos viewed in class or given as a class assignment) examining the inclusion of both genders in the course materials (see Appendix A and Appendix B).

Various methods of observational research can be used in the observation portion of this assignment. One observational tool for data collection is based on a design called INTERSECT, Interactions for Sex Equity in Classroom Teaching (Bauchner, Hergert, Sadker, & Sadker, 1982). INTERSECT is a complex analysis tool created to rate numerous classroom patterns such as interaction patterns, teacher assignment of classroom tasks, sex bias or equity language, sex segregation or integration, and discipline methods. However, a simpler method is suggested in order for students to get a "picture" of what is occurring in a classroom in regard to gender inclusion. Students use the tally approach to document faculty's interaction patterns with students, reviewing the following:

- which students are called on
- which students are allowed to interrupt
- which students, if called on, are asked probing questions to defend their position
- being cognizant of the gender dynamics and roles within the cooperative group setting, document if and how the instructor assigns group work, and note the gender interaction patterns within the groups

The use of this simple observation technique helps students to determine if all learners were being included in the class discussion and experience. (See Appendix C.)

Student's observation analysis papers are graded on syntax and content analysis using the Harvard Core Program Performance Criteria (http://bokenter.harvard.edu/doc/GradingPapers.html). Analysis in the paper includes rich descriptors from the teacher observation assignment including details of the amount of time and the day and hour of the observation. Students provide clear examples of the teacher's methods of instruction, stating if there was evidence of gender preference in the class interaction patterns. Also any group activities are mentioned, and full disclosure on the gender dynamics displayed within the cooperative group experience are noted and discussed.

The second part of the analysis paper is the evaluation of any curriculum material used in the class. Incorporating the data collected from the textbook review and video/film review, students provide an evaluation of whether females are equally represented in the course curriculum of the class they observed. Last, students summarize how they would improve the class they observed in areas of gender inclusion in the teaching methods, interaction patterns, and course curriculum.

By using the "connected model of education" philosophy, students can go beyond being the object of or subordinate to the material and/or teacher to becoming independent thinkers about education and social equity. Allowing students the opportunity to observe faculty and their teaching practices and review curriculum materials helps empower students and fosters the objectives of students demonstrating an understanding of gender-fair teaching practices. It is hoped once students are aware and have the knowledge of gender-fair teaching practices they will incorporate these skills in their own classrooms and lives. Empowering students to be active learners will allow them the opportunity to truly be change agents of their own learning and create positive change in their classrooms and communities.

## Conclusion

Many students enter college with the premise that all doors are open and all students have equal opportunity to succeed and enter the profession of their choice. Though the college classroom currently addresses numerous issue of inequities in society, missing from the conversation are the larger social constructs of gender, how gender inequities affect students both academically and emotionally, and the knowledge that these inequities begin as early as kindergarten through subtle messages students learn in the classroom (Carinci, 2002).

Research suggests that educators, once aware of gender equity techniques, are more than eager to implement such methods in the classroom (AAUW, 1999; Sanders, 2002, 2003). One study revealed that "the approaches taken to modify gender bias were effective supporting the need for increased teacher training in gender equity strategies" (Jones, Evans, Byrd, & Campbell, 2000). It is hoped that, after faculty are empowered with the information presented in this chapter and apply the knowledge firsthand in the college classroom setting, they will be inspired and will motivate college students who are future teachers to implement gender-fair teaching techniques in their own classrooms.

More faculty should encourage their students to examine other institutions within our society that contribute to the issues affecting gender role stereotyping and education practices (Title XI, assessment bias, computer and textbook bias, international concerns of women and education). Using the examined research and field experience, it is the hope of this author that faculty will be inspired from the data presented in this chapter to make changes in their own teaching strategies as well as support students to challenge stereotypes and biases in any form. One purpose of this chapter is to give faculty and their students the tools to feel confident enough to question the hierarchy of education, its influence on the learner, and eventually become agents of change and advocates of their own learning in and out of the classroom.

## Appendix A

### *Sex-Role Stereotyping in American Education*

*Textbook Review Worksheet*

1. List the name of the textbook being reviewed, subject of the book, and date of the publication.
2. List the authors and state sex (male/female), if possible.
3. What grade level is the book written for?
4. Review the textbook type (written word) for gender stereotyping. Please indicate what item(s) you found and why the item(s) is specific to sex-role stereotyping.
5. Review textbook photos. Are there any photos that portray male or females in gender-specific roles or behaviors? Please give examples of what you found and why you found the images specific to gender stereotyping.

6. Were the experts or authorities on the subject matter males or females, or both?

7. Is the textbook representative of females and their contributions to the subject matter? Please explain.

8. Overall, on a scale of 1 to 10, (10 being the highest), what score would you give the textbook you reviewed in representing females and including females in the subject matter? Please give justification for your score.

9. Do you think having a balanced representation of males and females in your education would have benefited you as a learner? How so?

## Appendix B

### *Sex-Role Stereotyping in American Education*

*Video/Film Review Worksheet*

1. List the name of the video/film being reviewed, subject of the film, and date of the production.

2. List the producers/creators or the film and state sex (male/female), if possible.

3. What grade level or age group was the film created for?

4. Are the protagonists, main characters, in the film male or female, or both? Give percentages.

5. If there is a narrator, is the narrator a male or female?

6. Review the film text (spoken word) for gender stereotyping. Please give examples of what you found and why you found the word usage specific to gender stereotyping.

7. Review the film visuals. Are there any visuals that portray males or females in gender-specific roles or behaviors? How might these images affect the viewer?

8. Do the activities represent both males and females in active roles? If not, explain.

9. Were the experts or authorities on the subject matter males, females, or both?

10. Does the film offer positive images of males and females? Please explain.

11. Overall, on a scale of 1 to 10 (10 being the highest), what score would

you give the film you reviewed in representing both males and females, and including females in the subject matter? Please give justification of your score.

12. Do you think it is important to have equal representation of males
and females in media presentation material? How would you think
this would affect you as a learner?

## Appendix C

### *Teacher/Class Observation Worksheet*

Teacher's Name _____

Teacher's Gender    Male    Female

Grade level of class observation _____

Subject being taught during observation _____

Observation Time:     Start time _____
                      Finish time _____

                      Total time of observation _____

**Using the space below, keep a tally of how many males and females experi-
enced the following types of interactions:**

**1. Teacher/Student Interaction**

Probing Questions                  Male Students      Female Students

Comments and Observation:


Feedback—Positive                  Male Students      Female Students

Comments and Observation: *(For example, what were the topics of the feedback that males and females received? Did you notice any patterns?)*


Feedback—Negative                  Male Students      Female Students

Comments and Observation: *(For example, what were the topics of the feedback that males and females received? Did you notice any patterns?)*

Allowed Interruptions           Male Students    Female Students

Comments and Observation:


Calling Students by Name      Male Students    Female Students

Comments and Observation:

## 2. Student/Student Interactions

Were there group activities performed during class    Yes    No
observation? If yes, describe the activity.


Were group locations assigned by the teacher? If not,    Yes    No
how did students arrange where the groups would
meet? Please describe.


Did the teacher assign roles to the students in the    Yes    No
groups? If not, what roles did the males and females
in each group take? Were there any patterns?


Choose one group to observe. Keep a tally of the following interactions.

Student to student interaction within
the group:                  male to male _____
                          male to female _____
                          female to female _____

## 3. Please note and describe the following behavior that might have oc-curred within the class or group interaction:

Interruptions between classmates or group members


Responding to student's suggestions


Showing preference for certain students' or a group member's ideas

Who led the group activity? How was the leader role chosen?

Sex segregation in seating arrangements.

Students or areas of the room that received a disproportionate amount of the teacher's attention.

Inclusive or exclusive language

Comments and notable quotes from students and/or teacher:

# References

American Association of University Women. (1991). *Stalled agenda: Gender equity and the training of educators.* Washington, DC: Author.

American Association of University Women. (1992). *How schools shortchange girls.* Washington, DC: Author.

American Association of University Women. (1999). *Gender gaps: Where schools still fail our children.* Washington, DC: Author.

Bauchner, J., Hergert, L., Sadker, D., & Sadker, M. (1982). INTERSECT (Interactions for sex equity in classroom teaching). Andover, MA: The Network.

Belenky, M., Clinchy, B., Goldberger, N., & Tarule, J. (1997). *Women's ways of knowing.* New York: Basic Books.

Bendixen-Noe, M., & Hall, L. (1996). The quest for gender equity in America's schools: From preschool and beyond. *Journal of Early Childhood Teacher Education, 17*(2), 50–67.

Block, J. (1984). *Sex role identity and ego development.* San Francisco: Jossey-Bass.

Brown, L. M., & Gilligan, C. (1992). *Meeting at the crossroads.* New York: Random House.

California Department of Education, Office of Gender Equity. (1992). *We are what we play.* Sacramento, CA: Author.

Campbell, D. (2004). *Choosing democracy* (3rd ed.). Upper Saddle River, NJ: Prentice-Hall.

Campbell, P., & Sanders, J. (1997). Uninformed but interested: Findings of a national survey on gender equity in preservice teacher education. *Journal of Teacher Education, 48*(1), 69–75.

Carinci, S. (2002). *Gender equity training in pre-service teacher preparation programs.* Unpublished dissertation, University of San Francisco, CA.

D'Ambrosio, M., & Hammer P. (1996). Gender equity in the Catholic elementary schools. Philadelphia: National Catholic Education Association.

Duffy, J., Warren, K., & Walsh, M. (2002). Classroom interactions: Gender of teacher, gender of student and classroom subject. *Sex Roles, 45,* 579–593.

Dweck, C. (1977). Learned helplessness and negative evaluations. *Educator, 19*(2), 44–49.

Edwards, R. (2004). You need to understand my gender role: Empirical test of Tannen's model of gender and communication. *Sex Roles, 50,* 491–505.

Fine, L. (1993). *Beyond silenced voices: Class, race, and gender in United States schools.* Albany: State University of New York Press.

Gilligan, C. (1982). *In a different voice: Psychological theory and women's development.* Cambridge, MA: Harvard University Press.

Goss, G. (1996). [Weaving girls into the curriculum.] Unpublished raw data.

Horgan, D. (1995). *Achieving gender equity: Strategies for the classroom.* Boston: Allyn & Bacon.

Karasik, R. (2006). Successful service learning. *Thriving in academe.* National Education Association, *23*(4), 6–7.

Jones, K., Evans, C., Byrd, R., & Campbell, K. (2000). Gender equity training and teacher behavior. *Journal of Instructional Psychology, 27*(3), 173–177.

Lee, V. (1997). Gender equity and the organization of schools. *Gender, equity and schooling.* New York: Garland.

Levine, E., & Orenstein, F. (1994). [Sugar and spice and puppy dog tails: Gender equity among middle school children]. Unpublished raw data.

Lips, H. (1989). Gender-role socialization: Lessons in femininity. *Women: A feminist perspective: Growing up female* (4th ed.) Mountain View, CA: Mayfield.

Noddings, N. (1992). *The challenge to care in school.* New York: Teachers College Press.

Orenstein, P. (1994). *Schoolgirls: Young women, self-esteem, and the confidence gap.* New York: Doubleday.

Owens, S., Smothers, B., & Love, F. (2003). Are girls victims of gender bias in our nation's schools? *Journal of Instructional Psychology, 30*(2), 131–136.

Pipher, M. (1994). *Reviving Ophelia: Saving the selves of adolescent girls.* New York: Ballantine.

Sadker, D. (1999). Gender equity: Still knocking at the classroom door. *Educational Leadership, 56*(7), 22–26.

Sadker, D. (2002). An educator's primer on the gender war. *Phi Delta Kappan, 84*(30), 235–240, 244.

Sadker, M., & Sadker, D. (1994). *Failing at fairness: How America's schools cheat girls.* New York: Macmillan.

Sadker, M., Sadker, D., & Klien, S. (1991). The issue of gender in elementary and secondary education. *Review of Research in Education, 17*, 269–334.

Sadker, M., Sadker, D., & Long, L. (1989). Gender and educational equality. In Banks & C. H. M. Banks (Eds.), *Multicultural education: Issues and perspectives* (pp. 106–123). Needham Heights, MA: Allyn & Bacon.

Sanders, J. (2002). Something is missing from teacher education: Attention to two genders. *Phi Delta Kappan, 84*(3), 241–243.

Sanders, J. (2003). Teaching gender equity in teacher education. *Education Digest, 68*(5), 25–30.

Serbin, L., & Connor, J. (1981). Sex-differential free play behavior: Effects of teacher modeling, location and gender. *Developmental Psychology, 17*, 640–646.

Tannen, D. (1994). *Talking from 9 to 5*. New York: William Morrow.

Tracy, D., & Lane, M. (1999, December). Gender-equitable teaching behaviors: Pre-service teachers' awareness and implementation. *Equity and Excellence in Education, 32*(3), 93–104.

Tyre, P. (2006, January 30). The trouble with boys. *Newsweek, 147*(5), 44–52.

Weiler, K. (1988). *Women teaching for change: Gender, class and power*. South Hadley, MA: Bergin & Garvey.

Wilbur, G. (1992). *Gender-fair curriculum*. Research report prepared for Wellesley College Research on Women. Washington, DC: American Association of University Women.

# 5

# FEMINISM, PUBLIC SOCIOLOGY, AND SERVICE LEARNING

## Issues of Gender in the Primary School Classroom

*Kristyan M. Kouri*

T he service-learning courses that I have developed at California State University, Northridge (CSUN) are partly founded upon social perspectives that stem from feminist theory and philosophy. Most feminists believe that the ultimate goal of one's teaching and research endeavors should be to create a more equitable society. While "a more equitable society" is usually thought of in terms of equality between women and men, many contemporary feminists have come to the conclusion that this can be accomplished only through the eradication of all forms of social inequality. This includes global inequality and inequities associated with race, age, social class, age, and sexual orientation.

But whatever the feminist orientation, making the link between theoretical thought and social action is one of the central tenets of feminist thinking (Thorne, 1993). Feminist philosophy is, therefore, entirely consistent with service-learning pedagogy in that both perspectives embrace what has come to be known as the pedagogy and scholarship of civic engagement. As a feminist sociologist, community activist, and educator, I hope that my personal and professional activities will serve to bring about positive social change. I see this service-learning program as a step in that direction, and it is my hope

The author wishes to thank Barrie Thorne and Jonathan Turner for reading an earlier draft of this chapter.

that the service-learning project brings us a small step closer to creating the kind of society that is free of inequities associated with gender, race, and social class.

The pedagogy of scholarship and civic engagement also aligns with a subfield of sociology called *public sociology*. Like feminists, public sociologists are actively involved in social projects in which they apply their theoretical and empirical knowledge with the goal of strengthening their communities. In his presidential address to the American Sociological Association, sociologist Michael Burawoy (2004) drew a clear link between service learning and public sociology. When engaging in the practice of public sociology with students, he stated, service-learning courses can be thought of as the ultimate prototype.

In keeping with this social theory/civic action connection, the inception of this service-learning program is also guided by the works of classical French social scientists Alexis de Tocqueville (1835/1969) and Émile Durkheim (1933/1964, 1897/1966), two theorists who believed that social solidarity was a hallmark of a healthy society. Societies made up of people who showed commitment and concern for those who lived around them, they asserted, were societies that functioned at an optimal level.

Drawing from this theoretical premise, students are asked to engage in tasks designed to enhance a child's standing, acts that will in turn promote the healthy functioning of our society.

The project also seeks to improve our community by providing our beleaguered public school system with some badly needed support. The fact that many of our local public schools are overcrowded and underfunded is common knowledge. It is virtually impossible for teachers working in the Los Angeles Unified School District to give their pupils all of the individual attention they need. With this in mind, I send CSUN students into the elementary school classroom to assist teachers in providing children with the in-depth attention and guidance needed to bolster academic achievement.

In both my Introduction to Women's Studies and Introduction to Sociology courses, key concepts associated with feminist/social theories are explored. A central tenet of both sociological and feminist theories is that gender roles are learned rather than biologically determined. One closely examined concept is the notion of *gender*—cultural assumptions made about the character of females and males, the rules they are expected to follow and the roles they are expected to play as a result of those assumptions. We explore other concepts that fall under the large social construction of gender umbrella: *gender differentiation* and *hegemonic masculinity*.[1] Gender differentiation refers to the tendency for women and men to alter their appearance in ways that make them look far more different than they would if they had done nothing at all. Some of these practices include shaving, makeup, hairstyles, and clothing. The hegemonic male, which has been the dominant male prototype for the past 100 years, is a rough and tough athletic man who scorns anything associated with frailty and weakness. Failure to live up to these rigid expectations will almost always result in shame and ridicule.

This investigation includes research put forth by feminist sociologist Barrie Thorne (1993), who conducted an extensive ethnography of girls and boys in elementary school. As Thorne observed children in the classroom and on the playground, she discovered that the girls and boys tended to separate themselves from each other. For example, if given the chance, girls would sit on one side of the classroom and the boys on the other. At recess, the children separated themselves once again with girls playing close to the buildings while boys, controlling as much as 10 times more space, played team sports in the field areas.

To gain a better understanding of the phenomenon, Thorne set about untangling the social processes that led to this gender divide. She noticed that when girls and boys did engage in friendly conversation, the other children who witnessed this event would chant, "She loves him," or "He loves her." In an attempt to guard against heterosexual teasing, she concluded, the girls and boys steered clear of each other. Sadly, this pervasive avoidance prevented the youngsters from coming to know each other as individuals, and from developing friendly, cooperative partnerships.

Thorne witnessed other social processes involving these girl/boy divisions. She saw that large numbers of children, who were interacting in a seemingly peaceful manner, would suddenly break into two opposing teams of boys against girls. She identified this social process as *borderwork*,[2] the tendency for girls and boys to come together in ways that drive them apart. Borderwork is thus a social situation where contact generates conflict. The three types of borderwork we focus on in class lectures are (a) chasing games, (b) pollution rituals, and (c) invasions.

In chasing games boys play the role of aggressive predator and the girls assume the role of screaming victim. Cooties games are likened to pollution rituals, often associated with menstruation, and are practiced by a number of cultural groups throughout the world. Thorne asserts that like other pollution rituals, the notion of cooties brings about images of unwanted touch and smell, and girls rather than boys are far more likely to be infected with the imaginary bugs. Invasions are carried out by small groups of boys who specialize in interrupting girls' highly coordinated games.

Borderwork, Thorne argues, encourages girls and boys to think of each other as members of two antagonistic and opposing teams rather than as individual children who share both differences as well as commonalities. Hence, when the social process of borderwork is enacted, stereotypes are perpetuated and the possibility for girl/boy platonic friendships is thwarted. Thorne asserts that these antagonist patterns of interaction persist into adulthood. If women and men continue to think of themselves as opposing teams, then their relationships may only be seen as romantic or competitive. And if women and men continue to draw upon this opposing team imagery as a way of guiding their adult interactions, men will work to maintain the more powerful winning team, leaving patriarchy largely intact.

Of course people are not robots and, as a result, do not always react to societal pressures in exactly the same fashion. Most people attempt to negotiate social rules, and a few manage to ignore them altogether. According to Thorne (1993), these behavioral exceptions are extremely important, for they suggest the possibility for change.[3] As a result, Thorne also searched for exceptions among children, documenting instances where children successfully crossed the gender divide.

In this attempt to bring course concepts to life through the process of service learning, I hope that the CSUN students will be able to identify some of these behavioral pattern processes while working at the elementary school site. I also want them to take note of the behavioral anomalies that are also sure to exist.

## Race and Social Class

The CSUN students are asked to look for the possibility of race and social class variations when analyzing the grade school setting. Like gender, these socially constructed categories of hierarchy affect people as they make their way through life, and it is always important to consider their impact when attempting to discern human behavior.

Sociologists have long demonstrated that a child's social class background is positively correlated with the social class background she or he falls into as an adult—an issue that is addressed in both my Introduction to Sociology and my women's studies courses. Social scientific research has shown that children from lower-social-class backgrounds will eventually find work similar to that of their parents (Correspondents of the *New York Times*, 2005; Featherman & Hauser, 1978; Grusky & Hauser, 1984). Since most of the children who attend our service-learning elementary school come from poor to working-class backgrounds, it is therefore likely that many of these children will grow up to be poor and working-class individuals. That said, there is still room for upward mobility, and when it comes to moving up the economic ladder, educational attainment is probably a person's best bet. Sociologists have long demonstrated that education has a strong impact on a person's income and occupation—the higher the educational attainment, the greater the likelihood of a higher income.

There is, however, more to this picture than academic achievement. Sociologist Pierre Bourdieu (1988) believed that the tendency for the social classes to replicate themselves is partially the result of culture. People at the higher echelons of the social stratification system, he contended, are endowed with *cultural capital*—proper attitudes toward education, and knowledge of cultural entities such as art, music, and literature. Middle-class parents, for example, provide their children with cultural capital with trips to concerts, museums, and the library. They also impart their beliefs about the importance of education to their children through direct discussion and by keeping a close eye on their children's educational progress. These social practices increase a child's chances of succeeding in school.[4] It therefore follows that, when it comes to one's ability to function within the context of the American educational system, the children who come from poor or working-class backgrounds may be at a disadvantage.

College students have acquired varying degrees of cultural capital, and it is my hope that they will not only augment the children's academic progress, but also impart some of their cultural skills to the working-class children they meet at the service-learning site. This extra amount of attention and guidance may induce a greater number of children to pay closer attention to their schoolwork and, in the long run, improve their chances of having a successful grade school career.[5] I also hope that their work in the elementary school will provide them with real-life examples of the kinds of inequities we talk about in the course.

## The Service-Learning Setting and Program

The service-learning site is an elementary school located in the southeastern region of the San Fernando Valley. The children who attend the school are typically English-language learners from lower-income families who qualify for Title I assistance and free or reduced-price meals. Over the course of the last five years, the general academic standing of the school has fluctuated, oscillating between below-average and acceptable standards.

Although the CSUN service-learning center has formed alliances with a number of community agencies, I instituted this particular program after a chance encounter with Leslie Walstedt (personal communication, November 14, 2005), a school counselor at a local elementary school. Because we both recognized that the elementary school teachers were overworked and that many of the schoolchildren were in desperate need of individual attention, we devised a program in which the CSUN students would provide teachers with assistance and the children with one-on-one time with a caring adult.

### *Student Scholar Program*

Creating and maintaining an ongoing service-learning program can take a great deal of a faculty member's time. As a result, the CSUN service-learning center crafted a Student Scholar Program in which particular CSUN students assist us with the implementation of our programs. I have been fortunate enough to work with five different student scholars who have been of tremendous help. Four of them were individuals who excelled in service learning while taking my courses and were enlisted to become scholars once their course work was completed.

The service-learning scholars help to facilitate the link between the university classroom and the elementary school site. Some of their tasks include supervising after-school programs and keeping track of the CSUN students who are in the process of completing their hours. In fact, three of my student scholars spoke Spanish, providing the elementary school teachers and children with additional in-depth assistance.

Approximately 200 of my students have chosen to take part in my service-learning program since its inception, and almost all of them report that their experiences were enjoyable. In addition, students who choose to participate in service learning while taking one of my courses (for example, sociology) will take another one of my courses (for example, women's studies) and involve themselves in the service-learning program yet again. This not only speaks to the success of the program but also provides continuity for both teachers and children.

## Training SL Students

At the beginning of each semester, my community partner, Mrs. Walstedt, travels to CSUN to speak to all my classes. The students are told that they can choose to participate in the service-learning program in exchange for taking their second midterm. To complete the assignment, they must assist teachers and/or work with children for a total of at least ten hours. When finished, they are required to turn in a journal that documents their experiences. Participating students receive a contract (Appendix A) that thoroughly explains what is expected of student assistants.

The contract was instituted as a result of difficulties experienced while implementing the program. Some students, for example, were enrolling themselves in the program but failing to meet their obligations. I have discovered that most students sign up for the program with good intentions, but some drop out because of unforeseen events. Whatever the case, broken promises leave children disappointed and teachers annoyed. So in an attempt to keep these occurrences to a minimum, we included an additional item (number 1a) in the contract emphasizing the importance of the commitment. It is important to recognize, however, that there will always be a few students who will be faced with difficulties that will prevent them from finishing the program in spite of precautionary measures.

## Troubleshooting

While most of the pairings of the service-learning students with the teachers have been successful, on a few occasions teachers have lodged complaints against the service-learning students. Two major incidents involved service-learning students dressing seductively while working in an elementary school setting and service-learning students refusing to take direction from the teachers they were assisting. As a result of these situations we included item number 3 in the contract (Appendix A), which states, "I will be working in a professional setting and I need to dress appropriately," and item 4: "The Glenwood Elementary School teacher I am assigned to will be my supervisor in the classroom, I am to follow the teacher's instructions, and I am to treat the teacher with respect."

## Culminating Paper Assignment

Upon completion of service, students are required to turn in a paper in which they not only describe their experience but also interpret their observations using the concepts and frameworks addressed in class. The students are asked to think of their assignment as a *participant observation research study* and are instructed to take note of what is going on around them as they participate in the service-learning program. This service-learning project lends itself particularly well to the introduction of qualitative research techniques.

When students enter college, the extent of their research training typically involves writing research papers that make use of secondary sources such as books and journals. Most students have very little experience conducting empirical research projects that require them to carefully observe human behavior. Working in an elementary school setting provides them with an opportunity to learn how to observe human behavior in a thoughtful and deliberate manner. Consequently, this service-learning assignment is an excellent way to introduce beginning students to empirical research methods.

I ask the students to do more than just describe their experiences when writing their journals; I also ask them to incorporate course terms and concepts about the behavioral patterns they may have witnessed. In doing so, the students learn to make the link between *description* and *analysis*. Instructions designed to guide them in this process are provided in Appendix B. These directions provide them with a number of questions designed to help the students link their observations with concepts discussed in class.

## Service-Learning Program Outcomes

In discussing the theories that serve to guide my decision to become involved in service-learning pedagogy, I have thus far presented my program objectives. This section discusses which of these community and learning goals have come to fruition. The data derived for this section come from three different sources: (a) reports from the elementary school teachers and counselors, (b) an open-ended questionnaire administered to a total of 60 service-learning participants at the end of the semester, and (c) data derived from the students' service-learning journals.

## Community Impact

While I cannot determine whether or not the CSUN students were able to imbue the elementary school children with any of their cultural capital, I can report that the CSUN students did help the children improve upon their standardized test scores. The academic standing, as determined by California Standards Based Tests, has fluctuated over the course of the past five years. In the 2002–2003 academic year the school's academic performance index (API) fell within the "acceptable range. But in the 2003–2004 academic year, the test scores dropped to an unacceptable level. As a result, the school district implemented an enrichment program with the aim of improving the children's academic skills. Teachers were enlisted to offer extra courses both after school and on Saturday mornings that were intended to enhance the children's reading, vocabulary, and math skills. The CSUN students participating in the service-learning program assisted these teachers every step of the way working at the elementary school during the week and on weekends. All of our efforts paid off: The elementary school children's test scores improved dramatically.

Leslie Walstedt, Glenwood's school counselor, explained it this way:

> Glenwood's academic performance index was 674 and it is now 702, a growth of 28 points. There were many interventions last year and the teachers were under the gun and worked exceptionally hard with the kids. Your CSUN program was one of the interventions. Although we cannot measure specifically which intervention did what for whom, we can safely assume that any extra help individually and in classrooms was helpful to our overall outcome.

In another instance, first grade teacher Pam Brown (personal communication, May 23, 2006) reported that one service-learning student was instrumental in helping the majority of her first graders pass their quarterly district math tests:

> The CSUN service-learning student worked with the entire group, small groups and one-on-on with students. She conducted lessons and reviewed

with students. The majority passed the test. I feel having another adult who can help with the specific needs of the students greatly improved their skill level and confidence in school.

## Evaluating Concepts and Theories Introduced in Courses

The open-ended questionnaire administered to the students at the end of the semester also included questions intended to ascertain whether the students believed they could link their service-learning experience to concepts and theories discussed in class. Of the 59 students who answered the question, 53 responded in the affirmative, while 5 students reported that they were unable to make a connection between their work duties and course materials. Two students indicated that they had difficulty applying course concepts to their experiences because they were assigned to a very small classroom consisting of three boys and one girl.

When the students listed examples of the course terms that they could discern, the terms most often mentioned were *gender differentiation, gender separation, gender roles, hegemonic masculinity,* and *borderwork.* Examples found in the student's service-learning journal also demonstrate their ability to frame their observations with the use of course concepts. To illustrate this point, I present the following written passages found among the students' service-learning journals.

### Gender Differentiation

The following statement drawn from a CSUN student's service-learning journal notes gender differentiation, one of the course concepts:

> The uniform that the kids wear is a mandatory requisite for every kid. The colors consist of blue and white without any other type of colors. But I noticed that most girls wore white shirts with a very feminine graphic design whereas most boys wore plain white shirts. It appears that the popular first grade hair cut for boys is the slicked-gel to the side hairstyle and the cool jazzy spiked hair. Most girls wear their hair in a loose ponytail. Evidently, boys and girls try to alter their appearance by wearing things which make them different or distinguishable from the opposite sex. Although the kids wore uniforms, gender differentiation was noticeable.

### Gender Separation

The CSUN students often witnessed the boys and girls separating themselves from each other in both the playground and classroom setting, as this student explained:

The kids were at lunch and had free play on the yard. I watched as the girls segregated themselves from the boys. They wanted to play girl games like handball and hopscotch. The boys wanted to play basketball and soccer.

But the CSUN students also noticed girls and boys working together cooperatively:

I noticed that there was not a separation between boys and girls, but rather a combination of both. For example, in a word puzzle play station there was a girl and boy interacting quite well with each other. It was rather intriguing to notice that the typical hegemonic boy was not intending to compete or challenge himself with the physical educational activities. The boy was instead working quite well with the girl.

This observation is consistent with what Thorne (1993) found while observing children in elementary schools in that girls and boys were more likely to work cooperatively when the activity was set up and supervised by an adult.

*Gender Roles*

After reading the student's journals, it became patently clear that even four- and five-year-olds were already playing their culturally scripted gender roles:

I talked to them about their Halloween costumes. Reina told me she wanted to be the pink power ranger. Angela wanted to be Cinderella. Angela told Reina that power rangers are for boys and she should be Snow White instead. Reina made it clear she did not want to be Snow White. Angela is falling into the role that girls are to live like a princess. By watching a lot of Disney movies she is being convinced that she could live like that also. Being that Angela is young, she does not know the difference between a fantasy and reality. Like the hegemonic male role, the majority of boys wanted to be either Batman or Superman. Boys want to take on the role of being strong and powerful. Superman and Batman are perfect characters for that.

The behaviors associated with gender roles took on a more serious bent as the children grew older, as a student who worked in a fifth grade classroom explained:

I did notice some gender roles while I was helping. I overheard one young girl saying to another girl that she did not eat most of her lunch because she was afraid of getting fat. She purposely eats less to keep her thin figure. I was not aware that these social pressures affect kids at such a young age. It somewhat disturbed me to overhear what she said. She is still a growing girl, and starving herself will cause more harm than it will do good.

## The Hegemonic Male Role

CSUN students found the elementary school boys playing the rough and tough hegemonic male role at all grade levels. A student observed the following behavioral pattern while working with a group of kindergarteners:

> I noticed the difference in gender by the games they played and the toys they used. The most anticipated feature of the outside world was tricycles. The boys seemed to be most amused by the bikes and would stop at nothing to get first chance on them. While they may not fit this description to the tee yet, (because of their age) many males showed signs of the "hegemonic male." Their want for racing the bikes and being the fastest was made obvious as they continued to go around the track. The boys would get mad and say mean things to one another when they did not get the bike they wanted. If attitudes like this persist, they may strive to become more rugged and dominant in their relationships with other people.

This second example came from a student assisting children in a third grade classroom:

> One boy in the class is a bit taller than the rest of the kids. He, as well as three other boys, appears to be the hegemonic male of the class. They hang in their own little sub group and are tuff [*sic*], rugged boys. They do not hug or display any kind of gentleness. They like to play around aggressively by pushing each other and telling each other to "shut-up man"! The boys do not display kindness to their peers that appear to be less intimidating than they are.

## Borderwork

Many students observed the schoolchildren engaging in the social process called *borderwork* while completing their service-learning hours. One such student, for example, witnessed an invasion while supervising six fourth grade girls playing handball:

> This boy came into the girls' game, knowing from the start that he just wanted to mess it up. This particular situation is called an *invasion* accord-

ing to the book *Gender Play* by Barrie Thorne. [The boy] also brought another boy over to the game with him, almost as though it gave him more power or influence to be with another boy rather than by himself.

## Behavioral Exceptions

The CSUN students were able to observe more than the typical behavior patterns often cited in the scholarly literature on gender; they were also able to identify behavioral exceptions. This is important because it demonstrates that the students are not simply forcing their observations to fit within the confines of a preconceived theory. It also shows the students that despite visible patterns, human behavior can also vary. Here is how one service-learning participant described an elementary school girl who did not play her culturally scripted feminine role:

> Almost every girl except one was very soft spoken and were always the ones [the teacher] would call on to do a specific task around the room. However, the one girl that didn't really follow the other girls had a very big difference from the others. Her physical characteristics were much different. For example, she was the tallest student in the room and was a thick boned girl. Because of these characteristics, I came to the conclusion that she isn't soft spoken because she knows she's bigger than all the boys, and she was not intimidated by the males in the classroom. She was the only one that broke the stereotype of how the young girls should act in the classroom.

Another student observed a group of first grade boys behaving in a fashion that American culture typically ascribes to girls:

> Since in our culture it is said or believed that girls are more talkative than boys, well then it is not true in Ms. Oh's class. At least eighty percent of the class talkers are boys and Ms. Oh made that distinction out-loud today.

## Cultural Capital

When asked in the end-of-semester outcome survey whether they could determine the children's social class backgrounds, the student responses varied. Some individuals believed that the children came from a variety of social class backgrounds including poor, working class, and middle class. Those who thought that the children were poor made this determination by the neighborhood the school was located in and by the fact the children did not appear to be wearing expensive clothes. Another set of service-learning students, however, indicated that they were not quite sure which social class backgrounds the children came from.

Quite a few students did, however, note that many of the schoolchildren had parents who were unable to speak English. The inability to speak the English language, they wrote, prevented parents from helping their children with their homework. With this, they likened their observations to Bourdieu's (1984, 1988) notion of cultural capital.

In regard to cultural capital, another student presented the following insightful passage:

> It was in this session with the kids that I noticed the liking and/or dislike for schoolwork, otherwise known as each pupil's individual cultural capital (proper attitudes towards various aspects of society). The assignment was to write their name three times and once without the help of the dotted lines. . . . I started with one student named David. This boy was working diligently and completed his work with ease. I asked the teacher about his personal background, and his response was no surprise. He comes from a family with no life altering problems. That is to say they don't necessarily have problems with money and/or divorce. This apparently gives him advantage [over] some of his classmates.
>
> Another girl I worked with named Carmen had a hard time completing her work and when help was there for her she refused the offer. Evidently her brother is very sick and her mother is poor. This reflected [on] her schoolwork and her concentration. Upon working on the computer she took longer and had trouble with the mouse. This contrasts with David who used the mouse effortlessly. To no surprise David has a computer at home, and Carmen doesn't. Cultural capital proves effective if one person has more experience and influences than another, they have an advantage.

## Concluding Comments

The data and passages presented in this chapter show that many student-learning goals are being met. Student journals demonstrate that they are able to make careful and deliberate observations while engaging in their service-learning activities, and that they are also able to link their observations with the concepts introduced in class. What's more, the students took note of behavioral exceptions and contemplated the ways in which social class may have affected the children's ability to learn within the context of a grade school setting. When one adds this finding to the fact that elementary school children's test scores improve with the help of the CSUN service-learning students, one can argue that this service-learning program does indeed meet the needs of both the classroom and the community. And in the end, this service-learning project is entirely in keeping with the philosophies of feminism, public sociology, and service learning in that we are using our academic knowledge to improve the lives of teachers and children living in our community.

## Appendix A

### *Service Learning Contract*

I understand that if I participate in this service-learning program:

1. If I cannot make my scheduled time, I need to call the office, give my name and provide the name of the teacher to let him or her know that I'm not coming.
   a. I will make every effort to complete my 10 hours, and that it is imperative that I am sure I will have the time to complete the program.
   b. I really need to think it through. Will I need a job and will the job interfere with my service-learning commitments? Is my course load heavy? Do I have transportation?
2. Teachers and students are depending on me, and they are at a loss when I don't show up, and/or I don't complete the program.
3. I will be working in a professional setting and I need to dress appropriately.
   a. I am not to wear short skirts, shorts, cropped tops exposing any part of my stomach, or low-cut blouses.
   b. I understand that if I come to the elementary school dressed inappropriately, I may be asked to leave.
4. That the Glenwood Elementary School teacher I am assigned to will be my supervisor in the classroom and I am to follow the teacher's instructions and I am to treat the teacher with respect.
5. I am to tutor children and/or help a teacher for a total of 10 hours.

6. I write a journal entry for each of those hours, so my journal must comprise 10 entries.

7. If I want to receive an A grade for the project I must complete the 10 hours and have course theories and concepts integrated into at least 7 of my journal entries.

8. My journals must be placed within a notebook.

9. I can hand write my journal entries as long as my writing is legible.

10. I need to have had a recent TB test, and I need to bring documentation of those results to the Glenwood school office. If I have not had a TB test I can get one for free at the CSUN Health Center.

I have read the contract and understand what is expected of me.

Print Name_____

Signature_____ Date_____

## Appendix B

### *Instructions for Service-Learning Journal*

1. Your service-learning assignment calls for you to spend 10 hours working with children at Glenwood Elementary School. Hence you must have a journal entry for every hour you put in. This means you must have 10 journal entries. Journal entries must consist of the observations you make working with children.

2. Your journal entries can be handwritten as long as they are legible.

3. It is important for you to integrate course concepts into your journal entries.

Listed below are a number of questions you might answer as you make your observations and write your journal entries:

a. Are the children engaged in *gender differentiation*, that is, do they dress in ways, or wear their hair in ways, or even move in ways that make them to appear more different than they really are?

b. Do boys attempt to follow the *hegemonic* male gender role? That is, do that attempt to play the role of a tough, rugged, athletic male who never cries or who never shows any emotions other than anger? Do you notice any boys who don't play this role? If so, how are they treated by their peers?

c.  Do you notice the girls playing any particular role?

d.  Do you notice any of the children, boys or girls, breaking traditional gender roles?

e.  Do you see any of the children engaging in *borderwork*, for example, chasing games, pollution rituals, or invasions? If they engage in chasing games do boys chase the girls, do girls chase the boys, or do boys sometimes chase girls while girls sometimes chase boys?

f.  Do you notice any close girl/boy friendships. Do you notice any children engaging in heterosexual teasing?

g.  Do the boys and girls separate themselves from each other when they are given the chance?

h.  Do some children display more cultural capital than others? That is, do some children have proper attitudes toward learning? Do they talk of music lessons, or art lessons? Do they talk of home computers? Do they talk of trips to museums?

*Remember*: "A" papers will be the ones that integrate course concepts into most of the journal entries.

## Notes

1.  Sociologist Robert Connell originally coined the term *hegemonic masculinity* in 1987.

2.  Thorne notes that the notion of borderwork comes from Fredrik Barth's (1969) study on the relationships between the Lapps and Norwegians. He notes that contact between the two groups actually strengthened ethnic boundaries.

3.  In keeping with the feminist goal of using research work to help to build a more equitable society, Thorne's book also provides parents and teachers with strategies for helping girls to build alliances. If girls and boys learn that males and females can have relaxed and friendly platonic relationships, she asserts they will have a greater opportunity for building alliances and working together cooperatively as adults. This mere act of cooperation between women and men is a solid step toward undermining our patriarchal social system.

4.  Bourdieu notes that parents from poor and working-class backgrounds are definitely not indifferent to their children's needs, for they too are concerned with their children's levels of educational attainment and achievement. He asserts, however, that many parents from lower-class backgrounds have failed to acquire the cultural skills needed to help their children navigate the world of academics.

5. The empirical evidence shows that these types of interventions are indeed effective. In 1995, for example, Tierney, Grossman, and Resch conducted what would come to be seen as a groundbreaking study with the Boys & Girls Clubs of America. The results of this study were resoundingly positive. Researchers found that the children with adult mentors missed half as many days of school as did the youngsters in the control group. These same children expressed more confidence in their ability to do their schoolwork, and as a result their grades rose at a modest level. Because the mentors did not engage in activities that might be thought of as explicit academic interventions, the researchers were quite impressed with this finding.

# References

Barth, F. (Ed.). (1969). *Ethnic groups and boundaries.* Boston: Little, Brown.

Bellah, R., Madsen, R., Sullivan, W., Swindler, A., & Tipton, S. (1985). *Habits of the heart: Individualism and commitment in American life.* Berkeley: University of California Press.

Bourdieu, P. (1984). *Distinction: A social critique of judgment and taste.* Cambridge, MA: Harvard University Press.

Bourdieu, P. (1988). *Language and symbolic power.* Cambridge, MA: Harvard University Press.

Burawoy, M. (2004). For public sociology. *The American Sociological Review, 70,* 4–28.

Connell, R. (1987). *Gender and power.* Stanford, CA: Stanford University Press.

Correspondents of the *New York Times.* (2005). *Class matters.* New York: Henry Holt.

Durkheim, É. (1964). *The division of labor in society* (G. Simpson, Trans.). New York: Free Press of Glencoe. (Original work published 1933)

Durkheim, É. (1966). *Suicide* (J. A. Spaulding & G. Simpson, Trans.). New York: Free Press. (Original work published 1897)

Featherman, D., & Hauser, R. M. (1978). *Opportunity and change.* New York: Academic Press.

Grusky, D. B., & Hauser, R. M. (1984). Comparative social mobility revisited: Models of convergence and divergence in 16 countries. *American Sociological Review, 49,* 19–38.

Thorne, B. (1993). *Gender play: Girls and boys in school.* New Brunswick, NJ: Rutgers University Press.

Tierney, J. P., Grossman, J. B., & Resch, N. L. (1995). *Making a difference: An impact study of big brother big sisters.* Philadelphia: Public/Private Ventures.

Toqueville, A. D. (1969). *Democracy in America* (G. Lawrence, Trans.). New York: Doubleday, Anchor Books. (Original work published 1835)

# SECTION THREE

## FEMINIST PEDAGOGY AND SERVICE LEARNING

# 6

# WOMEN AS SOCIAL WARRIORS

## A Framework for Community Service Learning Combining Amazonian Feminist Thinking and Social Justice Education Theories

*Veda E. Ward*

Embedded within the women's studies curriculum are numerous opportunities for both students and faculty members to engage in ongoing dialogue about the relevance of academic study beyond the classroom, the nature of intellectual growth, and the evolving complexity of feminist inquiry. In the last 10 years, community service learning has emerged as a popular integrative framework for many disciplines and preprofessional programs. Among the identified outcomes of a field-based, experiential learning approach is student cognitive development beyond increasing awareness and acquisition of knowledge about compelling issues toward commitment, passion, and true social activism.

Often, involvement in community service learning extends the focus of the student's actions not only outside the classroom but also beyond the student, her or his friends and family, and to community, state, and global issues. The shift in emphasis from *self* to *others* is powerful as the student moves from achieving individual/personal goals to facilitating the achievement of "collective" goals resulting in significant growth for the individual student, both as learner and as future citizen of the global community.

The purpose of this chapter is to investigate the "fit" between community service learning in women's studies as informed by social justice education and Amazonian feminist thinking and theory. The tripartite model presented here analyzes the intersection among Amazonian feminist thinking (theory), community service learning (pedagogy), and social justice (change). It suggests that feminist thinkers and educators have the potential to design and deliver powerful frameworks that can assist them with meeting the myriad challenges of contemporary education, while increasing efficacy among students enrolled in women's studies courses. The process outlined herein works equally well whether the desired outcome is engaged learning, institutional transformation, or societal change.

This chapter offers rich detail on each aspect of the triad, its relevance to student learning, and the necessity for using a powerful, conceptual "cement" to energize social consciousness through relevant community service-learning assignments.

## The Feminist Classroom Within a Social Justice Framework

A fundamental quality of the feminist classroom is that it creates an environment in which "a collaborative, decentralized style of teaching is designed to empower students to become active participants in the learning process (Agha-Jaffar, 2000, p. 1). Cohee et al. (1998) identify six tenets of feminist pedagogy, two of which are particularly relevant to this discussion: (a) Feminist pedagogy evolves from feminist social practice. It is therefore oriented toward social transformation, consciousness-raising, and social activism that is the translation of thought into action, and (b) feminist pedagogy is concerned for women students, both within and outside the classroom, and is committed to improving the lives of women (p. 3).

Faculty members embrace the challenge of creating learning experiences and environments that will result in accomplishing these aims. One framework that assists students in negotiating the transition between theory and practice can be found in social justice education, a perspective that incorporates the characteristics of student centeredness, collaboration, and experiential learning and is intellectual, analytical, multicultural, value based, and activist. According to Wade (2001), "high quality community service-learning activities share many of the same characteristics as social justice education" and include "care, relationship and responsibility" (p. 3). Feminists conscientiously include diverse perspectives in their classes looking at race, class, gender, ethnicity, and sexual expression as they inform experience and perspective. Ability, age, and religion have provided insight into how identity is formed and defined. For example, Patricia Hill Collins (1991) notes in *Black Feminist Thought*, "Black women's style of activism also reflects a belief that teaching people to be self-reliant fosters more empowerment than teaching them to follow" (p. 157). Familiar sayings attributed to African traditional tribal life, or other indigenous peoples' and wisdom, such as "it takes an entire village to raise a child" or "teach a person to fish," reflect the essence of this sentiment.

In addition to traditionally identified student traits or predictive measures that may be considered in the development of course learning outcomes and related assignments, new education research focuses on the "generations" of students one may encounter in the women's studies classroom. They may differ in learning styles, preferred pedagogies, preferred modes for delivery, and span the Boomer, Gen-X, and Millennial generations (Oblinger, 2003). An individual's worldview and priorities for social action (or inaction) are often influenced by one's peers and the need and desire to identify both theoretical and practical frameworks that present opportunities to share learning experiences while empowering multiple generations of students to take individual ownership of choices. This presents faculty members with a constant challenge. Creating opportunities for student interest to ignite by kindling a desire to apply course-based information to influence desired social change could become an important goal for the actively engaged instructor of community service-learning courses.

Community service learning intentionally extends the intellectual goals of the academy beyond the classroom and into the community. Students are moved to "unlearn" patterns of beliefs, for example, that one's education and learning are disconnected from that of other students or from the larger academic institution and external community. The faculty member must design ways to expedite the process of unlearning. Community service learning may be viewed as an emersion experience that offers potential to rapidly alter this limiting perspective in favor of one that is more synergistic. From registering new voters to advocating for (or against) stem cell research, organ transplantation, harvesting and freezing of eggs, cloning, organic farming, green building, and other "life-saving" practices, there can be a component of reinvention and perpetuation of oneself in others through "institutional" shifts. These attempts to intervene in "nature" may be described as searching for and unearthing the route to social justice in a warriorlike manner, whether head-on and overt or by taking a less direct but equally definitive means to an end through legislative reform.

As Haskell (2001) suggests, "Feminism . . . is a system of multiplicity and fluidity. Feminism is made up of many parts without clear boundaries separating them" (p. 8). Students, however, may expect, demand, or accidentally "discover" a theoretical framework that informs and grounds their work. At the same time, the community service-learning model requires attention to conceptualization as part of the learning cycle, and this is not always a favorite aspect of learning for students. Within this context, the following section summarizes one approach to engaging students participating in community service-learning projects by applying tenets of Amazonian feminism.

## Amazonian Feminism

Taking the time to connect current realities with ancient tradition is often essential to building confidence among students that they are, in fact, part of a long intellectual and cultural heritage. The depictions of warrior women exemplify feminist thinking as supported and enriched by other disciplines such as literature, history, foreign language, archaeology, and anthropology. As ever, the interdisciplinary focus, welcoming of many voices and multiple perspectives, is central to a womanist approach.

Although Osborne (1997) and others debate whether the centuries of scholarship devoted to researching matriarchies has amounted to anything "definitive," almost all feminist thinkers believe in the paramount need for women to reverse their "source of identity from outer-directed to inner-directed, which is achieved through 'metaphysical cannibalism'" (Donovan, 1996, p. 151). For this purpose, an approach based on "Amazonian feminism," a subarea within radical feminism, exemplified by Mary Shelly's work on vampires and symbolic transformation (see http://people.brandeis.edu/~teuber/shelleybio.html) and Ti-Grace Atkinson's 1974 work titled *Amazon Odyssey* (Donovan, 1996), can prove beneficial as students undertake the challenges of a field experience in women's studies. This approach is especially well adapted to activities with a social justice objective since "as the name implies, Amazonian feminism aims at empowering individuals, both men and women, to pursue self-exploration (physicality, psychology, sexual identity, gender performance) and fight for their rights in a form that is strong, relentless, innovative, but most of all, conducive to emancipation."[1] As with most feminist theories, Amazonian feminism opposes gender role stereotyping and discrimination based on assumptions that women are supposed to be or look or behave as if they were passive, weak, and physically helpless. Amazonian feminism vigorously rejects the idea that certain characteristics are inherently masculine (or feminine), and upholds and explores a vision of heroic womanhood by focusing on the images of the female heroes as expressed in fiction, art, and literature, in the physiques and feats of female warriors and athletes, and in sexual values and practices.[2] For example, in U.S. history, the settling of the West brought to the forefront female heroines like Annie Oakley and Calamity Jane, women who could fight, drink, and shoot "like men." Those legendary females were not only crafted to be equal to men in wit and ability but were somehow "superior" to their male counterparts. Resurrected from time to time in the themes of television miniseries are similar heroines, as in *Lonesome Dove, Dr. Quinn: Medicine Woman, Deadwood,* and others. Far beyond the Old West, current examples as in *Million Dollar Baby; Bend It Like Beckham; Whale Rider; Crouching Tiger, Hidden Dragon; Kill Bill 1* and *Kill Bill 2; The Matrix; Lara Croft Tomb Raider; Catwoman; Mean Girls;* and the occasional showing of delightful old *Wonder Woman* episodes, may be viewed as contemporary interpretations of Amazonian feminism that appear in multiple cinematic genres attracting quite a diverse audiences. Technology has not neglected the Amazon, as video games offer yet another version of animated comic-book-type warrior women, and either males or females may be handling the controls.

These contemporary examples spring from a rich history. Images of warrior women and goddesses have appeared throughout recorded history. While students have different amounts and types of knowledge about any phenomenon or topic introduced in the classroom, most come with some acquaintance with the woman warrior. While some recall the recurring, as well as powerful, yang/yin parallel worlds of myth and legend across time, others have read about Sarmatian/Amazon women as offspring born of Scythians who hunted, wore the same attire as men, and could not wed until they killed a man in battle (Silk Road Foundation, 1997–2000), as reported by Herodotus who said he saw Greek soldiers fight them in battle (Osborne, 1997). A few may recall the mention of Finkelshteyn's (1999) assessment of Brunhild as a possible counterpart to King Arthur or to Middle Eastern and Celtic versions of warring women, while others remember a reference to

Amdur's (2002) investigation of the women warriors of Japan who are described as hired mercenaries during the feudal period (1467–1568).

The contemporary world continues to provide myriad examples of the heroic behavior of women in war. During the war in Iraq, for example, students have received information about the roles and fates of female military personnel, reporters, and representatives of nongovernmental organizations. News reports of prisoner-of-war Jessica Lynch have been supplemented by the story of the woman who sacrificed her own life to save Lynch. Students may also be challenged by the tension generated in cultural differences in the meaning of women's heroism, as in the depictions of Middle Eastern mothers simultaneously grieving and celebrating the lives of their martyred children in the documentary *Women of the Hezbollah* (Abi-Samra, 2000) who gain status in some Islamic societies by making the ultimate sacrifice of having a child die as a martyr. Women's contributions to the war effort are culturally defined or mandated by religious doctrine, exemplified by giving one's own life in symbolic sacrifice for one's ideals, country, and commander.

The role of the Amazon warrior continues in contemporary social discourse as the appropriateness of women in combat remains highly controversial and widely debated (Kirkwood, 2003), and it is essential to recognize that women's fight to share the battlefield alongside males is still being fought along with other inequities and injustices. A similar struggle can be found in an analysis of female athletic participation. In Olympic sports, women's participation in wrestling, boxing, and other high-contact/violent sports, and particularly if engaged in with men, have been interpreted as bridging or breaking down structural barriers in an activity choice leading to social change. Combating social injustice or inequity is, in fact, a form of "warring" (waging war, e.g., the war on terrorism, the war on poverty, the war against AIDS/SIDA). Likewise, political campaigns often evoke the imagery of war or campaigning, including "beating" one's opponent, claiming "victory," or similar expressions. Female candidates seeking election to political office adopt and use these phrases and terms in their own quests for acquiring leadership and power that they believe will result (eventually) in changes for the collective good.

Traits such as physical strength, discipline, mental toughness, and leadership are interpreted in contemporary American feminism as not only those qualities essential for literal "soldiering," but also as those necessary for personal transformation and reinvention leading to activism. Women engage in warlike behavior for reasons ranging from protecting themselves or loved ones to safeguarding territory to establishing dominance, and even for more esoteric and symbolic reasons such as rites of passage or deconstructing social role stereotypes. The sacrifices that many women experience as they attack these stereotypes are a form of social activism. These highly physical and ritualized endeavors are sometimes described as "virtual" combat, as in women's participation in Tae bo as a form of health and fitness, or as reflected by the popularity (and artistic acclaim) of 2004's *Million Dollar Baby*. Both levels of combatlike involvement offer evidence of devotion to and interest in this aspect of the female experience as suggested by the training, competition, and discipline that lead to excellence in sports and athletics. Scenes of heroines defying internalized oppression, overcoming internalized domination, and improving visibility, pride, and solidarity among women, offer further evidence of the power of women's alliances (Pheterson, 1990). In a variety of ways, art imitates both real and surreal aspects of life, just as community service learning may be real or *too real* to our students, if they are not prepared to participate. Popular culture courses are often included in women's studies programs, and faculty can collaborate in a selection of media-based assignments that intentionally prepare students for the next level of academic challenge.

Today's students want evidence that what they are being taught is both meaningful and relevant. The instructor and the curriculum serve as training camps for student warriors entering the battlegrounds of community-based reality through community service learning. Similar to a unit of enlisted military personnel from various ages, ethnicities, and levels of education, the community service-learning experience can form a common arena for diverse generations of students to challenge each other to identify ways to connect classroom, community, and future commitment to civic engagement. The model is one of empowerment that allows women to share responsibility and practice strategies that lead to change.

## Community Service Learning and Women's Studies

Although experiential and community service learning in one form or another has complemented traditional instruction at a variety of academic levels for decades, the pedagogical approach has only recently been examined extensively in the context of those disciplines offering academic programs in women's studies, a body of knowledge that is increasingly valued as part of the general (core) education program available to all students. There is both increased *internal* and *external* pressure for academicians and campuses to reconnect and be accountable to the broader academic mission, so that both theory and practice must not only be scrutinized for *internal* validity among women's studies majors (or minors) but also for *external* relevance for educating the general student as an involved citizen.

While both perspectives contribute to the overall goals for student learning, feminist pedagogy challenges the community service-learning paradigm to maintain a social justice focus. Rahima Wade (2001) defines community service learning as "the integration of school or community-based service activities with academic skills and structured reflection, but which all too often neglects to focus on "whether some injustice has created the need for service in the first place" (p. 1). In some academic settings this omission can lead to a lack of understanding about the possible impact of student engagement beyond personal growth and fulfillment or program-specific learning outcomes. Students may therefore interpret community service-learning assignments as busy work or free labor that is irrelevant to course mastery, personal growth, or effecting positive change in the world.

While Agha-Jaffar (2000) recommends using guest speakers from the community to help "put a face on what otherwise might be an abstract issue" (p. 2), there are a variety of ways to introduce students to community service learning: assigning field research projects, preinternship practicum hours, or through visual media (news stories, videos, photo-essays, etc.). The university campus may also identify specific geographic areas or salient issues around which to intentionally focus community service-learning initiatives.

While some educators believe community service-learning assignments should be optional, others believe that *all* students in a department (or program) need to engage in this type of learning at some point in their academic program, whether to support campus goals, ensure common learning experiences among all majors, or to meet program accreditation requirements. Providing students options in the identification/selection of placements respects the student as an equal participant in the learning community, while ensuring some continuity across the curriculum. Abernathy and Oberchain's research (2001) reported that students with mild to moderate learning disabilities, and those described as passive learners, benefit from "instructional strategies and methods that more actively involve students and reduce teacher ownership" (p. 87), with the teacher assuming the role of facilitator rather than instructor.

Similarly, each student will come to understand the contribution of formal education as extending civic engagement beyond academic requirements, whether during or following college. To be certain, there is no single, one-size-fits-all approach, but there are a variety of social, political, and economic realities that serve as catalysts for student activism, and faculty can thereby seize the opportunity for effective use of community service-learning experiences. Women's studies students must understand, however, the broader context of these assignments.

## Practical Recommendations: The Devil Is in the Details

Each university has its own guidelines for designing course content, outlines, and syllabi. More and more attention is being paid to course objectives and learning outcomes since they alert the learner, the instructor, the academy, and institutional decision makers to the presence of measurable outcomes that provide evidence that learning has occurred or that marketable/transferable skills have been mastered. Reviewing and reframing course objectives, worksheets, and visual models (e.g., Howard, 2001) that could be incorporated into community service learning in an upper-division women's studies course will provide an integrated view of the rich, interconnectedness of course dimensions. Students will see something unexpected, challenging, and an opportunity for personal action in their own lives. In short, the attention to detail in course design, learning activities, and selection of materials is extremely important to the overall learning experience. Sample course information may either be appended or made available from the authors. The following is a sample course description:

> This course is devoted to the explorations, practice and understanding of the role of community service learning in Women's Studies. Specifically, students will examine the link between theories/ways of knowing and thinking common to the academic setting and those experienced in the "real" world. You, the students in the course, will apply your knowledge of Women's Studies and related disciplines reflecting the scholarship of women, to your work within a community-based organization whose

primary function is to provide services to women. This course builds on the traditional practicum/internship format where common class meetings provide a facilitated space to share student reports, participate in reflective exercises, discussions and problem solving, both among students and between students and the course instructor.

A next step assists students with making the connection or "leap" between theory and practice in the context. For example, instructors may design a matrix of theories commonly taught in departmental courses and use it to facilitate review and discussion of feminist theories/thinking. This will help students realize that their courses are interrelated and interdependent. Discussion may include implications of the theory for specific community service placements they might select.

Students contribute to the shared learning community as they orally review feminist theories ranging from the more traditional and familiar to the more esoteric such as ecofeminism and, as in this chapter, Amazonian feminism. Students may be asked to expand on this learning activity by discussing relevant campus events during Women's History Month, ethnic celebrations, goddesses-centered events, athletic competitions, and the like. Events "outside the course" are important for a variety of reasons but may be used as examples of how curricular and cocurricular activities may be linked to increase campus awareness or debate about desired sociopolitical outcomes, or center around perceived inequities for a given group.

Course requirements/assignments might include class attendance/active participation, community service-learning site attendance (minimum number of hours should be specified along with written verification from the placement on-site coordinator), journal entries, a midterm oral presentation connecting feminist/womanist theory with site selection, a work plan for the site (objectives or activities to be accomplished), periodic unannounced in-class reflections, and a final examination incorporating a comprehensive portfolio of learning activities and site-specific work to be shared with classmates, including a bona fide research paper on the role of community service learning in the discipline (women's studies).

Naturally, each academic program and instructor may adapt or tailor these basic approaches for their use based on the level of the course, curriculum focus, previous experience of students, and a variety of other factors. This section has merely provided brief examples to help add some flesh to the bones of the discussion.

## Assessment of Student Learning

As at many comprehensive universities, the impetus surrounding *assessment of student learning* has prompted the creation and inclusion of both formal and informal classroom assessment activities. Since for many students community service learning may present a new (and troubling) pedagogy, it is important to provide numerous ways for students to process, share, and even "vent" their experience. The assessment activities increase student interaction around what could be isolated learning experiences and can help the instructor identify both individual and common stumbling blocks that have become impediments to learning. Two of these are the Journal Entry Analysis (weeks 5–7 in a 15-week semester) and a final paper abstract. The reader is reminded that, although this is a junior-level course, many of the students postponed the course until their final semester, and two students enrolled were in the process of applying to graduate school in women's/gender studies or related fields.

The instructor designed several instructional aids for the class including the Journal Entry Analysis form. The form was used to analyze ongoing journal entries to be certain students were (a) keeping up with regular entries, (b) identifying activities at the site that would provide evidence of accomplishing their stated objectives, and (c) that there was evidence of application of a specific theoretical framework. The activity was preannounced, and during the identified class meeting the instructor distributed the form that had been copied on light-green paper. Students completed analyses of four of their own journal entries by filling in the form and then were asked to compare their entries to those of a course mate.

This activity took about 90 minutes of a three-hour class period to complete, including discussion. The instructor's review of journal comments suggested a variety of student emotions ranging from confusion to anger to rethinking to exasperation and eventually turning to acceptance, initiative, and a feeling of success. The final paper abstracts, submitted at the conclusion of the course, however, reflected cumulative growth throughout the semester, although for some progress was slow. The following are excerpts:

### *Final Paper Abstracts*

Some students showed a sophisticated understanding of the intersection of the models presented in class, as one student stated:

The service-learning model constructs a markedly different learning environment for students. As a unique pedagogical tool, this model gives students a practical experience with theoretical frameworks designed to describe reality and identify problems. As a Feminist approach, this model is particularly valuable. The author of this work identifies one such example of a service learning experience in which such learning takes place. Specifically, the student learner was able to experience the way in which internalized gender roles influence the actions of individuals within a patriarchal construct. The example forwarded illustrate [*sic*] how the service-learning model functions to bolster an education in Women's Studies.

Other students gained insight regarding the challenges of community service and the need for creative approaches to resolve difficulties, for example:

> When providing community service, service is only effective when the community welcomes the service that is being offered. If the community does not welcome the service, then the service will be rejected and ultimately pointless. . . . I provided my service from a Marxist Socialist Feministic and Multicultural Feministic perspective. . . . I decided to attend the [site] on various days to receive a general idea of how many people do in fact utilize the [site]. . . . After the creation and launching of the page I found that more people were aware of whom [*sic*] I am. People wanted to get a hold of me asking about the web page and indirectly that helped the [site]. . . . In conclusion, it still holds true that anything well advertised can create a great difference. It does not matter what product is being sold as long as if you can market it the right way, anything can be sold, in this case the utilization of the [site].

Students were able to demonstrate their grasp of the connection between course material and the community work they engaged in, as stated in the following:

> Service learning is a concept relatively new to many people. However, it is increasingly taking the place of traditional community service projects. Community service learning can be seen as beneficial to Women's Studies classes in particular. Reasons for this may include essential feminist perspectives such as the call for women to become agents of changes. . . . For my service-learning project, I have analyzed the feminist perspective of women's service as talked about in Denise Chavez's novel *Face of an*

*Angel.* . . . She tells the next woman "Never forget that the work you do is important and full of lessons." I have taken that and applied it to all my work at the [site]. I chose to try to create more of a sense of community within the volunteers themselves. I did this by having events just for the volunteer[s] that were aimed at thanking them for all the work that they do at the [site]. I emphasized that all work, [is] important, however small it is perceived to be.

The effectiveness of service-learning pedagogy to reinforce core concepts was also illustrated in the comments of several students, for example:

My community service-learning experience has taught me more about Global Feminism than my Theory class could through various speakers at the [site]. I was able to hear from at least two Global Feminists about the effects of globalization in Argentina and the United States. I learned more about the International Monetary Fund and its damaging activities than I ever [k]new before.

The challenge of finding feminist friendly modes of pedagogy for application to Women's Studies curriculum has faced educators since the inception of Women's Studies academic programs. In particular feminists have sought modes of conveying information that do not replicate or otherwise promote the patriarchal and hierarchical methods of the traditional academy. This paper looks at how current critical theories regarding both Community-based service learning (CSL) and feminist thought illuminate the possibility that CSL is a pedagogical tool that may be particularly suited to feminist classrooms. . . . The case study for this analysis is based on my own experience with the [site] observing how race, class and gender impact Hospice patients, families and other caregivers.

## Discussion

The examples demonstrate the engagement students experienced both with the core material of the course and their experiences applying insights from theory to practical community activism. The comments also reflect a level of uncertainty and anxiety about introducing a new pedagogy in women's studies. Some of the students were quite negative about the community service-learning course requirement as part of the major. The course was also available for upper-division general education credit to nonmajor students. The first few weeks were definitely only the beginning of a long journey on a bumpy road as students examined and confronted their community service-"learning curve" demons.

So what's a professor to do? The instructor adopted three proactive strategies to smooth the way that provided (a) a specific example of theory as it applied to the course and resulted in the theme of Amazonian feminism discussed in this chapter, (b) more discussion (processing and problem solving) and reflective exercises *in class* so students could receive more frequent feedback on their progress, and (c) an invitation to the department chairperson to observe the class, listen to student concerns, and offer constructive feedback.

As a result of this process the following three recommendations were made to the department that both the students and the faculty member agreed upon. First, the department faculty (advisory board, alumnae, students) might preidentify a set of sites that met departmental goals, and through which the community service-learning experience could connect theory to the needs of the external community. Second, the "seeds" of community service learning would be planted in lower-division course work (e.g., special events, shorter-term community service-learning assignments, introduction of the concept and Howard's model in lower-division courses, giving CSL examples from previous women's studies students of how social justice education principles were applied and the resulting effect on the community served). Third, the community service-learning course needed to be "owned" by the department, significantly modified, or dropped. The 20-hour commitment placed numerous constraints on the host sites and on the students, but was viewed as "reasonable" for working students, since it extended over a 15-week semester.

This process, similar to that of a community meeting, became another lived example of practicing those actions needed for change, but in this case it was within the context of pedagogy. Faculty members must be committed to this process, and those who are not used to being challenged may wish to seek more traditional instructional assignments. Faculty must also be prepared to respond to the concerns of students.

Students need to be assured that the difficult work of community service is fundamental to course mastery, useful in personal skill development, and instrumental to effecting positive social change. The students raised important questions about the validity of "making them volunteer" and whether this was in direct conflict with feminist perspectives suggesting that women have all too long done invisible and undervalued, as well as unpaid, work (Dunn, 1997). Again, the instructor can answer this in part by raising the image of the warrior woman wielding the sword and armor of social justice, education, and civic engagement, which is far from the passive, disempowered image of the oppressed woman who has been socialized to believe her only legitimate use of time is to volunteer with her faith-based community, child's school, or at the voter registration booth. Students can also be assisted in resolving the issues raised by volunteerism versus feminist empowerment by examples that show how volunteering may itself be a route to empowerment. Activism is work, and volunteering may be the first step in a process of social change, as Pardo (1998) describes Josie Howard's efforts to keep her son out of gangs in east Los Angeles:

> She observed that "somehow the kids seemed to have some respect when parents were around" so they got permission to maintain presence in and around junior high schools. . . . Soon after Josie became a member of the Concerned Parents group, she volunteered to work with other community groups. Through her community work she learned much about obtaining support from Chicano agencies, such as the Mexican American Legal Defense and Education Fund (MALDEF). Later when she confronted other community issues in Monterey Park, she sought assistance from these and other public agencies created to fight discrimination and promote Mexican American political representation. (p. 84)

An interesting reversal of the argument that volunteer work is unpaid exploitation of women's labor can be made by challenging the students to embrace a given community service-learning project as a way to seize power in the community in a powerfully proactive and integrative way. While it is important to give students some choice in placements and projects, doing so requires significant up-front preparation, ideally before the course meets. When this has not occurred, time to sort through placements has to be done within the course and can cause anxiety. In the present example, some students were clearly taken beyond their comfort zone as they sought a placement, worked with the field placement site staff to identify desired outcomes, chose a framework for delivering or realizing outcomes, followed through on implementation, and reconnected their work to prior learning through reflection and evaluation. In spite of these challenges, most students were able to make the desired connections among academic work, civic engagement, and field experience. Learning is not without risk taking, and can definitely become an adventure. Parson's (1996) reflection on community service learning states that "for the students, what was once a 'chore' or 'do-gooding' becomes a true learning experience" (p. 4).

The final paper abstracts produced in the course serve as evidence that students were, in fact, able to pull it all together by the conclusion of the course, as is indicated by the excerpts presented in this chapter. The course provided an important transition from lower- to upper-division expectations for students to "think outside the box" creatively, or at least to *apply* course concepts in ways not normally experienced in the humanities (where women's studies is housed on the campus).

As Eyler (2000) concludes, "There is a belief in the power of real world experience, but little guidance on how to increase the ability of students to learn from experience and integrate it with other sources of information." To say the least this remains a challenge across the disciplines.

## Conclusion

The Amazonian feminist approach provides a wide range of empirical identification and testing. Community service-learning models support the method of critical inquiry as simply, albeit superficially, presented in this chapter. Certainly, the experience of this instructor is that service learning can be and often is best viewed as a critical pedagogy (Wink, 2000) of challenging and testing assumptions and realities of oneself, as well as those of institutions and individuals one encounters. The payoff for the learner can be figuratively transformative—just like our radical, whirling Wonder Woman!

This approach to learning changes both instruction (from directive to facilitative) and learning from classroom to the social context of daily life, and reinforces the need to infuse community service-learning assignments with the realities of social justice, righting wrongs, and becoming vigilant citizen-warriors. In the end, it is a rewarding exercise in meaningful learning since students "act upon and use their generated knowledge for self- and social transformation" (Wink, p. 129). The social war for lifelong learning is one that is ongoing and appropriately examined in the framework of Amazonian feminist thought.

# Notes

1. Amazonian Feminism Web site: http://www.glbtq.com/literature/
amazons.html
2. Definitions of various branches of feminism may be found at http://
www.cs.uu.nl/wais/html/na-dir/feminism/terms.html

# References

Abernathy, T. V., & Oberchain, K. M. (2001). Student ownership of service-learn-
    ing projects: Including ourselves in our community. *Intervention in School and
    Clinic, 37*(2), 86.
Abi-Samra, M. (Director). (2000). *The Women of Hezbollah* [Documentary]. United
    States.
Agha-Jaffar, T. (2000). From pedagogy to praxis in women's studies: Guest speakers
    and service learning as pedagogy. *Feminist Teacher, 13*(1), 1–11.
Amdur, E. (2002). *Women warriors of Japan: The role of arms-bearing women in Japa-
    nese history.* Retrieved from http://www.koryubooks.com/Library/wwj2.html
Cohee, G. E., Daumer, E., Kemp, T., Krebs, P. M., Lafky, S. A., & Runzo, S.
    (1998). *The feminist teacher anthology: Pedagogies and classroom strategies.* New
    York: Teachers College Press.
Collins, P. H. (1991). *Black feminist thought: Knowledge, consciousness, and the politics
    of empowerment.* New York: Routledge.
Donovan, J. (1996). *Feminist Theory: The intellectual traditions of American feminism.*
    New York: A Frederick Ungar Book.
Dunn, D. (1997). *Workplace/women's place: An anthology.* Los Angeles: Roxbury.
Eyler, J. S. (2000, Fall). What do we need to know about the impact of service-
    learning on student learning? [Special issue]. *Michigan Journal of Community Ser-
    vice Learning,* 11–17.
Finkelshteyn, N. J. (1999). *Warrior Women.* http://www.geocities.com/Athens/
    Olympus/3505/wmnarmor.html? 200415.
Haskell, R. (2001). Vampirism as the feminine in Anne Rice's *Interview with the
    Vampire.* Retrieved from http://www.bactroid.net/article.php/177
Howard, J. (2001). *Service learning course design workbook.* Ann Arbor, MI: Univer-
    sity of Michigan OSCL Press.
Kirkwood, R. C. (2003). *What kind of nation sends women into combat?* Retrieved
    from http://www.lewrockwell.com/orig3/Kirkwood3.html
Oblinger, D. (2003, July/August). Boomers, Gen-Xers, Millenials: Understanding
    the new students. *Educause Review, 38*(4), 37–47.

Osborne, L. (1997). *The women warriors.* Retrieved from http://www.icubed.com/ ~ljg/wwarriors.html

Pardo, M. S. (1998). *Mexican American women activists: Identity and resistance in two Los Angeles communities.* Philadelphia: Temple University Press.

Parsons, C. (1996). How to make service into service learning [Electronic version]. *The Journal of Volunteer Administration*, 14(3), 35–38. Retrieved from http://ener gizeinc.com/art/jser.html

Pheterson, G. (1990). Alliances between women: Overcoming internalized oppression and internalized domination. In L. Albrecht & R. Brewer (Eds.), *Bridges of power: Women's multicultural alliances* (pp. 34–48). Philadelphia: New Society Publishers.

Silk Road Foundation. (1997–2000). *The women warriors: The Sarmatians.* Retrieved from http://www.silk-road/artl/sarmatian.shtml

Wade, R. (2001). . . . *And justice for all: Community service-learning for social justice.* Denver, CO: Education Commission of the States. Retrieved from http://www .ecs.org/clearinghouse/29/13/2913.htm

Wink, J. (2000). *Critical pedagogy: Notes from the real world.* New York: Addison-Wesley/Longman.

# 7

# THE YOUNG WOMEN'S STUDIES CLUB

## Placing Gender and Multicultural Competence at the Center

*Susan E. Cayleff and Angela J. LaGrotteria*

[The Young Women's Studies Club] has showed me so much of women and has changed my view of how women should be treated. We are not just anything but something. We have a value.

—Female high school club member, fall 2004[1]

T he student who wrote these words spoke of her own increased knowledge of women's history, her own improved self-esteem, and the valuable lessons she learned from girls' and women's lives. This was made possible by the mentoring she received from university undergraduates in an upper-division American Women's History class. By being affiliated with the Young Women's Studies Club (YWSC), the college students gain knowledge of women's issues, concerns, and rights that were previously unfamiliar to them. For the college students, this Community-Based Service Learning (CBSL) experience helps enrich their knowledge of diverse communities locally and globally. It also allows them to take the materials and analyses provided in their women's studies college course(s) and aid high school students in learning. For the high school students they mentor, this collaboration fosters a proud articulation of their worth as young women and men.

Both the college students and the high school club members connect these insights as they examine the importance of other women's lives. In this chapter, we argue that the work done by San Diego State University (SDSU) undergraduates with the YWSC at Hoover High School in San Diego exemplifies a successful CBSL program by implementing experiential approaches to teaching and foregrounding women's studies. This approach differs significantly from the traditional university or high school classroom and is most beneficial for multicultural students.

## Theoretical Overview

The experiential approaches we have implemented are connected to principles of feminist, multicultural, and nondominant pedagogy. Paulo Freire's *Pedagogy of the Oppressed* (1921/2000) was influential in our pedagogical approach; it delineates strategies of teaching that transcend lecturing. In his article "The Adult Literacy Process as Cultural Action for Freedom," Freire (2001) suggested critical pedagogy that used innovative ways to teach adults to read and write. He argued that adults' ability to learn these skills would increase if they were engaged "in the constant problematizing of their existential situations" (p. 344). In short, if the words they are learning have direct meaning in their lives they will be more motivated to learn reading and writing. We also use this approach with the YWSC. The material and activities are always relevant to the students' lives and social locations. They are introduced to feminist theories and opportunities for activism, which they apply to their own circumstances.

This parallels the classroom experiences the college-level CBSL students encounter in the year-long American Women's History class. In 2000, Susan Cayleff officially listed her introductory undergraduate course as a CBSL option. It appears in the course catalog as such and alerts college undergraduates that they can earn (partial) course credit through on-site activism. The undergraduates are selected during the first week of class. The American Women's History class syllabi discuss the CBSL option on page one. Students are told they can apply to work with the YWSC, and if accepted they will be exonerated from the 8- to 10-page, annotated bibliography, final paper assignment. The syllabi also explain that more detailed instructions will be given orally within the first two to four class meetings. Interested students fill out an application form that asks them to state their year in college, major, previous relevant experience, and why they want to participate in the club.

The graduate student advisor and professor-liaison as a team evaluate the college undergraduates. Grades are assigned based on their minimum 20 hours of involvement, the analytic content of their journal and final paper, and their willingness and ability to function appropriately within this multi-layered group context. Usually 20-plus students apply, and 8 to 12 are selected because the ratio of college to high school students must facilitate much small-group interaction. A greater number of college students would make their presence dominating and defeat the goal of mentor–student balance. The students are selected based on the strengths of the answers they give in their applications. Diversity among the college students is a priority, and the selection process takes this into consideration as well. Students' contributions to the project cover a wide range of activities; they have suggested events such as the college mentoring session, speakers they know, creative projects, and museum visits. Meshing the college students' interests with those of the YWSC members necessitates employing feminist pedagogy in both settings.

This is no small task since the members of YWSC represent a broad range of ethnicities and nationalities in an inner-city public high school in Southern California. The club, like the school, contains almost equal numbers of Asian, African American, Latino/a, African, and Middle Eastern students who come from diverse cultural belief systems. Thus, we incorporate multicultural pedagogy, which necessitates honoring difference while working on a shared goal. bell hooks (1994), a feminist scholar greatly influenced by Freire, addressed the importance of multicultural pedagogy in *Teaching to Transgress*. According to hooks, "All students, not just those from marginalized groups, seem more eager to enter energetically into classroom discussion when they perceive it as pertaining directly to them" (p. 87). The key is to encourage students to examine their experiences from a critical standpoint and consider other ways of knowing. This strategy creates a safe environment for diverse students to share their opinions and perspectives.

Engaging students from a critical standpoint is a crucial aspect of non-dominant pedagogy. According to Robert A. Rhoads in "Critical Multiculturalism and Service Learning":

> [Critical multiculturalism] combines the conditions of cultural diversity
> with the emancipatory vision of critical educational practice borrowing

from postmodernism, critical theory, and feminism. . . . [This] liberatory
form of pedagogy [has as] a goal . . . education [that] challenge[s] students
to become knowledgeable of the social, political, and economic forces that
have shaped their lives and the lives of others (Freire, 2001; Giroux, 1992;
hooks, 1994). (p. 41)

Informed by these theoretical precepts, we implement a nonhierarchical
learning environment framed by feminist pedagogy and gender, race, geographic origin, and socioeconomic positions.

At its heart, feminist pedagogy calls for an egalitarian classroom in which
gender issues are openly acknowledged, explored, analyzed, and critiqued.
Then resourceful steps are taken to suggest remedies for these social ills. A
powerfully effective way to do this is to link theory with activism and classroom with community. As Carolyn M. Shrewsbury asserts in "What Is Feminist Pedagogy?": "Feminist pedagogy includes teaching strategies that are
based on a reconceptualization of community with a richness that includes
autonomy and individuality of members who share a sense of relationship
and connectedness with each other" (p. 13). This integration of feminist,
multicultural, and nondominant pedagogical practices in a community-
based classroom fosters inclusive social change.

## Teaching and Learning Objectives/Process of the
## CBSL Project

The college students are enrolled in the American Women's History course.
The objectives for their learning focus on the lives of diverse women in the
following realms: familial relations, work roles, sex-role expectations, examples of resistance and accommodation, health practices, political involvements, and bonding among women. They are also taught to consider
changes over time and larger cultural influences (i.e., war, economic down-
turns, colonized communities, shifting federal policies, and so on). The undergraduates are trained by two distinct approaches. The first is the course
materials they learn in Women's Studies 341A and B. The second level of
training occurs on site through the directions, role modeling, and leadership
of the graduate student coordinator.

The joint partnership between SDSU and Hoover High School began
in the early 1990s when the SDSU undergraduate women's studies class So-

cialization of Women linked with a class of high school seniors. The high school students constituted and named the club themselves. In its 12 years of existence, the YWSC has grown to a seven-level collaborative effort: the Department of Women's Studies at SDSU, the ongoing cooperation of the high school principal, college professor(s), undergraduate students in an upper-division women's studies course, high school teacher/advisor, master's women's studies student coordinator, and club officers and their high school peers. Communication and decision making flows from the SDSU faculty advisor (Cayleff) to the graduate student coordinator (Angela LaGrotteria) to the college students to the high school faculty advisor and to the participating high school students. But this communication process can just as easily originate with the high school members or college undergraduates and flow from that starting point.

We all work collaboratively to plan activities. There are several that are particularly successful and popular. For the Women in Sports night, YWSC members attend a slide show presentation on women in sports, go to an SDSU women's basketball game, and meet the team afterward. Other events include participation in Hoover High's Homecoming Parade, replete with a decorated vehicle sporting feminist messages and images; a Women's History Month poster contest; and guest speakers drawn from women's studies faculty, graduate students, and community activists on several topics, such as violence in relationships, understanding Islam, sexual abuse, teen pregnancy, and the experiences of new immigrants to America, among others. Further creative projects include "Media Constructed Women," "Photographing Female Role Models," and the antiviolence "Clothesline Project." The calendar is rounded out with field trips to the San Diego Museum of Art to view artwork by women, SDSU student-led college application mentoring sessions, participation in Hoover High's multicultural food fair, and an annual softball game and picnic. The SDSU undergraduates, drawn from a variety of majors and both female and male, participate in all of these events and the weekly meetings with the high school students.

The college students are carefully versed in dress code, language, punctuality, display of identification badges, and their place as role models, mentors, and learners. They also are instructed to mingle among the high school students and facilitate discussion and elicit ideas for future events from the students. Their learning experiences, as they report in end-of-semester evaluations, chronicle several recurrent themes: This experience has clarified for many the grade level of students they want to teach in K–12; it has increased their multicultural competence on issues of immigration, race, ethnicity, and social class; it has enhanced their ability to assume a leadership role; and it has fostered a commitment to continue doing this kind of community-based work.

There is a fluid exchange of ideas and leadership with little discernible hierarchy among the seven levels of participants. For example, when a work group of Club members presents their poster board projects or text/Web-based research on a topic, they become the teachers. When the club projects are displayed in the school's media center, hundreds of students, teachers, counselors, and administrators see and discuss the work of the YWSC. As we participate in the homecoming parade, chanting feminist slogans, our voices are mixed with the football chants. During softball games in the park, professors, teachers, and students of varying levels have called encouragement to each other and demonstrated a friendly competitive spirit. At SDSU sporting events we have cheered, snacked, and watched our team together. These activities, in which leadership roles are exchanged, foster both the undergraduates' and the high school students' learning of feminist principles. They experience empowerment, consensus decision making, nonhierarchical dynamics, increased cross-cultural awareness, and actual knowledge about women's roles in history (through the projects that are research and speaker based).

Even the "mechanics" of gathering are shared: A few minutes prior to a weekly club meeting ending, everyone helps tidy the classroom, put away supplies, and articulate the goals of the next meeting. Following multicultural pedagogy, we listen and consider all opinions and perspectives. Instead of asking the club to accept a particular position, we ask that we respect each other and the different perspectives we bring. During discussions after a brief film clip or guest speaker, everyone has an equal voice. Most club members easily share their experiences and/or beliefs in this safe and nonconfrontational environment.

Feedback from the college students highlights the equality they experience. Collectively they have noted their sense of accomplishment in helping design successful projects, their growing comfort with serving as mentors who help guide discussions, their ability to accept opinions and ideas that contradict their own, and the need for them to listen and learn from the high school students. Anne A. comments in her reflection paper that "the two most important skills that I acquired are the ability to speak with and listen to high school students and the ability to take initiative."

The high school students have noted their excitement at helping create the semester's schedule of activities, their ability to question speakers and to conceptualize a research project alongside a college student, and at the decisions they make autonomously. These decisions include the following: which theme to adopt for their homecoming float, which activities are a priority to them, how the club wants its leadership to be configured (solo president, two presidents, or run by a circle of leaders), and who should take the lead on any given meeting.

## Assessment: Overall Learning Outcomes/Experiences of the University Undergraduates

We have elicited written reflective journals, final papers, end-of-semester evaluation sheets, and oral presentations from the college students that articulate the impact of this collaboration on them. From the undergraduates' analyses, we receive many helpful suggestions, all of which we consider and some of which we successfully integrate into the club. Undergraduates have expressed to both of us on several occasions—and in their written and oral reflections—that they feel empowered by the YWSC, that they have furthered their own knowledge of women's studies and issues, and that they wish there would have been such a club in their high schools.

The following quotes taken from undergraduates' journals and reflection papers support our aforementioned argument. Beth M. remarks: "I learned from the [high school] students as well. These young people weren't just coming to club meetings for pizza. They were seeking a place where they could find support, information, and encouragement in the company of other women, as well as some men, all who were gathered for the same reason." Alicia discovers: "[The YWSC high school members] had so many opinions and ideas, things that I did not even think about at the ages of fourteen and fifteen. . . . I began to wonder why I never spoke the way these [young] women did and I realized that I had been silenced." Mary proclaims: "I am forever learning more at every meeting I go to. My brain feels like it has been on overdrive this past month, and I love it!" Patty muses: "When I was in high school I don't think I really gave any sort of thought to issues pertaining to women's rights. . . . I think it's really amazing that Hoover

High School has this women's studies club and even more so that so many girls are this interested in it."

Specifically, the undergraduates learn how to work in a group setting. While they do not meet formally outside the club, they are asked to remain after their women's studies class on occasion to strategize about logistics for an upcoming event. At these times the professor-liaison makes suggestions and asks for feedback. They also communicate by e-mail constantly with the graduate student mentor on planning, bringing in needed materials, transportation needs, reflections on projects just completed, and plans for the upcoming event. The undergraduates learn how to serve as educators in a nontraditional environment and how to honor varied cultural traditions. Alicia comments on the remarkable diversity of the club: "I looked around [the room] and discovered that most of the young women in the club were of non-Caucasian descent. As a Mexican-American woman I felt very closely linked to some of the girls." Also, undergraduates learn how to conceptualize, organize, and implement a project, how to function within a consensus-building environment, how to communicate effectively with high school students with this demographic mix, how to facilitate a valuable learning experience that emphasizes "process" as much as it does knowledge, and how to reciprocally learn from students whose life experiences often differ from their own.

Quotations from the undergraduate journals reveal what was of benefit to them. As Jamie T. wrote: "Our group was diverse in the way they looked, the way they acted, and the way they spoke, but the magazine activity let us all come together. We shared a common concern for the way women (and men) are represented in the media. . . . I wish I had had such an opportunity [in high school]." Similarly, as Mario M., a male undergraduate, said: "We attended the Sally Ride night, and it enriched my knowledge by learning more about women and their triumphs. This entire program wasn't only beneficial for the [Hoover] students, but for me as well." And Sian R., an international student from Wales, said that her mentoring the YWSC "was extremely valuable to both my personal and my educational development. . . . After completing this, I hope to continue onto a teaching qualification. . . . so I feel that the opportunity I was offered at Hoover was significant to my future." Finally, Tricia G. talked about the satisfaction of demythologizing pressures put on young women: "It makes me feel really good to know that I might have helped them to understand that nobody has a perfect body and you'll only make yourself miserable trying to be something that you are not."[2]

At semester's end the YWSC CBSL students organize a presentation for their college classmates about their experiences. Here they report on the various activities, discuss what was of value for them, articulate discoveries they made about themselves and the high school students, and display projects that they and club members created. They also offer critiques that stress the following: the constraints of a short meeting, the difficulties of drawing a large contingent for off-campus weekend activities, and their frustration that they discovered the value of CBSL so late in their undergraduate studies.

## Assessment: Overall Learning Outcomes/Experiences of YWSC Members

We ask club members to discuss what they liked/didn't like, what they would change/keep the same, what they had learned, and how the club had affected their lives. These critical reflections are necessary. Jeff Claus and Curtis Ogden assert in *Service Learning for Youth Empowerment and Social Change* (1999), "Service experience, when set in a framework of substantive reflection, can also motivate and empower young people to think critically about their world and to act on it with a growing sense of purpose, agency, and optimism" (p. 1). In addition, a spring 2004 doctoral student at the California School of Professional Psychology selected the YWSC as her dissertation topic. Trained as a clinical psychologist, Jennifer C. Joseph's (2005) thesis was titled "Adolescent Girls' Experiences Receiving Early Feminist Education Through Participation in a Young Women's Studies Club." Over the course of the year she interviewed 16 young women ranging in age from 14 to 18 whose membership in the club spanned three months to three years. Their races/ethnicities were the following: three African Americans, two Somali Africans, one Ugandan African, eight Mexican Americans, one European American, and one Caucasian Mexican. Her findings offer a clear and positive assessment of the club's benefits to its participants.

Through an interview format (some were done in groups, a few individually) Joseph found that the young women identified two major themes that affected their lives. The first of these was obstacles. They described their own experiences with male privilege (e.g., "girls are put second"), a sexual double standard that benefited boys and limited girls' choices, body self-hatred exacerbated by objectification and sexual harassment, restrictive social mobility imposed on them by their families because they are female, and physical and sexual abuse. Demonstratively, Jaida talked about the sexual double standard: "When it comes to sex and stuff like that . . . Girls and guys—it's very different. If a girl is with a guy or she's intimate with him or whatever, she's a ho. She's this. She's that. You know, versus . . . a guy—he get glorified for it. He gets a pat on his back for doing certain things." Similarly, Julia shared how the club helped her realize restrictive gender roles within her own family: "My brother lives in Arizona . . . whenever he comes down . . . my mom . . . never lets him touch the dishes . . . and when I'm cleaning . . . I'll have to fold clothes and I'll ask my brother for help, she goes, no you can't ask him for help, he's a boy. . . . I think it's unfair. . . . just because we were born females doesn't make us slaves or anything." A third female club member who became aware of obstacles said:

> I used to blame myself for all the abuses I went through. And when I learned about this woman speaking [at the club] about domestic violence and emotional and sexual stuff like that, I was like, hmmmm. . . . It's not my fault. Cause the guy took advantage of me. And it wasn't my fault. And that's when, at that point, I know it wasn't my fault.

According to Joseph the second major theme that emerged for them as a result of the club was empowerment. They noted that the role models (graduate students, college undergraduates, college faculty) were positive influences that helped them realize they had choices. They identified claiming and developing their voices. They spoke of learning healthy resistance to oppression and being provided with tools for a better life. They also spoke of forging self-determination. Vanessa said:

> For me it's scary. Cause I'm the oldest girl. . . . My grandma had my mom when she was fifteen and my mom had me when she was fifteen. And it was really scary cause they're all expecting me to be pregnant too. And that's why yesterday on my birthday was a, how you want to say it? An achievement for me. That I turned seventeen and I wasn't pregnant.

Many young women expressed comfort and pride in claiming or developing their own "voice." As Alicia explained: "In class I usually don't answer questions out loud, but when I'm in the Club I give my opinion. . . . I'm more comfortable, I guess, because it's with all girls." These themes of empowerment abounded in the interviews. As Vanessa said: "We're strong. People might think we're weak sometimes, and in reality we're stronger than they think. I mean, girls, girls might seem weak sometimes, but we're strong." For Roni, the club helped her recast obstacles she had faced: "Getting hassled, kinda, makes you stronger, like being able to brush things off and being able to ignore something and get past it." The Joseph study revealed that participation in the club fostered empowerment and enhanced adolescent girls' self-esteem—for example, some participants who had been abused stopped blaming themselves. Their education about oppression (manifested in sexism, racism, and classism) contributed to their greater intellectual freedom. Finally, club members said they felt less compelled to conform to strict gender roles.

Assessment revealed that students' participation within the club provided them with a place for healthy resistance and the intellectual tools to reconsider their prescribed sex roles. These critical thinking skills might lead to increased civic engagement as the club members mature. It is clear at this time that club members share their insights with nonclub members at the high school. In many instances these "reported-to" friends come to the club and become members themselves. One final thought: Because so many of the club's activities are project oriented, its efforts and perspectives are displayed throughout the high school over the course of the year. This in and of itself is a form of civic engagement, consciousness-raising, and collective self-assertion.

This learning environment benefits all involved with the club, especially the undergraduates and high school students. The undergraduates serve as mentors to the high school students and facilitate their learning experiences by offering guidance and ensuring that the YWSC is a fun and safe environment. In events such as the Women's History Month poster contest, the undergraduates integrate the CBSL component by linking academic knowledge with participation in activism. This integrative approach is frequently discussed, analyzed, and lauded in women's studies classes. The undergraduates are able to experience firsthand the positive effects of consciousness-raising and community activism that complements historical study. The undergraduates come to see that young people can and do make change in their community. Women's studies' class content asserts that the personal is political and that both individual and community action are crucial to improving social conditions. The undergraduates participating in YWSC realize these ideals.

The high school students overwhelmingly express their appreciation for and satisfaction with the club. In their regular end-of-semester feedback comments, they articulate several favorite aspects of belonging to the club: Self-esteem and community involvement were increased as was knowledge of students from different cultures/countries, and the creation of and participation in activities fueled their feminist ideals. As one Hoover student wrote, "I like the fact that as a young woman there is a program that helps me know more of who I am." Another student commented that she "really like[s] that we have a diversity of girls in the club." Our experience with the YWSC has shown that amid the cultural diversity, the members share one pervasive commonality: the belief that difference does not imply exclusion from global feminisms.

One guest speaker was a college-age woman who talked to the YWSC about her experience as the only female football player on her high school's team. One high school member (perhaps overoptimistically) exclaimed about the discussion: "Women can do anything males can (no limitations), like football. We're equal!" Over two meetings, a speaker from the Center for Community Solutions (a San Diego–based activist organization) discussed healthy teen relationships and warning signs of trouble, such as a male's insistence that the female wear a piece of his clothing as a visible sign that she "belongs" to him. One Hoover student, commenting on this presentation, said it made her think differently about herself as a young woman: "[I must] . . . respect myself and make myself valued like [read apart] from my boyfriend and other boys." Further, a male graduate student in women's studies guest lectured on "Gender, Culture, and Sexual Assault." He focused on men's and women's parts in prevention of sexual assault and emphasized that it is *never* a woman's fault if she is sexually assaulted/raped. One club member reflected: "I've learned a lot [in YWSC] about sexual harassment and valuing that 'No means no,' and that women's opinions mean a lot."

We positively maintain that increased feelings of self-awareness, self-esteem, and confidence are a direct result of the CBSL experience with the YWSC. As one Hoover student said, "I am a young woman and that is beautiful, and I should enjoy it and embrace it." Another YWSC member commented: "I like the fact that we get to discuss the issues that most female teenagers have." And, when asked what she had gained from the YWSC, another student wrote, "I can definitely say that I see things differently, and that I have a greater respect for other women."

## Problem-Solving Advice

Of course, the club has its unique challenges that require problem-solving strategies. First, we are constrained by working within the public school K–12 system. These difficulties include the following: holding meetings in a rushed 35-minute block of time, securing permission slips from parents so that club members can participate in off-campus trips, securing and providing adequate transportation from the high school to field sites and returning in time for students to catch their buses home, an insecure budget (this has been ameliorated in recent years by a financial commitment from the Department of Women's Studies at SDSU), a high school campus concerned with violence and gang prevention that requires a very tight movement-by-written-permission-only pass system during the school day, and working with a population (largely) of minors (this necessitates permission slips, a carefully planned drop-off to a common site at the event's end, or driving students to their homes). One other problem that has emerged of late involves the high school faculty sponsor of the club. In previous years we were fortunate to work with feminist, highly interactive teachers who brought their enthusiasm and leadership to the club meetings and activities. When one such advisor left San Diego to take another job, a colleague-friend of hers assumed the position. Unfortunately, it has not been as smooth a "fit." The new advisor chooses to participate less, and this is problematic because the club's high school teacher-advisor is crucial for securing parental permission slips, helping advertise club activities on campus, and generally instilling a positive tone in interested students.

We have addressed these problems in the following ways. The 35-minute time block is immutable. We have learned to be extremely well organized by handing out the food as the students enter, calling the meeting to order immediately, having tight and engaging agendas, and previewing the next week's activities. Securing permission slips takes a collective effort from the club's student president, the high school teacher-advisor, and the graduate student coordinator. To get these back in time for a scheduled event we use midweek prompts from the club's on-site advisor, print flyers reminding students, and mention it throughout the 35-minute meetings. Still, this issue can be a stumbling block if only 6 students are able to go to a museum, but 25 signed up expressing their interest. We have learned to value the size of the group, whatever it is. College faculty and graduate students with the appropriate insurance provide transportation. One year a grant made it possible to offer small honorariums for these expenses to graduate students, but it is almost always an expense they bear.

Two other problems emerged: personality issues among club members and the inability of the high school student president to be an effective leader. We have long encouraged copresidents so that the club can function effectively if one of the students is absent. Dual leadership can be challenging if one student is more verbal and directive than the other. In those instances we have worked with both to balance the participation of each. During those rare semesters when we have only one president, the results are far less beneficial. At present we are planning to bring in a "coordinating committee" of sorts to assist the president with advertising club activities, securing permission slips, running the meetings, and preparing for and attending activities. Given the nature of their high school schedules and familial demands, it is too much labor and responsibility for one student to handle comfortably.

While the public inner-city high school location for women's studies is challenging and at times frustrating, it is exhilarating and always electric. The high school location is important to CBSL participation in higher education, as Terry Pickeral (2003) comments in "Partnerships With Elementary and Secondary Education," because "as service-learning pedagogy and practice increase in elementary and secondary schools, it has become clear that students' pre-college experiences will, for better or worse, shape their attitudes toward collegiate service-learning" (p. 175). In fact, three YWSC members who have graduated from Hoover High have taken Cayleff's class and gone back to their high school as CBSL mentors. All three expressed how rewarding it was for them to return to their high school and be a part of a club that empowered them just a couple years earlier. Nan wrote:

> Being a [Hoover student] once myself, I have seen how some of my peers had negative influences from other people and they ended up dropping out of high school. So I believe that positive influence is a very important thing for teens at their age because they can easily be guided in the wrong direction.

Further, our experience shows that the multicultural high school location fuels cultural understanding, promotes and affirms feminist consciousness, and bridges divergent backgrounds among an internationally and ethnically/racially diverse student population. As Paula A. Roy and Molly Schen (1993) argue in their essay "Feminist Pedagogy: Transforming the High School Classroom," "the high school may be more receptive to feminist teaching than the college lecture hall. . . . the high school may be the pivotal place where powerful ideas and practice can converge" (pp. 142, 146). Years of experience with the YWSC high school location demonstrate this contention: CBSL learning outcomes are positive, exciting, and necessary in the search for social justice.

## Reflection

For Cayleff, this is the single most innovative and rewarding program that she has worked with in 23 years of university teaching. It delivers feminist process and issues to young, diverse women and men. It honors the origins of women's studies, which in the early 1970s were seen as vehicles for social change. It also has immediate rewards when a project or task is done; we see the excitement and understanding blossom before our eyes. This type of tangible response is welcome to a career that is frequently achieved in quasi isolation amid archives and long hours of scholarly writing. It offers a certain sense of "being alive" and involvement in our contemporary world that is similar to classroom teaching but unique for the ages served and approaches used. It is also a reciprocal learning environment. We have learned about geographic dislocations, cultural belief systems, adjustments to American life, sex role expectations within diverse cultures, and countless other invaluable aspects of the club members' lives. Cayleff has taken these insights back into her university classroom and her own research interests. The graduate student coordinator, Angela LaGrotteria characterized her paid assistantship as immeasurably fulfilling and meaningful. With each meeting and event she learned more about women's issues and felt an overwhelming pride and satisfaction in her involvement with the YWSC. Clearly the environment rewards us.

SDSU undergraduates' journals/final papers about their YWSC experiences and YWSC high school students' evaluations demonstrate a successful CBSL program. When practicing experiential learning objectives, one is at risk of facing resistance, misunderstanding, even animosity. We are delighted that this CBSL environment has yielded such positive outcomes for the undergraduates amid these challenges. We have seen firsthand that community activism, outside the walls of traditional academia, has long-lasting, important effects. It has further convinced us that there need not be a split between theory and activism, nor between university and community.

The undergraduates' impact on the community is significant. We know that many undergraduates feel inspired to continue community service work after being a club member. Alison comments: "This experience has definitely made me want to volunteer at other places and get involved in things that I normally wouldn't have gotten involved in. It's really challenged me to go above and beyond the things that I normally do and to think about other people besides myself." Do CBSL courses inspire more students to become involved in their communities and feel inspired to make a difference in young people's lives? We believe it does, as Van notes: "After being involved in this Club I also made time to volunteer by helping at freshman orientation . . . assisting kids with reading and math . . . mentoring and helping kids with homework . . . and supporting the elderly at a local residence."

The undergraduates help bridge the distance frequently felt by nondominant groups concerning the potential for college education for their youth. Hanh, who was in the YWSC as a high school student and served as an undergraduate mentor, commented that it helped her decide to attend a four-year university:

> During my senior year in high school, when I was in the YWSC, an SDSU college student shared her college experiences with me and what the SDSU campus environment was like. Before, I was not planning on attending SDSU at all, even though I already applied and was admitted. My first choice was a community college, but her experiences at SDSU made me want to experience what she did and so I decided to attend SDSU after all.

This student is currently a nursing major.

## Future Directions

Changes we would make to enhance the experiences of the undergraduates working with the YWSC would be (a) expanding what we do as a group, (b) increasing their involvement with parents and within the community, (c) working to expand the amount of time the college students could share with the high school students, and (d) sharing the mechanics of this project so that it can be used as a model elsewhere. Of course, these goals are constrained by time and monetary resources. Greater resources would allow for field trips beyond a 10-mile radius, participation in leadership workshops for the undergraduates and club members, and the ability to buy reference books that could "live" at the high school for club-related research.

Some specific questions are: How did membership in a high school feminist club affect its members later in life? Do they carry with them explicit concerns for women's issues? Are they active in women's organizations, clubs, and so forth, after high school, during college, and/or after college? (We have evidence that this is true via the "generational" mentoring.) Also, do they continue to demonstrate cultural competence?

The club creates an atmosphere of awareness, inclusiveness, and acceptance for the college and high school students. Evidence to date shows the undergraduates take their classroom and experiential knowledge and translate it into living feminist theory/activism while valuing cultural diversity. As J. Dwyer, an SDSU undergraduate, wrote: "This experience has affected my life in such a positive way. . . . As a future teacher, I can take all of these one-of-a-kind [YWSC] experiences and apply them to bettering the lives of future generations."

## Notes

1. YWSC high school students' comments are taken from Cayleff's end-of-semester evaluation forms from 2004–2005.

2. Quoted undergraduate comments are taken from Cayleff's SDSU student reflection papers 2001–2005.

## References

Claus, J., & Ogden, C. (1999). Service learning for youth empowerment and social change: An introduction. In J. Claus and C. Ogden (Eds.), *Service learning for youth empowerment and social change* (pp. 1–7). New York: Peter Lang.

Freire, P. (2000). *Pedagogy of the oppressed* (M. B. Ramos, Trans.). New York: Continuum. (Original work published 1921)

Freire, P. (2001). The adult literacy process as cultural action for freedom. In S. W. Beck & L. N. Oláh (Eds.), *Perspectives on language and literacy: Beyond the here and now* (pp. 335–351). Harvard Educational Review Reprint Series No. 35. Cambridge, MA: Harvard Educational Review.

hooks, b. (1994). *Teaching to transgress: Education as the practice of freedom.* New York: Routledge,

Joseph, J. C. (2005). *Adolescent girls' experiences receiving early feminist education through participation in a Young Women's Studies Club.* Unpublished doctoral dissertation, California School of Professional Psychology at Alliant International University, San Diego.

Pickeral, T. (2003). Partnerships with elementary and secondary education. In B. Jacoby & Associates (Eds.), *Building partnerships for service-learning* (pp. 174–191). San Francisco: Jossey-Bass.

Rhoads, R. A. (1998). Critical multiculturalism and service learning. *Academic Service Learning: A Pedagogy of Action and Reflection, 73,* 39–46.

Roy, P. A., & Schen, M. (1993). Feminist pedagogy: Transforming the high school classroom. *Women's Studies Quarterly, 21*(3/4), 142–147.

Shrewsbury, C. M. (1993). What is feminist pedagogy? *Women's Studies Quarterly, 21*(3/4), 8–16.

# LEARNING ABOUT PREJUDICE, OPPRESSION, AND HATE

## Reversing the Silence

*Silvina Ituarte*

While scholars and educators recognize the complexities of the socialization process and the roles of privilege and disadvantage in the existence of social inequities, these concepts are often difficult for students to comprehend within a classroom setting without a real-life context to frame their foundation. Without these real-life contexts, the concepts embody a surreal or abstract dimension that does not translate well into the type of effectual learning necessary for provoking interest in, or understanding of, social justice. In order to support student appreciation for the complexities of prejudice, oppression, hate crimes, and gender inequities students enrolled in a Prejudice, Violence, and Criminal Justice course participated in a campus-based service-learning project. The project included designing visual displays throughout the university as well as promoting dialogue, in the form of role plays, concerning the silencing effects of prejudice and bias-motivated violence.

## Theoretical Underpinning

According to Bobbie Harro's (2000) "Cycle of Socialization," one is born with no prejudices, stereotypes, traditions, or biases. Through interactions with those whom one trusts (i.e., family, friends, educators), he or she is socialized regarding the norms, expectations, values, and roles ascribed to specific individuals within a given culture, including one's gender roles. Each person is exposed to value-laden beliefs about the way "things are" as well as the way things "ought to be." These beliefs and norms are subsequently reinforced through institutions, such as schools and religious places of worship, as well as cultural practices, language, and the media. These institutional and cultural messages are then enforced through a process of rewards and punishments that ostracize unpopular behaviors and reward the norm. For example, boys who play with dolls may be scolded for acting outside the socially defined expectations of what it means to be male, and girls may be praised for wanting to baby-sit. In this process, some are rewarded with privileges, while others are persecuted for deviating from the norm. Harro (2000) believes this translates into responses including but not limited to guilt, anger, self-hatred, stress, and dissonance that lead to silence by those who are disadvantaged, as well as acceptance by those with privilege who frequently do not recognize the inequities. For example, couples may not recognize the heterosexual privilege of having access to the legal recognition of marriage during important health-related emergencies or in making arrangements after death. Harro (2000) explains that people have a choice either to maintain the status quo by doing nothing about these inequities or to raise the consciousness of others by taking a stand with their words and actions.

## The Service-Learning Project

While enrolled in a 16-week course, students learned about the relationship between oppression, gender bias, inequality, discrimination, and bias-motivated offenses; the role of privilege and allies within the socialization process; the normative assumptions about various groups according to sex, age, ethnicity, race, sexual orientation, and ability; as well as the connections between the socialization process and bias-motivated offenses. For their project, the students worked on a consciousness-raising event designed to draw attention to those who have been silenced by oppression and hate. The objectives of the project were to formulate an activity that would inform the campus community, as well as the community at large, about discrimination and oppression; demonstrate the importance of creating allies; show support for marginalized groups; and demonstrate a commitment toward ending oppression.

For their project, the students coordinated an event called the Day of Silence, modeled after a national event that originated with a paper written by an 18-year-old student at the University of Virginia protesting the silencing of lesbian, gay, bisexual, and transgender people within mainstream culture. While this project expanded the original concept to embrace all oppressed groups including but not limited to those dealing with gender disparities, poverty, ableism, and victims of hatred and prejudice, the emphasis remained on the premise of forming alliances and promoting dialogue. The project was called the Day of Silence to symbolize the silencing effects of oppression as experienced by those exploited on the basis of sex, harassed for their immigrant status, estranged as a result of their religion, scrutinized for their race, alienated as a result of their sexual orientation, or mistreated because of a disability. Throughout the day, participants made a vow to remain silent for a specified amount of time (e.g., from 12:30 p.m. until 1:00 p.m.) and distributed cards explaining their advocacy for oppressed groups stating the following, which is adapted from the Day of Silence Web site at http://www.dayofsilence.org:

> Please understand my reasons for not speaking today. I support the rights of everyone including women; people of color; ethnic and religious minorities; lesbian, gay, bisexual, and transgender people; those who are differently abled; economic minorities; and all other oppressed persons. People who are silent today believe that laws and attitudes should be inclusive of people of all backgrounds. The *Day of Silence* draws attention to those who have been silenced by hatred, oppression, and prejudice. Think about the voices you are not hearing. What can you do to end the silence?

At the end of the silence (1:00 p.m.), the participants gathered, reflected, and participated in educational role plays and personal accounts that explored the meaning of the day's events and the need for future involvement in social and civic issues. This provided an opportunity to explore the meaning behind the silence and the significance of speaking out against oppression.

With the premise that the voices of victims of abuse and prejudice are often *silenced*, a blue ribbon (which has come to represent efforts to raise awareness regarding child abuse and neglect) was thought to be an appropriate symbol for the Day of Silence. On this day, wearing this ribbon was intended to raise awareness not only for those silenced by child abuse and neglect, but also for those who are silenced by prejudice, bias-motivated aggression, and domestic violence, sexual abuse, and all other forms of oppression. Members of the campus community were encouraged to consider participating in the Day of Silence in a manner that best suited them. For those whose campus responsibilities may have made it impossible to remain silent for an extended period of time (e.g., therapists at the counseling center), support for the event was encouraged in a number of creative ways. Some ideas included wearing the ribbons distributed on the day of the event, recording a voice mail message stating one's silence during a designated time frame, or taking three minutes at the beginning of a course to explain the day's event.

## In the Classroom

Throughout the semester, students examined social constructs, theories, historical events, research findings, and statistical analyses that comprehensively provided a context for academically understanding discrimination and violence. For the purpose of this monograph, this chapter will particularly emphasize the activities, readings, and issues related to gender. Students learned that bias crimes, regularly referred to in the media as "hate crimes," comprise a range of offenses committed in response to a victim's actual or perceived race, religion, ethnicity, national origin, gender, gender identity, sexual orientation, or disability.[1] By focusing on innate characteristics of the victim, bias-motivated acts of vandalism, defamation, harassment, intimidation, assault, arson, and homicide broadcast a threatening message to all members of the community and affect not only the victim but also the group to which the victim belongs. Often, these bias-motivated behaviors originate from what some perceive as benevolent pranks or comments. Nationally, the largest proportions of bias-motivated crimes reported to the Federal Bureau of Investigation (FBI) frequently include acts of intimidation, vandalism, and assault.

Despite the fact that this course was taught at a diverse and multicultural campus, the concept of privilege often raises considerable amounts of anxiety and resistance. Boatright-Horowitz (2005) have found that "many students seem to believe that they are already fairly well informed regarding racism (Khan, 1999), and they are likely to be resistant to having their 'assumptive worlds' challenged (Millstein, 1997)" (p. 35). Since discussing prejudice, oppression, and privilege are not easy, especially not in a classroom setting in which students may hesitate to speak for fear of saying the wrong thing, students were introduced to the course content in a gentle manner. "Building bridges between people from different social backgrounds becomes increasingly important as our society becomes more diverse and socially stratified. One way we can foster learning and understanding across difference is to bring college students together to talk and learn from each other, to find ways to communicate, and to understand why it is not always easy to get along or to identify common ground" (Zuniga, 2003, p. 8). Past experience in teaching similar topics revealed that students experience the greatest difficulty and resistance when attempting to empathize with the concepts of "skin privilege." In order to approach the concept of privilege in a gentle manner, the concept of "male privilege" was introduced first. In class, the students listened to a parallel description of a woman and man at work with varying meanings attached to the same behaviors written by Natasha Josefowitz in 1980 (see Appendix A). Despite "Impressions From an Office" having been written in 1980, students still recognize the truth that exists in Josefowitz's depictions of how different meanings are attached to the same behaviors when performed by women and men. She explains:

> His desk is cluttered. . . . He's obviously a hard worker and a busy man: Her desk is cluttered. . . . She's obviously a disorganized scatterbrain: He is talking with his co-workers. . . . He must be discussing the latest deal: She is talking with her co-workers. . . . She must be gossiping: He's leaving for a better job. . . . He knows how to recognize a good opportunity: She's leaving for a better job. . . . Women are undependable. (Josefowitz, 1980, p. 60)

The concepts of male privilege were further developed through exposure to various writings depicting the subtlety of a male-centered culture. While there have been numerous advances in recent years, both language and culture continue to view men as the norm of society. Women's groups have drawn attention to these issues through repeated requests for gender-neutral language (e.g., firefighter instead of fireman), yet these changes have been relatively slow and fairly recent. For centuries, "men's social bodies [have been] the measure of what is 'human.' *Gray's Anatomy*, in use for 100 years, well into the twentieth century, presented the human body as male [and] the female body was shown only where it differed from the male" (Laqueur 1990, pp. 166–167).

While learning more about the social construction of gender, students examined how "biological differences are given real meaning by the ways in which a culture interprets and uses them" (Bem, 1994, p. 31). In an assignment, students were asked to examine how the color of the boxes and packaging used in a local toy store differed according to specifically assigned gender roles. The toys prescribed for young girls were typically packaged in pink boxes, while many of the toys designed for boys were encased in camouflage colors. In order to provide a more comprehensive historical context for the meanings associated with the social constructions of race, class, and gender, students read about women's struggle to gain access to higher education in the 19th century at a time, according to Hubbard, when "scientists initially claimed [women] could not be educated because [their] brains are too small" (as cited in Rothenberg, 2001, p. 46). As these claims remained unsubstantiated, the focus of the debate shifted to whether women *should* be educated. Hubbard said that those supporting the exclusion of women from higher education

> based their concerns on the claim that girls need to devote much energy to establishing the proper functioning of their ovaries and womb and that if they divert their energy to their brains by studying, their reproductive organs will shrivel, they will become sterile, and the race would die out. . . . The notion that women's reproductive organs need careful nurturing was used to justify excluding upper class girls and young women from higher education but not to spare the working class, poor, black women who were laboring in the factories and homes of the upper class. (as cited in Rothenberg, 2001, p. 46)

The social construction of race, class, and gender become painfully evident as cultural practices are used to discriminate and divide oppressed groups according to race, sex, and economics. Still today, the social construction of gender aids in maintaining the status quo in situations in which some young women and men are afraid to attempt particular activities for fear of violating an expected gender role. For men, that may involve denying an interest in cooking for fear of being labeled a sissy, while women may refrain from participating in particular sports for fear of being called a tomboy. While some individuals may perceive these fears as relatively insignificant, acts of bias-motivated harassment can begin with acts of name-calling to intimidate the victim into conformity.

In relating these discoveries to Harro's "Cycle of Socialization" (2000), students began exploring the concepts of "normative thinking" and questioning their own expectations and privileges. Students were asked to consider the following situations with regard to social constructions of gender. In their experience with their parents (assuming situations with both a male and female parent), which parent did the majority of the driving? Which parent cooked versus which parent was responsible for barbecuing? Also, male students were asked about their feelings regarding changing the language to include the term *woman* as the new all-encompassing term for people. While many students could not see the problem with using male-centered terms like *man* or *policeman* to address all people or police officers, many expressed their discomfort in using the terms *woman* and *policewoman* to include all male and female individuals. Although many changes have taken place during the 20th century and the beginning of the new millennium, awareness of the subtle inequities resulting from the social constructions of race, class, and gender provide the foundation necessary to examine various forms of privilege.

Once students were able to understand, and accept, the existence of male privilege, then Peggy McIntosh's (1998) foundational article about "skin privilege" was introduced. In her chapter, "White Privilege: Unpacking the Invisible Knapsack," McIntosh equates the concept of skin privilege to a person possessing a backpack complete with maps, compasses, and various other essential tools necessary to navigate through life's journey. Those holding an essential tool—*privilege*—experience an advantage over those who have an empty backpack. In examining the following examples from McIntosh's descriptions, it is evident that people of color are disadvantaged in a culture that uses the experience of those possessing skin privilege as the norm:

> I can turn on the television or open the front page of the paper and see people of my race widely represented; I can be sure that my children will be given curricular materials that testify to the existence of their race; I can do well in a challenging situation without being called a credit to my race; I am never asked to speak for all the people of my racial group; and I can easily buy posters, postcards, picture books, greeting cards, dolls, toys, and children's magazines featuring people of my race. (McIntosh, 2004, pp. 105–106)

In preparation for this class session, students had been asked to bring a copy of their favorite magazine (e.g., *Marie Claire*, *Fitness*, *Sports Illustrated*,

*Ebony, Newsweek, Esquire, Vogue, Details,* etc.) in order to examine the images of men and women while also paying attention to issues of race, ethnicity, social economic status, disability, age, and sexual orientation. As the students laid the magazines next to each other, it instantly became evident that only two magazines had people of color on the covers. No images were found of people with disabilities, and every person on the cover was young, healthy, and affluent. Through the use of these brief exercises, students began to recognize that "in our current society, inequity exists and people come from places of privilege and disadvantage" (Zyngier, 2003, p. 43).

After comprehending the concepts of male privilege and skin privilege, students were familiarized with the notion of "heterosexual privilege." Students viewed a scene from the HBO special *If These Walls Could Talk 2* (Kane, 2000) depicting the challenges faced by two elderly women, who despite their partnership of over 20 years, had no legal rights to one another during emergency hospital visits, memorial service arrangements, or possession of shared property. While the video provided a basis for students to witness illustrations of the inequalities faced by gay and lesbian couples, the video could not fully convey the pressure experienced by many to conceal their identity in order to avoid an array of repercussions. In order to pseudo-experience the social impact of heterosexual privilege, students are asked to make a choice: They could write about their experience and feelings after wearing a button stating I Support the Rights of Lesbians, Gay Men, and Transgender Individuals around their families, friends, and public settings for 24 hours, or they could choose not to wear the button and write an explanation of their reasons for making this choice (activity adapted from Adams et al., 2000). In either of these scenarios, students typically recognized their feelings of unease from having strangers question their sexuality (verbally or through glances) or from having family raise objections to their public statement.

## Empowerment Through Action: The Project

When determining the type of service-learning project appropriate for a course on bias crimes, the instructor heeded the comments of critics who "argue that service-learning may actually reinforce prejudice and replicate power differentials between those conferring and those receiving the service" (King, 2004, p. 123). As pointed out by King, "to be in a position to 'provide service' to another party may itself be a mark of privilege" (p. 123). While various community groups would have been appropriate community partners, the instructor chose to focus on a campus-based event in order to have all the students working on the same student-centered and student-driven project. The project provided a forum for students to learn from one another, engage in dialogue about the course readings, reflect on the experience of the assigned activities, and participate in developing a community event based on the course readings and personal experiences.

In creating the Day of Silence displays and role plays, students were "applying their classroom knowledge to the living community" (Jakubowski, 2003, p. 24) in which they socialize and attend class. By learning from one another's experiences, sharing viewpoints on various quotes and images, and developing role plays pertinent to the campus community and the community at large, students gained insight beyond the text and "cultivate[ed] their appreciation of diversity by actually experiencing it" (Jakubowski, 2003, p. 24). This project engaged students in active learning as opposed to passive acceptance of definitions and abstract concepts that appear meaningless without an experiential contextual framework.

Because students sometimes find it difficult to convey their thoughts and feeling through the use of words, images in the form of photographs, statistics, and quotes were used to spawn ideas and provide a context that could be understood at both a scholarly and emotional level. With the intention of raising questions, invoking curiosity, and generating a passion for social change, the students were encouraged to gather images that challenged conventional expectations (e.g., marathon winners in wheelchairs, female airplane mechanics, male nurses, etc.) and provoked critical thought. While educators aspire to promote analytical skills, "critical thinking is understood to be the process that occurs among adults in their everyday interactions . . . by choosing to regularly question and explore the most commonsensical details of their social experiences—in relationships, at work, in political involvements—when interpreting mass media (Brookfield, 1987, p. 12), critical thinking represents 'a lived activity, not an academic pastime' " (Jakubowski, 2003, pp. 25–26). For this assignment, critical thinking extended beyond the readings and into the social context in which students interact.

Throughout this project students synthesized their classroom learning within the living context of news stories, historical events, and personal experiences. They recognized the material they were learning was more than facts to be remembered. As is the goal of all service-learning experiences, this project provided students with an opportunity to understand the course content within a real-life context: a context that matters to students. For the students, the course material was learned at a deeper level, because it became relevant and therefore meaningful. While students described experiences with discrimination or disagreed on what to include on the displays, they heard the points of view from "real" students as opposed to abstract theories from philosophers with whom students feel they cannot relate. While emphasizing the value of experience, it also allowed students to "recognize their own personal resources; how much they can learn from each other; how much they already know about a theme" (Jakubowski, 2003, p. 26). While hate crimes and prejudice represent social issues pertinent to everyone, this project allowed students to recognize their own concerns with oppression. The project created awareness of one another's similar and different experiences, and prompted a deeper understanding of one's personal responsibility in tackling social issues.

## Envisioning the Role Plays

Writing the role plays for the universitywide performance was a collaborative effort among all the students. Students selected examples of campus situations that incorporated the concepts of privilege, allies, prejudice, and bias-motivated violence. Since the majority of bias-motivated offenders consist of young men in their late teens and early twenties (FBI, 2003) who commit their crimes in groups not affiliated with organized hate groups (Finn, 1988; Herek & Berrill, 1992; Levin & McDevitt, 1993), the role plays emphasized the challenge of coping with peer pressure and provided techniques for becoming allies of oppressed groups. The concept of forming allies was emphasized throughout the event, with the hope of encouraging students to "move from thinking of racism as something individual, malicious, overt, and possibly exaggerated by people of color, to seeing it as a pervasive reality that they themselves have a responsibility to address" (Miller & Harris, 2005, p. 224).

Too often, students feel overwhelmed by larger social issues such as discrimination, poverty, abuse, prejudice, and violence, and they are paralyzed from taking any action at all. "Students must be empowered to inquire, act and reflect on the issues that are of concern to them and to positively transform situations where they see disadvantage or unfairness in their own and

other's lives" (Zyngier, 2003, p. 43). As the scenarios developed from continuous dialogue, a few students chose to divulge examples of occurrences they
had experienced at this, or another, campus. Students from the Sikh and
Muslim communities explained some of the harassment they experienced
after the attacks of September 11th, African American students affirmed the
experiences described in Peggy McIntosh's "Invisible Knapsack" (1993), female students described the experience of harassment, and one student described a bias-motivated assault. As a group, everyone agreed that the role
plays should inspire reflection and promote a sense of empowerment. Each
role play was accompanied by narrations that described the role play, explained its meaning, and raised questions. While the final role plays included Muslim students receiving disparaging comments while walking to
class, a student becoming an ally, a student refusing to work with a peer
of color, a young woman being sexually assaulted in response to her sexual
orientation, and a student in a wheelchair resisting an attacker, this chapter
focused solely on the role play related to gender. The following represents
the various scenes within this particular role play and the details of each
scene:

Narrator 1:
   When students enter their chosen institution of higher education, they
may not have been exposed to a vast array of backgrounds, nationalities,
and experiences. With some effort, patience, and time, students can work
together and learn from one another. This project represents an initial step
toward promoting dialogue and awareness. These images and role plays
will depict possible situations you may encounter, and inform you about
some most useful campus resources available.
   While in college, we don't just learn from our classes, but also through
our interactions with others. The role play you will see depicts the encounter between a young woman and two male students who feel a need to
scrutinize her after feeling their advances were disregarded. What you will
see next happens nationally across campuses. What do you think could be
done to prevent this from happening?

**Scene I:**

• **(Elysia)** Woman is walking to class and two male students pass by.
• **(Ryan)** One of them says, "Hey, babe, you shouldn't be walking to class
  alone at night. How about me being your bodyguard?"

- (**Howard**) "No, dude, you're not her type if you know what I mean." (giggling as he walks away)
- (**Ryan**) "So is that right? You're into chicks? I'd love to come over and watch sometime."
- (**Elysia**) She walks away, "I don't have time for this. I have class in five minutes."
- (**Ryan**) "I'm not done with you yet. You'll change. I'll show you what you've been missing." We see Ryan grab her bag from behind and push her behind the stage. (**LIGHTS OFF**)

**Scene II:**

- (**Elysia**) Hair messed up, shirt torn, walks into police station.
- (**Sam**) Officer at the desk looks up and says, "Oh my, what happened to you?" with a concerned look
- (**Elysia**) "I was raped by a student who was harassing me."
- (**Sam**) "OK, now. Let's write it all down. What was he harassing you about?"
- (**Elysia**) "Well he was upset that I turned him down, so he started making comments about me being gay"
- (**Sam**) "OOOhhh! (putting down the pen and not willing to write further). Are you gay?"
- (**Elysia**) "What?!"
- (**Sam**) "Well if you are, then what do you expect?"
- (**Elysia**) "Are you kidding me? Are you going to do anything?"
- (**Sam**) The officer turns around and begins shuffling papers. I don't have time for this, I have *real cases* to deal with."
- (**Elysia**) (sees a flyer and walks out reading it) She says, "Well if the police are not going to help me, I'll help myself."

Narrator 2:

The young woman portrayed in the role play was not only victimized by the assailants, but also by a member of the system. The homophobia displayed by the police officer is not uncommon, and therefore many victims of crimes such as sexual assault or antigay hate crimes remain *silent* instead of reporting the offense. A fellow student has made the choice to share her real-life experience with you and speak out against this type of violence. What can we all do to make sure prejudice does not silence anyone else?

(Real-life narrative)

**Scene III:**

- After the real-life narrative, several students are in the background practicing martial arts.
- (**Elysia**) The rape survivor walks in and sees a desk. She looks for some information and Joe comes up to her.
- (**Joe**) "Hi, do you need some help?"
- (**Elysia**) "Well, I was thinking of taking some self-defense classes, but I don't know if I can do this. It looks hard, and I've never done anything like this before."
- (**Joe**) "You should not limit yourself. Every person in every situation has potential. All it takes is realizing that potential and going for it.
- (**Joe**) "These are Vanessa and Chris. They've been my students for three years. (speaking to Vanessa and Chris) Could you give a brief demonstration of a technique or two?"
- (**Vanessa** in wheelchair) "Sure."
- (**Joe**) "Be aggressive and don't hold back. Yame."
- (Demonstration) Vanessa flings her attacker in the air despite being in a wheelchair.
- (**Joe**) (to Elysia) "Are you ready to get started?"
- (**Elysia**) "Yeah! This is great! Thank you."

Narrator 3:

Whether one is differently abled, a woman or man, young or old, American born or an immigrant, a person of color or Caucasian, or a member of an oppressed religious group, no one should have to endure the silencing effects of prejudice. Today this group has gathered here to share personal stories, views, and ideas in order to assist in ending prejudice and hate. The members of this team represent diverse backgrounds, beliefs, and campus groups including several clubs, sororities, and first-year seminar peers. This is an attempt to raise awareness so that each person can find a way of working toward eliminating hate by speaking out against prejudice.

## Conclusion

Frequently, students feel helpless and overwhelmed when faced with tackling social issues. In order to foster further contemplation, several class sessions began with a reflection of Abraham Lincoln's quote, "The greatest tragedy of our social transition is not the noisiness of so called bad people; it is the appalling silence of so called good people." This quote not only reinforced the meaning of ending the silence against prejudice, but also reiterated the personal choice each person assumes in Harro's "Cycle of Socialization" (2000). This project involved students in an event that empowered them to recognize the impact of their actions (good or bad). The event allowed students to take a step toward fighting prejudice, recognizing their role in society's safety and welfare, and acknowledging they have a choice in their words and behaviors.

Throughout the semester, students reviewed social constructs, theories, historical events, and scholarly research examining the role of privilege, allies, prejudice, and the cycle of socialization within the context of bias-motivated offenses. For their campus-based service-learning project, the students prepared visual displays and an array of role plays for a consciousness-raising event designed to draw attention to silencing effects of bias-motivated violence. The Day of Silence event provided all the students enrolled in the course with an opportunity to work on the same student-centered and student-driven project. The students were assessed according to their participation in any of the various parts of the project as well as in their understanding of the course content. While some students became more involved in preparing the visual displays for the university, others preferred to perform in the role plays. Because the Day of Silence event provided students with an opportunity to understand the course material within a context that mattered to them (the university community), the course content had meaning. After the role plays were complete, it was not just the students who learned from the course, but also the audience members who attended the role plays, the passersby who viewed the campus displays, the campus community members who read the posters explaining the event, and the professor who took note of the student interactions regarding which images to include in the displays and what to incorporate in the role plays.

# Appendix A

## *He Works/She Works*

From Josefowitz (1980)

| | |
|---|---|
| The family picture is on his desk:<br>Ah, a solid, responsible family man. | The family picture is on her desk:<br>Umm, her family will come before her career. |
| His desk is cluttered:<br>He's obviously a hard worker and a busy man. | Her desk is cluttered:<br>She's obviously a disorganized scatterbrain. |
| He is talking with his co-workers:<br>He must be discussing the latest deal. | She is talking with her co-workers:<br>She must be gossiping. |
| He's not in the office:<br>He's meeting customers. | She's not in the office:<br>She must be out shopping. |
| He's having lunch with the boss:<br>He's on his way up. | She's having lunch with the boss:<br>They must be having an affair. |
| The boss criticized him:<br>He'll improve his performance. | The boss criticized her:<br>She'll be very upset. |
| He got an unfair deal:<br>Did he get angry? | She got an unfair deal:<br>Did she cry? |
| He's getting married:<br>He'll get more settled. | She's getting married:<br>She'll get pregnant and leave. |
| He's having a baby:<br>He'll need a raise. | She's having a baby:<br>She'll cost the company money in maternity benefits. |
| He's going on a business trip:<br>It's good for his career. | She's going on a business trip:<br>What does her husband say? |
| He's leaving for a better job:<br>He knows how to recognize a good opportunity. | She's leaving for a better job:<br>Women are undependable. |

## Notes

1. The individuals included as "protected groups" vary according to the state. Many states include race, religion, and ethnicity as protected categories, yet gender, sexual orientation, and disability are protected categories in a few states.

## References

Adams, M., Blumenfeld, W. J., Castaneda, R., Hackman, H. W., Peters, M. L., & Zuniga, X. (2000). *Readings for diversity and social justice: An anthology of racism, anti-Semitism, sexism, heterosexism, ableism, and classism.* New York: Routledge.

Bem, S. L. (1994). In a male-centered world, female differences are transformed into female disadvantage. *The Chronicle of Higher Education*, August 17, (B1–B2).

Boatright-Horowitz, S. L. (2005, September). Teaching antiracism in a large introductory psychology course: A course module and its evaluation. *Journal of Black Studies, 36*(1), 34–51.

Federal Bureau of Investigation. (2003). *Uniform crime report.* Washington, DC.

Finn, P. (1988). Bias crime: A special target for prosecutors. *Prosecutor, 21*(4), 9–15.

Harro, B. (2000). Cycle of socialization. In M. Adams, W. J. Blumenfeld, R. Castaneda, H. W. Hackman, M. L. Peters, & X. Zuniga (Eds.), *Readings for diversity and social justice: An anthology on racism, anti-Semitism, sexism, heterosexism, ableism, and classism* (pp. 15–20). New York: Routledge.

Herek, G. M., & Berrill, K. T. (1992). *Hate crimes: Confronting violence against lesbians and gay men.* Newbury Park, CA: Sage.

Hubbard, R. (1990). *The politics of women's biology.* New Brunswick, NJ: Rutgers University Press.

Jakubowski, L. M. (2003). Beyond book learning: Cultivating the pedagogy of experience through field trips. *The Journal of Experiential Education, 26*(1), 24–33.

Josefowitz, N. (1980). *Paths to power.* Reading, MA: Addison-Wesley.

Kane, M. (Producer). (2000). *If these walls could talk 2.* United States: HBO Home Box Studios.

King, J. T. (2004). Service-learning as a site for critical pedagogy: A case of collaboration, caring, and defamiliarization across borders. *The Journal of Experiential Education, 26*(3), 121–137.

Laqueur, T. (1990). *Making sex: Body and gender from Greeks to Freud.* Cambridge, MA: Harvard University Press.

Levin, J., & McDevitt, J. (1993). *Hate crimes: The rising tide of bigotry and bloodshed.* New York: Plenum.

McIntosh, P. (2004). White privilege: The invisible knapsack. In M. Andersen & P. H. Collins (Eds.), *Race, class, and gender: An anthology* (5th ed., pp. 103–108). Belmont, CA: Thomas Wadsworth.

Miller, A. N., & Harris, T. M. (2005, July). Communicating to develop white racial identity in an interracial communication class. *Communication Education, 54*(3), 223–242.

Zuniga, X. (2003, January/February). Bridging differences through dialogue. *About Campus, 7*(6), 8–16.

Zyngier, D. (2003). Connectedness—Isn't it time that education came out from behind the classroom door! *Teacher Learning Network, 10*(2), 4–7.

# SECTION FOUR

## WOMEN AND VIOLENCE

# 9

# USING AN ECOLOGICAL PERSPECTIVE TO UNDERSTAND AND ADDRESS SEXUAL ASSAULT ON CAMPUS

*Courtney E. Ahrens and Patricia D. Rozee*

The ecological perspective provides an interesting model for community service-learning practitioners because it forces us to consider the dynamic interplay between the individual and the environment. Neither exists in isolation or without the influence of the other. In the case of community service it provides a direct pathway to exploring the larger social context in which the service occurs. Social issues such as rape cannot be accurately examined without considering how the context of individual, family and small group, organizational, community, and societal levels all have an impact on both etiology and intervention. For the community service learner this may result in interventions that go well beyond simply serving. Instead the goal might be to have an effect on the issue through social change activities intended to transform belief and behavior in the interest of social justice.

In this chapter we will explore social action projects at each ecological level. To frame these social action projects, we begin by providing information about the legal definition of rape and the prevalence of rape. We then use an ecological perspective to organize research about several potential causes of rape. Social action projects designed to address these causes are then described in detail. These social action projects form the core of the community service-learning interventions in the course. The intent is to influence the social issue of rape through social change interventions at multiple levels. These converging solutions can have profound implications for social change outcomes on campus.

## Legal Definition of Rape

Legal definitions of rape vary from state to state. In California, rape is defined by a series of penal codes. According to Penal Codes 261 and 262, rape is an act of sexual intercourse that occurs against a person's will under any of the following conditions: by means of threat or force, when a person is intoxicated and cannot resist, when a person is unconscious of the nature of the act (e.g., the person is asleep or the act was misrepresented), through the threat of future retaliation, or through the threat of official action (e.g., incarceration, deportation). Similar codes restrict unwanted oral copulation (Penal Code 288a) and penetration by an object (Penal Code 289). In each case, any sexual act that was not fully consented to is included in the definition. According to subsection 261.6, a person must voluntarily and actively cooperate in the sexual act—if a person has not consented in word and deed, it may be considered rape.

## Prevalence of Rape

Prevalence statistics vary widely. Studies that define rape in behavioral terms (e.g., have you ever given in to sexual intercourse because someone threatened to hurt you?) find higher rates than studies that use the word *rape* or are based on police reports. As a result, there is great controversy about how to define rape for research purposes (DeKeseredy & Schwartz, 2001; Kilpatrick, 2004; Koss, 1996). To obtain an understanding of how common rape is, it is therefore necessary to look at the findings of multiple studies. Among the most commonly cited national-level studies is the Federal Bureau of Investigation's (FBI) Uniform Crime Reports (Federal Bureau of Investigation, 2005), which only includes instances of forced penile-vaginal intercourse that were *reported* to the police in a given year. The most recent statistics from the UCR indicate that 94,635 women were forcibly raped in 2004. Most researchers estimate that reported rapes comprise only a small portion, perhaps one in eight, of actual rapes. The Bureau of Justice Statistics' National Crime Victimization Survey (NCVS) is more comprehensive. This survey includes any form of unwanted sexual penetration against men or women through psychological or physical coercion. The most recent statistics from the NCVS indicates that 209,880 people were raped in 2004. These statistics are still considered somewhat low by most experts, however, because the methodology used to elicit rape reports from victims does not facilitate disclosure (Kilpatrick, 2004; Koss, 1996). To remedy these methodological problems, the National Violence Against Women Survey (NVAWS) used more behaviorally based screening questions. The NVAWS found that 302,100 women were raped in the 12 months prior to the survey (Tjaden & Thoennes, 2000) and 18% of women had been raped in their lifetime. Similarly, the National Women's Study used behaviorally based questions and found that 12.65% of women had been raped in their lifetime (Resnick, Kilpatrick, Dansky, Saunders, & Best, 1993).

Other studies have focused on more specialized populations. An early study of rape among college students found that 15% of college women had been raped in their lifetime (Koss, Gidycz, & Wisniewski, 1987). The National Survey of Adolescents focused on youth ages 12 through 17 and found that 13% of the girls had been sexually assaulted in their lifetime (Kilpatrick, Saunders, & Smith, 2003). A nationally representative sample of U.S. Navy recruits found that 36% of the women had been raped in their lifetime (Merrill et al., 1998). Finally, a national telephone survey found that 34% of married women had been threatened or forced into having unwanted sex with their spouse or previous romantic partner (Basile, 2002). After a review of these and other prevalence studies, Rozee and Koss (2001) concluded that the rate of rape has remained at a consistent 15% lifetime prevalence over the last quarter century, despite various prevention efforts.

## Etiology of Rape

Rape is a complex social phenomenon that is prompted by a variety of conditions. To gain a fuller understanding of why rape occurs, it is necessary to take a comprehensive view. This chapter will use the ecological perspective to help organize a vast array of research findings on the etiology of rape.

### Ecological Perspective

Adapted from the study of ecology, the ecological perspective suggests that there is a dynamic interplay between individuals and the environment they inhabit (Kelly, 1966; Kelly, Ryan, Altman, & Stelzner, 2000). Individual behavior is thus influenced by the settings and culture in which the individual operates; the settings and culture are, in turn, influenced by the individuals who inhabit them. Urie Bronfenbrenner (1979), a developmental psychologist, was one of the first theorists to propose a model that captured this inherent complexity. His basic approach has since been integrated with a systems-level approach that views systems (e.g., people, organizations, societies) as hierarchically nested such that each higher-level system comprises lower-level systems (e.g., societies comprise social groups that comprise individuals; Miller, 1978). The resulting framework includes five mutually influential levels that must be taken into account when understanding or intervening in any social problem. The individual level focuses on individual people's beliefs, behaviors, and experiences. The family and small-group level focuses on interaction patterns in families and peer groups. The organizational level includes the structure, policies, and procedures of organizations. The community level focuses on community characteristics, assets, and deficits. The societal level includes cultural values and state or national laws and policies.

The ecological model has been applied to research and interventions ranging from health promotion (Barrera, Toobert, Angell, Glasgow, & Mackinnon, 2006), to child abuse (Zielinski & Bradshaw, 2006), to mental illness (Perkins, Born, Raines, & Galka, 2005), to academic performance (Mahoney, Lord, & Carryl, 2005), to women's career development (Cook, Heppner, & O'Brien, 2005). Indeed, faculty teaching about nearly any topic could adapt this approach to suit their needs and should feel free to borrow from this chapter and modify the recommended action plans accordingly.

The remainder of this chapter will use this basic framework to organize community-based research and action projects on rape. For each level, a review of potential causes will be provided, and an action project will be described. While the literature reviews are by no means comprehensive, some of the more robust findings have been selected and can be used for class lectures.

For the social action projects, an effective strategy is to divide the action projects among the students so that one-fifth of the class is assigned to each project. In this way the overall effect of converging solutions enacted at the five levels of intervention can be readily assessed. These are semester-long projects, so students should be assigned to groups at the beginning of the term. Although class discussion time should be devoted to organizing and reflecting upon these projects throughout the semester, each group should make a formal presentation at the end of the semester about its specific action project. Such oral reflections will allow all the students to see the powerful effects of their social change initiatives at each level of intervention. It also facilitates thinking about social issues at multiple levels, preventing the tendency of students to focus solely on individual-level solutions.

## Individual Level

The individual level focuses on the beliefs, behaviors, and experiences of perpetrators that may lead them to commit rape. The focus here is on the rapist, not the victim. This point will need to be made to the students who will be inclined to focus on what the victim did wrong. Studies of victim characteristics have shown that the most reliable predictor of being a rape victim is gender—being a woman (Rozee & Koss, 2001). Students need to understand that no matter what the victim did, what she wore, or how vulnerable she may have been, the rapist was the one who decided to commit the crime. There is nothing that a victim can do that would *cause* a perpetrator to commit rape. The rapist always has the option of choosing to rape or not—rape is a behavioral choice. Understanding why the rapist might choose to commit the crime is the focus of this level.

*Individual-level causes.* There are a variety of individual characteristics that appear to be linked to rape. Most research in this area suggests that particular combinations of characteristics are most predictive of rape. For example, Malamuth, Sockloskie, Koss, and Tanaka (1991) proposed a confluence model of sexual aggression that proposes two paths. In the first path, family conflict, such as domestic violence or child abuse, may affect children's attachment. Children who do not feel connected to others and have little trust in the world may engage in a variety of antisocial behaviors and may develop more short-term, promiscuous relationships as they grow older. A promiscuous and impersonal sexual orientation has been found to be predictive of committing rape (Malamuth, 1998). In the second path, individuals who hold attitudes that support violence toward women ultimately develop a sense of hostile masculinity. Hostile masculinity includes a hostile and distrustful orientation toward women and gratification from dominating and holding power over women (particularly when the individual feels rejected or powerless). The resulting hostility toward women is predictive of rape (Cowan & Mills, 2004; Malamuth, 1998). However, the likelihood to commit rape may be reduced by specific personality characteristics. Empathy, nurturance, and the ability to feel compassion for others may reduce the likelihood of committing rape (Dean & Malamuth, 1997; Malamuth, Linz, Heavey, & Barnes, 1995).

Similar findings have emerged in a variety of studies. Hypermasculinity, hostility toward women, acceptance of violence, adversarial sexual beliefs, promiscuous sexuality, sexual entitlement, and lack of empathy have all been found to predict rape (Abbey, McAuslan, & Ross, 1998; Abbey, Zawacki, Buck, Clinton, & McAuslan, 2004; Kanin, 1985; Koss, Leonard, Beezley, & Oros, 1985; Malamuth, Linz, Heavey, Barnes, & Acker, 1995; Ryan, 2004). Other researchers have focused on the role of rape myth acceptance and the related role of sexual misperception. According to this research, rapists may believe that they have the right to rape if the victim was flirting or leading them on (Abbey et al., 1998; Muehlenhard & Linton, 1987; Ryan, 2004; Shotland, 1989). Such misperceptions may be particularly likely when the perpetrator has consumed alcohol (Abbey et al., 2004).

*Individual-level action project.* To address the causes described above, a subset of students formed a Speaker's Bureau on campus. The goal of the Speaker's Bureau was to conduct educational presentations in classrooms, residence halls, fraternities and sororities, and at campus events. These presentations ranged from 15 to 60 minutes depending on the needs of the sponsoring organization.

To design these presentations, students are encouraged to first research existing prevention programs. Information about such programs can be obtained through the research literature and prevention-education manuals (contact the California Coalition Against Sexual Assault's Web site for help on obtaining manuals: http://www.calcasa.org). The Women's Center on campus and the local rape crisis center are also valuable resources. Rape crisis centers typically have their own Speaker's Bureau and are often willing to either collaborate or share materials and resources. These resources help students develop their own presentations. These presentations include information on the definition and prevalence of rape (as described above). They also include exercises aimed at reducing the individual-level causes described above (e.g., hostility toward women, hypermasculinity, rape myth acceptance, viewing sex as conquest, and lack of empathy). Students also develop handouts describing rape myths and facts, a description of healthy relationships, information on what to do if someone they know is raped, and a list of community resources.

Once their presentation materials are finalized, students begin marketing the Speaker's Bureau to faculty, resident assistants, and student groups on campus and scheduling presentations. At the end of the semester, the students give a sample presentation to the entire class and then discuss the impact they believe the Speaker's Bureau had on attendees. This presentation is followed up with a discussion of what they have learned from the experience and how it connects to course concepts.

## Family and Small-Group Level

The family and small-group level focuses on interaction patterns in families and small groups. Once again, the focus is on the rapists' families and peer circles.

*Family/small-group causes.* Familial violence is related to later sexual aggression (Hunter, Figueredo, Malamuth, & Becker, 2003; Malamuth et al., 1995; White & Smith, 2004). Such familial violence includes domestic violence between parents as well as physical and sexual abuse of children. In one study, being sexually victimized as a child, being physically punished as a child, and witnessing domestic violence all doubled the likelihood of committing rape (White & Smith, 2004). It has been suggested that children exposed to such situations may accept these behaviors as normal (Ryan, 2004) and may subsequently enact them on others (particularly in the case of noncoercive sexual abuse; Hunter et al., 2003). Even when the family is not overtly violent, families high in rigid, traditional gender roles may be associated with rape perpetration (Koss & Dinero, 1988; Malamuth et al., 1995). This may be because the patriarchal structures inherent in such families may contribute to the development of hypermasculinity and hostility toward women (Ryan, 2004).

Peer groups may also make rape perpetration more likely. Peers who share similar beliefs about violence, hostility toward women, and patriarchy are likely to support one another in these beliefs (Schwartz & DeKeseredy, 1997). Sexual violence can become normalized in such groups when women are viewed as objects to be sexually conquered (Koss & Dinero, 1988; Martin & Hummer, 1989). This may be particularly likely in fraternities and athletic teams that promote hostility and degrading treatment of women (Humphrey & Kahn, 2000).

*Family- and small-group-level action project.* This project should be limited to male students. These students are encouraged to create a prevention program that targets male fraternities and sports teams. These sessions involve males talking to males about sexual violence. This format is designed to reduce the defensiveness that often occurs in mixed-gender groups. Sometimes our students have teamed up with a male police officer or counselor to make their presentations. This strategy can make the presentation a bit less daunting for the students.

This intervention emphasizes men's roles as allies in the fight against sexual assault. Efforts are made to help men see that rape is a problem for everyone—not just women. Men are hurt when the women they love are traumatized. Men are hurt when the actions of some men perpetuate the idea that all men are rapists. And men are hurt by rigid gender roles that promote violence at the expense of their full humanity. Men therefore have a stake in ensuring that rape does not continue—and men are in a unique position to do something about this. As men, they can stand up to one another and not tolerate degrading treatment of women. They can work to create social environments based on respect, not violence. They can promote healthy relationships based on trust and communication. Many men are open to these ideas, but it takes an organized effort to promote this kind of dialogue.

To help develop an intervention for male fraternities and sports teams, students can use the Men Can Stop Rape Project Web site (http://www .mencanstoprape.org). This Web site has a wealth of information and ideas about how to engage men as allies in the fight against rape. The local rape crisis center is also a good source of information as is the Women's Center on campus. Based on these resources, students develop a series of group activities and handouts to use in their interventions. Interactive and discussion-based activities are more effective than lectures, so emphasis is given to audience participation.

At the end of the semester, the students who participated in this action project present their workshop for the class. This demonstration is followed by a description of the benefits their group had for the actual participants. Students discuss what they have learned from this experience and how it relates to course concepts.

## Organizational Level

The organizational level includes the structure, policies, and procedures of organizations. This level focuses on problems in organizational operations that may enable rape to continue.

*Organizational-level causes.* Organizations affiliated with the criminal justice system, the medical system, and universities all have practices and procedures that may inadvertently enable rape. Police procedures have been given a great deal of scrutiny over the last 10 or so years resulting in considerable reform. However, there are still a great many rape myths involved in founding cases (deciding the validity of the allegations). This is especially problematic in the case of date and acquaintance rape where the principle defense is that the sexual contact was consensual (Campbell & Johnson, 1997). Rape myths also affect prosecutorial decisions. Prosecutors receive promotions based primarily on their win-loss ratio. This organizational structure prompts prosecutors to pay more attention to convictability than to actual violations of the law. In the case of rape, legal system personnel may base decisions to pursue a case on their perceptions of how juries would respond (Frazier & Haney, 1996; Frohmann, 1997; Martin & Powell, 1994; Spohn, Beichner, & Davis-Frenzel, 2001). Thus, despite legal reforms, police and prosecutors may continue to reference rape myths when evaluating victims' claims (Campbell & Johnson, 1997) and when deciding whether to proceed with prosecution (Martin & Powell, 1994). As a result, less than 25% of reported cases are ever prosecuted (Frazier & Haney, 1996). Even when cases are prosecuted, defendants often choose jury trials, knowing that rape myths will work to their advantage. As a result, less than 12% of cases result in a guilty verdict (Frazier & Haney, 1996).

Similar problems have been noted with the medical system. Martin and Powell (1994) argue that the organizational framework guiding medical systems' activities are oriented toward the needs of the organization rather than the needs of victims. Whereas the victim needs to feel safe and supported, the emergency room needs to treat emergent patients. Because rape victims rarely have life-threatening injuries, they are often required to wait for hours before receiving care and the care they receive is often hurried and inadequate (Ahrens et al., 2000; Campbell et al., 1999). Such negative treatment may make victims less likely to disclose the rape to authorities (Ahrens, 2006).

University procedures may also play a role. By law, colleges and universities are required to make campus rape rates public (Clery Act, 1990). But, concern about the impact on student recruitment often leads universities to handle cases internally, reclassify cases, and even discourage victims from making reports (Bohmer & Parrot, 1993). The lack of official response to rape on campus creates an environment where rape is functionally tolerated.

*Organizational-level action project.* To address organizational causes on campus, a subset of students researched and reported on university policies on sexual assault, procedures for filing a complaint, and rape statistics on campus. Information about these topics can be obtained via official documents and interviews with university police, campus judicial boards, residential hall staff, and student life personnel. During these interviews, students ask about the overall procedures and what each specific informant does in cases of rape. They also ask about aspects of the procedures informants would like to see changed. Interviews are also conducted with students. These interviews inquire about student awareness of university policies on rape and their suggestions for change.

The goal of this research is to identify existing policies, determine if there is any confusion or disagreement about what those policies are, and obtain suggestions for change. These findings are written up as a report with accompanying recommendations that can be distributed to university police, the campus judicial board, residential hall directors, and relevant administrators. At the end of the semester, students present this report to the class. Students also discuss what they have learned from this experience and how it relates to course concepts.

## Community Level

The community level focuses on community characteristics, assets, and deficits. The focus is on the presence and absence of characteristics that make rape more likely.

*Community-level causes.* Communities that are high in social disorganization generally have higher rates of crime (Almgren, 2005). Such communities are characterized by a lack of formal and informal social monitoring, disintegrating facilities, and the presence of gangs and other illegal behavior. These characteristics may all enable rape. Similarly, the presence of strip clubs, nightclubs, and bars may encourage negative attitudes toward women and disinhibit aggressive behavior, leading to higher rates of rape (Buddie &

Parks, 2003). College campuses may also facilitate rape when they do not provide adequate lighting, call boxes, open spaces, or escort services that can make rape less likely (Day, 1995).

Rural communities may have their own unique difficulties. The large service areas may mean that victims must travel great distances to obtain medical, advocacy, and mental health assistance, and that police response time may be seriously delayed (Logan, Evans, Stevenson, & Jordan, 2005). Rural residents may also have fewer resources for accessing services such as transportation or public phones (Ruback & Ménard, 2001). Furthermore, rural areas often have social norms against reporting. In small, close-knit towns there may be intense pressure to not report crimes committed by community members, fear of bringing shame on the family, and fear of retaliation by the perpetrator (Logan et al., 2005). In African American communities there may be a special reluctance to solicit help because of distrust of the police. African American women report community pressure to not report black perpetrators to avoid further jeopardizing the black community in the criminal justice system (Sorenson, 1996; Wyatt, 1992). All of these community characteristics may make it less likely that victims will report the crime and that rapists will be prosecuted.

*Community-level action project.* To address community causes on campus, a subset of students conduct an observational survey of the campus safety infrastructure. Students walk around the campus and document areas with poor lighting, lack of call boxes, or areas with obstructed views. They also conduct several tests of the escort service to determine how long it takes for them to show up, if they ever fail to show up, and any factors that appear to affect their service (e.g., time of night, area of campus). Students supplement the results of their environmental scan using focus groups with students about safety concerns on campus.

Students use this information to write a report about current safety-related conditions, concerns, and recommendations for improving safety on campus. This report is then shared with university police and relevant campus administrators. At the end of the semester, students present the report to the rest of the class. They also discuss what they learned as a result of this experience and how this relates to course concepts.

Two students commented on their community experience: "Thank you for empowering us and thank you for giving us the opportunity to help make a difference in our community."

## Societal Level

The societal level includes cultural values and state or national laws and policies. The focus is on broader influences that transcend community boundaries.

*Societal-level causes.* Cultural beliefs about gender and rape play an important role in enabling rape. Patriarchal societies that hold men in higher regard and give men more power than women have been found to have higher rates of violence against women worldwide (Rozée, 1993; Sanday, 1981). In such societies, women are supposed to be submissive and subservient while men are expected to be dominant and aggressive. Rape is both a product of male entitlement and a tool for "keeping women in their place" (Brownmiller, 1975; MacKinnon, 1987).

Cultural acceptance of rape myths may also play a role. Widespread beliefs about victim accountability help exonerate perpetrators of responsibility in the eyes of the perpetrator, the victim, and society (Burt, 1980; Lonsway & Fitzgerald, 1994). If perpetrators are not held responsible, they will remain free to continue raping. Similarly, stereotypical beliefs about what does and does not constitute rape may limit the number of crimes that are reported to the police in the first place. Indeed, less than 25% of rapes are reported to the police (Bachman, 1998), often because victims do not think their case qualifies as rape (Layman, Gidycz, & Lynn, 1996).

Media portrayals of women may also play a substantial role. Women are consistently portrayed as sexual objects in the media. Such depictions dehumanize women and promote the idea that they are less intelligent and less powerful in society (MacKinnon, 1987). This is particularly likely in pornography. A growing body of literature suggests that pornography is related to rape (see Malamuth, Addison, & Koss, 2000, for a review of this literature). A series of meta-analytic reviews have found that exposure to both violent and nonviolent pornography increases rape myth acceptance and behavioral aggression in experimental settings (Allen, D'Alessio, & Brezgel, 1995; Allen, Emmers, Gebhardt, & Giery, 1995). Similar findings have been found in correlational studies of convicted rapists and noncriminal populations alike (Malamuth et al., 2000). This effect is particularly prominent among men who have high levels of sexual promiscuity and hostility toward women, suggesting that pornography increases sexual violence among men already predisposed to such violence (Malamuth et al., 2000) perhaps by reducing inhibitions against violence (Russell, 1998).

Finally, laws and public policy on rape affects what types of rape are reported and prosecuted, how criminal trials proceed, and what types of punishment rapists receive. In the not-so-distant past, rape victims were legally required to produce witnesses, show substantial levels of injury, and have virtually spotless reputations in order for prosecution to proceed (Bohmer, 1998). Such requirements still exist in many countries throughout the world (El-Mouelhy, 2004). Even in the United States, ambiguity in some state laws still permit rape once sexual intercourse is initiated (Lyon, 2004) and rape-shield laws (which prohibit the victims' psychological and sexual history from being admitted into court or the identity of the victim from being revealed to the media) are often disregarded (Murphy, 2002). Sentencing regulations also often minimize the importance of lesser sexual offenses, allowing plea bargains or imposing minor fines in lieu of prison sentences (Koss, Bachar, Hopkins, & Carlson, 2004).

*Societal-level action project.* To address some of the rape myth and media causes described above, students work together to create a campuswide anti-rape demonstration. To help design the demonstration, students collaborate with the campus Women's Center and their local rape crisis centers. Rape crisis centers often host marches, rallies, or other antirape demonstrations and may be able to provide information and assistance. Agency staff can also provide evaluations of student performance in organizing the event.

Students display the Clothesline Project during the day. The Clothesline Project allows rape survivors to decorate T-shirts that depict the impact that rape has had on them (http://www.clotheslineproject.org). Most rape crisis centers have sets of T-shirts on hand or can gain access to T-shirts for display. Students then host a Take Back the Night (TBTN) march on campus. The TBTN Web site provides helpful implementation advice (http://www.takebackthenight.org). This Web site can walk students through the process of lining up guest speakers, getting permits to hold a march, advertising the event, and leading the march. Students may also hold a speak out at the end of the march.

The speak out provides an opportunity for survivors of sexual assault to tell their stories. This helps break the silence for survivors and is an incredibly moving experience for everyone present. Coordinating with the local rape crisis center to have trained crisis counselors on hand is a must.

At the end of the semester, the students who worked on this project describe the effect they think it had on participants. They also discuss what they learned and how this related to course concepts. For example, one student discussed the impact of helping organize the Clothesline Project:

> When it was "dead-time," I myself began reading all the shirts. Some of them were so moving that I wanted to cry either because I felt their pain or because I was so happy that they overcame their suffering. It was a wonderful experience and I am grateful to have been a part of it. I admit, my sole purpose was to get course credit, but after being exposed to this, new doors have opened. My outlook has totally changed.

## Assessing Student Learning

Structured reflection is the defining feature of any community service-learning course. It is important that reflection is continuous throughout the semester and that it requires students to critically analyze the relationship of the field experience to the course content. There are several methods of incorporating reflection into a course. The types of reflection that we have used in the above activities are weekly reflection questions, periodic oral reflections, and midterm and end-of-the-semester reflection papers.

Reflections can be oral, written, or both, but a key aspect of strengthening students' reflections is the student's ability to see and hear other students' thinking on their experiences. To enable this collaborative learning, we have had students post their responses to weekly reflection questions on the class Web site discussion board. The importance of in-class oral reflection is that students can learn from the experiences of other students—both their joys and challenges. This has often resulted in students becoming aware that the issue they are experiencing is not unique. This helps to demystify and normalize difficult experiences in the field. Careful attention should be paid to the questions that are posed to the students. These questions should not be too broad and should help students make connections between specific course concepts and their experiences in the field. The following are some examples of reflection questions that we have used for the TBTN exercise:

1. One of the basic tenets of feminism is that inequalities between men and women should be challenged. How does this emphasis on social change relate to organizing TBTN or working at a rape crisis center?
2. Stereotypical characteristics of women vary across cultures, but most

women experience some restrictions on their movements. How do such restrictions relate to TBTN?

3. Women are generally considered to be weaker and more passive while men are considered stronger and more active. How do these stereotypes affect the likelihood of rape?

4. Institutional oppression occurs when the practices and policies of the dominant institutions facilitate the subjugation, marginalization, or exclusion of the targeted group. Which U.S. institutions facilitate violence against women? How do TBTN and rape crisis centers work to counter this?

5. Teachers encourage boys to solve problems while they encourage girls to watch. How might this affect girls' sense of power and ability to make a difference in the world? How might this relate to participation in TBTN or working at a rape crisis center?

6. Sexual scripts dictate which sexual acts are considered acceptable and how sexual interactions are expected to play out. How do U.S. sexual scripts contribute to violence against women? How do Latino concepts of machismo and *marianismo* contribute to violence against women?

7. Homophobia enforces rigid, traditional gender roles. What impact does this have on violence against women?

8. Men who score high in masculinity tend to view male–female relationships as adversarial. How might this affect violence against women?

The final reflection paper is somewhat more global in its approach in that it asks students to reflect upon the overall community service-learning experience and how it has affected their learning of course materials and also their perceptions of the community and the student's role as an engaged citizen. The final reflection is intended to let students see their fieldwork in the larger context of the ongoing community and assess their contribution to the larger social issue of rape. The following is an example of the instructions the students receive:

> Final Reflection Paper: This is the portion of your final report where you summarize your progress as a service learner. Some questions to help you in your reflection and that can be included in your final oral and written report:

1. What has this community service experience meant to you, personally and professionally?
2. What new skills have you learned, or what skills did you have a chance to practice and perfect, that will enhance your future educational or career goals?
3. What will you take with you from this semester into your future career?
4. What have you learned about yourself in the context of your community (e.g., socially, emotionally, intellectually, professionally) that contributed to your own development?
5. Has this experience changed the way that you think about social issues or "women's" issues?
6. In what ways has your community service enhanced your understanding of the course material and making abstract concepts real?
7. In what way did combining service and learning in the course change the way you view the process of learning?
8. How does this service-learning course compare to other more traditional courses in terms of your own education?
9. What do you feel you were able to contribute to the community as a result of your placement?
10. How did your experience contribute to your understanding of yourself in the context of community, as a citizen of the community?
11. Do you feel your experience with volunteering in the community made it more likely that you would do so again in the future?
12. What are your suggestions for enhancing the community service-learning experience for future students?

The impact of using a community service-learning approach is also evident in student comments. While students are often resistant to the perceived "extra work" at the beginning of the semester, it is typical for students to refer to their community service-learning activities as the "best experience of my life" by the end of the semester. These students describe both the empowerment that comes from being actively involved in promoting social change as well the ways in which community service learning enhanced their learning. As one student put it, "It's like a pop-up book. You see course concepts displayed before your eyes."

The benefits of community service learning are not limited to the students. After a group of students examined the policies and procedures of the residence halls at the University of Illinois at Chicago, the residential life director was able to implement several substantive changes in the training of staff and the education of students. In this way, the activities in which the students engage have a real potential for enabling sustained social change.

## Conclusion

Rape is a complex social phenomenon that is influenced by a myriad of causes. This chapter has attempted to review some of the more robust findings at the individual, family/small group, organization, community, and societal levels. Related community-based action projects were also described for each level. Assessment of the combined effects of these multiple-level interventions is expected to create a greater impact than any one intervention on its own. It is hoped that this information will be helpful to anyone teaching a community psychology class, a class on contemporary social issues, psychology of women, or on violence against women. A similar approach is also appropriate for faculty interested in a variety of psychological issues.

## References

Abbey, A., McAuslan, P., & Ross, L. (1998). Sexual assault perpetration by college men: The role of alcohol, misperception of sexual intent, and sexual beliefs and experiences. *Journal of Social & Clinical Psychology, 17*(2), 167–195.

Abbey, A., Zawacki, T., Buck, P. O., Clinton, A. M., & McAuslan, P. (2004). Sexual assault and alcohol consumption: What do we know about their relationship and what types of research are still needed? *Aggression & Violent Behavior, 9*(3), 271–303.

Ahrens, C. (in press). Being silenced: The impact of negative social reactions on the disclosure of rape. *American Journal of Community Psychology.*

Ahrens, C., Campbell, R., Wasco, S., Aponte, G., Grubstein, L., & Davidson, W. (2000). Sexual assault nurse examiner programs: Alternative systems for service delivery for sexual assault victims. *Journal of Interpersonal Violence, 15*, 921–943.

Allen, M., D'Alessio, D., & Brezgel, K. (1995). A meta-analysis summarizing the effects of pornography II: Aggression after exposure. *Human Communication Research, 22*(2), 258–283.

Allen, M., Emmers, T., Gebhardt, L., & Giery, M. A. (1995). Exposure to pornography and acceptance of rape myths. *Journal of Communication, 45*(1), 5–26.

Almgren, G. (2005). The ecological context of interpersonal violence: From culture to collective efficacy. *Journal of Interpersonal Violence, 20*(2), 218–224.

Bachman, R. (1998). The factors related to rape reporting behavior and arrest: New evidence from the national crime victimization survey. *Criminal Justice and Behavior, 25*(1), 8–29.

Barrera, M., Toobert, D., Angell, K., Glasgow, R., Mackinnon, D. (2006). Social support and social-ecological resources as mediators of lifestyle intervention effects for type 2 diabetes. *Journal of Health Psychology, 11*(3), 483–495.

Basile, K. C. (2002). Prevalence of wife rape and other intimate partner sexual coercion in a nationally representative sample of women. *Violence and Victims, 17*(5), 511–524.

Bohmer, C. (1998). Rape and the law. In M. E. Odem & J. Clay-Warner (Eds.), *Confronting rape and sexual assault* (pp. 247–262). Wilmington, DE: SR Books/ Scholarly Resources.

Bohmer, C. & Parrot, A. (1993). *Sexual assault on campus: The problem and the solution.* New York: Lexington Books.

Bronfenbrenner, U. (1979). Contexts of child rearing: Problems and prospects. *American Psychologist, 34*(10), 844–850.

Brownmiller, S. (1975). *Against our will: Men, women, and rape.* New York: Simon and Schuster.

Buddie, A. M., & Parks, K. A. (2003). The role of the bar context and social behaviors on women's risk for aggression. *Journal of Interpersonal Violence, 18*(12), 1378–1393.

Burt, M. R. (1980). Cultural myths and supports for rape. *Journal of Personality and Social Psychology, 38,* 217–230.

Campbell, R., & Johnson, C. R. (1997). Police officers' perceptions of rape: Is there consistency between state law and individual beliefs? *Journal of Interpersonal Violence, 12*(2), 255–274.

Campbell, R., Sefl, T., Barnes, H., Ahrens, C., Wasco, S., & Zaragoza-Diesfeld, Y. (1999). Community services for rape survivors: Enhancing psychological well-being or increasing trauma? *Journal of Consulting and Clinical Psychology, 67,* 847–858.

Campbell, R., & Wasco, S. M. (2005). Understanding rape and sexual assault: 20 years of progress and future directions. *Journal of Interpersonal Violence, 20*(1), 127–131.

Clery Act, 20 U.S.C. § 1092(f) (1990).

Cook, E., Heppner, M., & O'Brien, K. (2005). Multicultural and gender influences in women's career development: An ecological perspective. *Journal of Multicultural Counseling and Development, 33*(3), 165–179.

Cowan, G., & Mills, R. D. (2004). Personal inadequacy and intimacy predictors of men's hostility toward women. *Sex Roles, 51*(1), 67–78.

Day, K. (1995). Assault prevention as social control: Women and sexual assault prevention on urban college campuses. *Journal of Environmental Psychology*, *15*(4), 261–281.

Dean, K. E., & Malamuth, N. M. (1997). Characteristics of men who aggress sexually and of men who imagine aggressing: Risk and moderating variables. *Journal of Personality and Social Psychology*, *72*(2), 449–455.

DeKeseredy, W. S., & Schwartz, M. D. (2001). Definitional issues. In C. M. Renzetti, J. L. Edleson, & R. K. Bergen (Eds.), *Sourcebook on violence against women* (pp. 23–34). Thousand Oaks, CA: Sage.

El-Mouelhy, M. (2004). Violence against women: A public health problem. *Journal of Primary Prevention*, *25*(2), 289–303.

Federal Bureau of Investigation. (2005). *Crime in the United States 2005*. Washington, DC: U.S. Department of Justice.

Frazier, P. A., & Haney, B. (1996). Sexual assault cases in the legal system: Police, prosecutor, and victim perspectives. *Law & Human Behavior*, *20*(6), 607–628.

Frohmann, L. (1997). Convictability and discordant locales: Reproducing race, class, and gender ideologies in prosecutorial decision-making. *Law & Society Review*, *31*(3), 531–556.

Humphrey, S. E., & Kahn, A. S. (2000). Fraternities, athletic teams, and rape: Importance of identification with a risky group. *Journal of Interpersonal Violence*, *15*(12), 1313–1322.

Hunter, J. A., Figueredo, A. J., Malamuth, N. M., & Becker, J. V. (2003). Juvenile sex offenders: Toward the development of a typology. *Sexual Abuse: Journal of Research and Treatment*, *15*(1), 27–48.

Kanin, E. J. (1985). Date rapists: Differential sexual socialization and relative deprivation. *Archives of Sexual Behavior*, *14*(3), 218–232.

Kelly, J. G. (1966). Ecological constraints on mental health services. *American Psychologist*, *21*(6), 535–539.

Kelly, J. G., Ryan, A. M., Altman, B. E., & Stelzner, S. P. (2000). Understanding and changing social systems: An ecological view. In J. Rappaport, & E. Seidman (Eds.), *Handbook of community psychology* (pp. 133–159). New York: Kluwer Academic/Plenum Publishers.

Kilpatrick, D. G. (2004). What is violence against women? Defining and measuring the problem. *Journal of Interpersonal Violence*, *19*(11), 1209–1234.

Kilpatrick, D. G., Saunders, B. E., & Smith, D. W. (2003). *Youth victimization: Prevalence and implications* (National Institute of Justice Publication No. 194972). Washington, DC: National Institute of Justice.

Koss, M. P. (1996). The measurement of rape victimization in crime surveys. *Criminal Justice and Behavior*, *23*(1), 55–69.

Koss, M. P., Bachar, K. J., Hopkins, C. Q., & Carlson, C. (2004). Expanding a community's justice response to sex crimes through advocacy, prosecutorial, and public health collaboration: Introducing the RESTORE program. *Journal of Interpersonal Violence, 19*(12), 1435–1463.

Koss, M. P., & Dinero, T. E. (1988). Predictors of sexual aggression among a national sample of male college students. *Annals of the New York Academy of Sciences, 528*, 133–147.

Koss, M. P., Gidycz, C. A., & Wisniewski, N. (1987). The scope of rape: Incidence and prevalence of sexual aggression and victimization in a national sample of higher education students. *Journal of Consulting and Clinical Psychology, 55*(2), 162–170.

Koss, M. P., Leonard, K. E., Beezley, D. A., & Oros, C. J. (1985). Nonstranger sexual aggression: A discriminant analysis of the psychological characteristics of undetected offenders. *Sex Roles, 12*(9), 981–992.

Layman, M. J., Gidycz, C. A., & Lynn, S. J. (1996). Unacknowledged versus acknowledged rape victims: Situational factors and posttraumatic stress. *Journal of Abnormal Psychology, 105*(1), 124–131.

Logan, T. K., Evans, L., Stevenson, E., & Jordan, C. E. (2005). Barriers to services for rural and urban survivors of rape. *Journal of Interpersonal Violence, 20*(5), 591–616.

Lonsway, K. A., & Fitzgerald, L. F. (1994). Rape myths: In review. *Psychology of Women Quarterly, 18*(2), 133–164.

Lyon, M. R. (2004). No means no?: Withdrawal of consent during intercourse and the continuing evolution of the definition of rape. *Criminal Law & Criminology, 95* (1), 277–313.

MacKinnon, C. (1987). *Feminism unmodified: Discourses on life and law.* Cambridge, MA: Harvard University Press.

Mahoney, J., Lord, H., & Carryl, E. (2005). An ecological analysis of after-school program participation and the development of academic performance and motivational attributes for disadvantaged children. *Child Development, 76*(4), 811–825.

Malamuth, N. M. (1998). The confluence model as an organizing framework for research on sexually aggressive men: Risk moderators, imagined aggression, and pornography consumption. In R. G. Geen & E. Donnerstein (Eds.), *Human aggression: Theories, research, and implications for social policy* (pp. 229–245). New York: Academic Press.

Malamuth, N. M., Addison, T., & Koss, M. (2000). Pornography and sexual aggression: Are there reliable effects and can we understand them? *Annual Review of Sex Research, 11*, 26–91.

Malamuth, N. M., Linz, D., Heavey, C. L., & Barnes, G. (1995). Using the confluence model of sexual aggression to predict men's conflict with women: A 10-year follow-up study. *Journal of Personality and Social Psychology, 69*(2), 353–369.

Malamuth, N. M., Sockloskie, R. J., Koss, M. P., & Tanaka, J. S. (1991). Characteristics of aggressors against women: Testing a model using a national sample of college students. *Journal of Consulting and Clinical Psychology, 59*(5), 670–681.

Martin, P., & Hummer, R. A. (1989). Fraternities and rape on campus. *Gender & Society, 3*(4), 457–473.

Martin, P., & Powell, R. (1994). Accounting for the "second assault": Legal organizations' framing of rape victims. *Law and Social Inquiry, 19*, 853–890.

Merrill, L. L., Hervig, L. K., Newell, C. E., Gold, S. R., Milner, J. S., Rosswork, S. G., et al. (1998). Prevalence of premilitary adult sexual victimization and aggression in a Navy recruit sample. *Military Medicine, 163*(4), 209–212.

Miller, J. G. (1978). *Living Systems.* New York: McGraw-Hill.

Muehlenhard, C. L., & Linton, M. A. (1987). Date rape and sexual aggression in dating situations: Incidence and risk factors. *Journal of Counseling Psychology, 34*(2), 186–196.

Perkins, D., Born, D., Raines, J., & Galka, S. (2005). Program evaluation from an ecological perspective: Supported employment services for persons with serious psychiatric disabilities. *Psychiatric Rehabilitation Journal, 28*(3), 217–224.

Resnick, H. S., Kilpatrick, D. G., Dansky, B. S., & Saunders, B. E. (1993). Prevalence of civilian trauma and posttraumatic stress disorder in a representative national sample of women. *Journal of Consulting and Clinical Psychology, 61*(6), 984–991.

Rozée, P. D. (1993). Forbidden or forgiven? Rape in cross-cultural perspective. *Psychology of Women Quarterly, 17*(4), 499–514.

Rozee, P. D., & Koss, M. P. (2001). Rape: A century of resistance. *Psychology of Women Quarterly, 25*(4), 295–311.

Ruback, R. B., & Ménard, K. S. (2001). Rural-urban differences in sexual victimization and reporting: Analyses using UCR and crisis center data. *Criminal Justice & Behavior, 28*(2), 131–155.

Russell, D. E. H. (1998). *Dangerous relationships: Pornography, misogyny, and rape.* Thousand Oaks, CA: Sage.

Ryan, K. M. (2004). Further evidence for a cognitive component of rape. *Aggression and Violent Behavior, 9*(6), 579–604.

Sanday, P. R. (1981). The socio-cultural context of rape: A cross-cultural study. *Journal of Social Issues, 37*(4), 5–27.

Schwartz, M. D., & DeKeseredy, W. S. (1997). *Sexual assault on the college campus: The role of male peer support.* Thousand Oaks, CA: Sage.

Shotland, R. L. (1989). A model of the causes of date rape in developing and close relationships. In C. Hendrick (Ed.), *Close relationships* (pp. 247–270). Thousand Oaks, CA: Sage.

Sorenson, S. B. (1996). Violence against women: Examining ethnic differences and commonalities. *Evaluation Review, 20*(2), 123–145.

Spohn, C., Beichner, D., & Davis-Frenzel, E. (2001). Prosecutorial justifications for sexual assault case rejection: Guarding the "gateway to justice." *Social Problems, 48*(2), 206–235.

Tjaden, P., & Thoennes, N. (2000). Prevalence and consequences of male-to-female and female-to-male intimate partner violence as measured by the National Violence Against Women Survey. *Violence Against Women, 6*(2), 142–161.

White, J. W., & Smith, P. H. (2004). Sexual assault perpetration and reperpetration: From adolescence to young adulthood. *Criminal Justice and Behavior, 31*(2), 182–202.

Wyatt, G. E. (1992). The sociocultural context of African American and White American women's rape. *Journal of Social Issues, 48*(1), 77–91.

Zielinski, D., & Bradshaw, C. (2006). Ecological influences on the sequelae of child maltreatment: A review of the literature. *Child Maltreatment, 11*(1), 49–62.

# FROM "NO MEANS NO" TO COMMUNITY CHANGE

The Impact of University-Based Service Learning
Related to Intimate Violence Prevention

*Elena Klaw and Marilyn C. Ampuero*

Intimate violence is a major public health problem in the United States (Centers for Disease Control and Prevention [CDC], 2005; Melton, 2002). Nearly 25% of American women report having been raped or physically assaulted by an intimate partner (Tjaden & Thoennes, 2000). Consistently, young women between the ages of 16 and 24 make up the group most at risk for intimate abuse (Tjaden & Thoennes, 2000). Of teens enrolled in grades 9 through 12, 9.1% of girls report having been physically assaulted and 21.3% sexually assaulted (Smith, White, & Holland, 2003). By the time they graduate from college, up to one in four women report having been sexually assaulted (Brener, McMahon, Warren, & Douglas, 1999; Fisher, Cullen & Turner, 2000; Koss, 1993). Women who were sexually and physically victimized in high school are at significantly greater risk for physical and sexual victimization in their undergraduate years (Smith, White, & Holland, 2003). Further, youth who have been exposed to or experienced intimate violence are far more likely to become involved in abusive relationships as adults (Carr & VanDeusen, 2002; Frias-Armenta, 2002; Widom & Maxfield, 2001). According to the CDC, nearly two million injuries and 1,300 deaths result from intimate violence annually (CDC, 2003).

Adolescence and young adulthood represent the ideal window of opportunity for ending the intergenerational cycle of violence (Wolfe et al., 2003), yet a paucity of dating violence programs exist. Of the prevention programs that have emerged, most involve providing prevention education through a single workshop. A growing body of research indicates that such efforts are useful in changing beliefs and attitudes that correlate with involvement in intimate partner violence, but the longevity of the effects of such brief programs is uncertain (Smith, White, & Holland, 2003).

In response to the alarming rates of acquaintance rape consistently found on college campuses, for example (Brener, McMahon, Warren, & Douglas, 1999), universities have made increasing efforts to implement educational programs aimed at preventing sexual assault. Most early interventions focused on teaching skills related to self-defense and communication and paid little attention to challenging the cultural norms that perpetuate violence (Drieschner & Lange, 1999). To the extent that intimate aggression is rooted in firmly entrenched social attitudes and institutions, such programs have demonstrated limited effectiveness in reducing the rates of abuse that college students experience (Lonsway, 1996). Further, the duration of most interventions, ranging from 30 minutes to two hours, appears to be insufficient to produce lasting change in behaviors and attitudes (Anderson et. al., 1998; Lonsway, 1996).

In contrast, a growing body of evidence (Fonow, Richardon, & Wemerus, 1992; Foubert, 2000; Klaw et al., 2005) suggests that education focused on the societal context of antiwoman violence may reduce participants' adherence to beliefs that support intimate assault (for example, the belief that women deserve and enjoy rape and physical abuse; Burt, 1998). Toward that end, service learning represents a potent approach for engaging undergraduates in applying critical analysis toward addressing a pressing social problem. Research suggests that involvement in service learning increases civic engagement, satisfaction with college, and leadership. Applying school-based knowledge to community problem solving also increases both critical thinking skills and knowledge retention (see Eyler, Giles, Stenson, & Gray, 1999). Service learning as a model for both undergraduate education and community intervention is based on several assumptions relevant to current research and discussion pertaining to higher education reform. Such an approach assumes that institutions of higher education have a responsibility to help solve societal problems (Eisen, Cimino, Aparicio, Marstteller, & Kushner, 2003) and that students actually learn more effectively when academic material is connected with hands-on community problem solving (Markus, Howard, & King, 1993).

In this chapter, we will discuss two innovative service-learning efforts. First, we will present a program called Love, Sex, and Power (LSP) that is offered at an urban, comprehensive West Coast university serving a diverse body of largely commuter-oriented students. This program is contained within a capstone seminar offered by the psychology department and involves training senior psychology majors to serve as intimate violence peer educators.

## The LSP Service-Learning Course

Modeled after a successful campus rape prevention effort that will be described later, the LSP course focuses primarily on preventing domestic violence and dating abuse. As peer educators, students enrolled in the LSP course provide scripted intimate partner violence prevention workshops (see Appendix B for the workshop script that is provided to all LSP students) to community members and student groups. Workshops review the differences between healthy and unhealthy relationships, discuss types of intimate partner abuse, provide statistics related to intimate violence, and explain how to help someone involved in an abusive relationship. All students who take the LSP class are required to provide at least one prevention workshop during their semester of course participation, in addition to participating in two other service-learning activities, such as marching in an antiviolence rally or disseminating information about intimate partner violence at local health fairs.

In addition, the LSP course requires that students write an American Psychological Association–style report based on a critical synthesis of primary research related to one aspect of intimate violence. Students present their research reports and recommendations in the context of a campus-community dialogue session and research poster fair held at the end of each semester. Objectives for the course as stated in the syllabus are to (a) increase understanding of prevention psychology, a key area of community psychology, (b) critically examine current research related to prevention and to build skills in conducting literature reviews, (c) critically examine current preventive interventions related to relationship violence, (d) increase understanding of social contexts for relationship violence, (e) inform students about resources available to assist when abuse or sexual assault occurs, (f) build skills related to public speaking and effective written communication, and (g) develop a sense of respect, responsibility, and community among students.

To meet these objectives, the course integrates empirical, theoretical, and current topical perspectives related to preventing intimate violence. Course material is presented through a wide range of readings, guest speakers, and films. Students demonstrate their understanding of prevention programming, domestic/dating violence, and sexual assault through three distinct integration assignments that involve responding to essay questions. Additionally, to participate in the required service-learning aspect of the course, students must first present a "practice workshop" to an audience of peers and volunteer evaluators. Students are evaluated on the basis of their accuracy in presenting the scripted workshop material, clarity of communication, and ability to handle questions from the audience. Students who do not receive approximately 80% of points possible for essay assignments and practice workshop presentation are required to meet with the professor or teaching assistant to review course materials prior to serving as peer educators.

Although LSP workshop scripts are provided to students to ensure the accuracy and quality of all presentations, LSP students contribute to the program far beyond their role as presenters. To meet the needs of the immigrant residents of this city, for example, LSP students have translated program materials into Spanish, Vietnamese, Tagalog, and Russian and have successfully provided educational workshops in these languages. As a result of the efforts of LSP students, the number of Spanish-language workshops provided increases each semester. Further, former LSP students stay involved in the program in important ways. Each semester, former LSP students who work for social service agencies serve as guest speakers, practice workshop evaluators, and community dialogue participants. Further, as social service program coordinators themselves, former students provide opportunities for current peer educators to provide prevention workshops to social service agency clientele.

## Outcomes of the Service-Learning Program

To date, LSP students have provided over 100 workshops in the community, supplying information and resources related to intimate violence to over

1,500 residents. Recently, the program has received recognition and support from the city and county as a model initiative for preventing intimate abuse. As the director of the program, Elena Klaw has been invited to join Comm UniverCity San Jose, an innovative university–city partnership for service learning and empowerment focused on downtown San Jose. Faculty and administrators have recognized LSP as a model service-learning effort through the Provost's Award for Service-Learning. Students themselves have celebrated campus violence prevention efforts through a V Day event on campus, providing further campus support for the program. Most important, service-learning students who have participated in the LSP program over the past four years now serve as key community leaders in the area of intimate violence. They help with developing and implementing programs, such as the La Familia Program,[1] that expand prevention efforts to underserved ethnic-minority local residents.

Preliminary research about the LSP program suggests that participating in the LSP course has significant effects on undergraduate peer educators. Existing data indicates that as a result of course participation, LSP students decreased their belief in domestic violence supportive myths, reduced their support for interpersonal violence, and experienced increased academic engagement. In contrast, no significant mean differences were found between pre- and posttest responses in a comparison group of undergraduates. Taken together, these findings suggest that semester-long initiatives may be integral to challenging the beliefs that increase the likelihood of intimate violence. Feedback from LSP students provides further support for the contention that the course alters students' knowledge and beliefs related to intimate aggression.

## The Campus Acquaintance Rape Education (CARE) Program

The success of LSP is not surprising since the program stems from Klaw's involvement with a well-established antiviolence program with a record of demonstrated effectiveness in another large public university. CARE is a model rape prevention initiative sponsored by the Office of Women's Programs of a large Midwestern residential university.[2] At the center of the CARE program is an academic course offered by the community health department that trains undergraduates to serve as peer educators on the issue of sexual assault. Framed by an explicitly feminist approach, the course connects the dynamics of sexual assault to a cultural context of inequality. Thus, the class considers racism, sexism, heterosexism, and ageism as interlocking forms of oppression and focuses on the practices of institutions that affect students' lives, such as university athletics and the media. Following completion of the CARE course, about 50% of CARE students become peer educators, receiving academic credit to provide scripted, interactive workshops in campus settings such as fraternities, sororities, residence halls, and classes. These workshops focus on definitions, laws, and resources related to acquaintance rape on college campuses. In response to the documented success of the CARE program, the university mandated that all first-year students participate in a CARE workshop as part of the orientation to the university (see Klaw et al, 2005; Lonsway et al, 1998; Lonsway & Kothari, 2000).

As described elsewhere, an evaluation employing standardized measures of support for victim-blaming myths revealed that students who participated in the CARE class were less accepting of cultural rape myths than students who participated in a general course on human sexuality. This finding remained consistent even two years following course participation (see Lonsway et al., 1998). Based on responses to a videotaped sexual conflict scenario, CARE students demonstrated improved skills in sexual communication following course participation compared to prior course involvement. Qualitative results based on interviews, focus groups, and anonymous reaction papers demonstrated that the process of attitude change through CARE involved fundamental shifts in thoughts, feelings, and behaviors related to intimate aggression (see Klaw et al., 2005). Awareness was described as the first step in developing "rape consciousness," an identity shift that incorporates an active understanding of the link between patriarchy and relationship violence.

Although LSP and CARE share many features, there are key distinctions. First, CARE efforts focus on the campus community while LSP provides the majority of its services beyond the walls of the university. Second, unlike the CARE class, the LSP program involves peer education as service learning within the context of course participation itself. Most significantly, the LSP program lacks the basic resources that support the CARE Program, which is housed within the University Office of Women's Programs, an office containing full-time program coordinators/student advocates, a secretary, and graduate assistants.

## Challenges in Implementing the Service-Learning Program

Gaining structural support for implementing LSP has been challenging. First, social problems such as intimate violence are complex, and addressing them requires an interdisciplinary approach. Thus, it was important for Klaw to justify why and how a course about intimate violence fits within the curriculum of a traditional psychology department. Second, even a "shoestring" program such as LSP requires some resources, and some creative solutions were necessary. The LSP program was initially developed as a result of a grant from the campus Center for Service Learning (CSL) that released Klaw, as a new faculty member with a full teaching load. Since no designated office exists to provide administrative support, funding, or workspace for the LSP program, all materials for implementing peer education programming are stored in a cardboard box located in a supply closet in the main office of the psychology department. Maintaining the service-learning aspect of the program has required one teaching assistant per semester to serve as the primary contact person coordinating all peer education workshops. In the earliest stages of the project, CSL generously funded such assistance. Current support has come out of the psychology department's budget and a small discretionary fund allocated by the university for work with the city–university collaborative. The Cross Cultural Center on campus has sponsored the community forum each semester, and the psychology department and CSL together have been able to provide parking passes to the many community leaders who serve as guest speakers in the course. Despite these allotments, however, the instructor has funded many of the videos used for the peer education program out of her own pocket. Significant time has been spent each semester scrambling for monies for needs ranging from small items, such as refreshments for the campus-community dialogue session and parking passes for agency leaders who serve as trainers, to the more substantial need of support for a teaching assistant. Thus, future directions for the program include the pursuit of more sustainable funding, either through grant submission or the acquisition of revenues from the city or county to increase local violence prevention efforts. In keeping with the program's mission to expand access to intimate partner violence education, the current focus of the LSP course is understanding intimate violence across the globe (see Appendix A for the current syllabus). In this semester's course, we focus on cultural instantiations of intimate partner violence in hopes of providing more expansive, culturally tailored services to the distinct ethnic communities in our locality.

## Conclusion

Preventing intimate violence by involving undergraduates as peer educators remains a worthwhile and rewarding endeavor. The results of a growing body of research suggest that such intensive programs may lead to a change in violence-related attitudes that is sustained over time (see Lonsway et al., 1998). More research on the effects of a service-learning curriculum is needed. Such research might explore the influence of course participation on students' choice of major, grade point averages, college retention and satisfaction, career choice, community involvement, and a sense of social responsibility. Readers might consider ways to employ multiple methodologies (e.g., random assignment, surveys, interviews, focus groups, and behavioral observations) to better understand the unique effects of service-learning participation. Survey-based research conducted with the CARE class as well as with the LSP class provides evidence that attitude change occurs as a result of participation in an intensive course about intimate violence. Qualitative findings from interviews, reaction papers, and responses of CARE students to videotaped sexual conflict scenarios suggest that students increase their awareness and understanding of sexual assault and alter their behaviors related to dating, specifically by developing empathy and learning to communicate more assertively.

Finally, in the case of intimate violence prevention efforts, it is necessary to employ longitudinal examinations of behavior to examine whether such courses ultimately influence aggression. Research about CARE indicates that in contrast to the results of short-term interventions, semester-long courses may lead to long-lasting changes in attitudes and behaviors (see Lonsway et al., 1998). Building on current findings drawn from qualitative and quantitative examinations, readers are urged to explore innovative ways to assess whether prevention efforts actually reduce rates of intimate abuse experienced by college students. Although our own research has not measured reductions in abuse, we are encouraged by findings related to school-based child sexual abuse prevention programs. In a sample of more than 800 women, for example, Gibson and Leitenberg (2000) found that women who had attended a school-based child sexual abuse prevention program as children were almost half as likely to report experiencing sexual abuse.

In terms of implementation and expansion, we remain frustrated by the uphill struggles to institutionalize service-learning approaches. Klaw's experience implementing service learning at a comprehensive, commuter-oriented, metropolitan university suggests that for effective wide-scale curricular innovation to occur, support from university administrators is essential. Faculty and students involved in this approach must be recognized and rewarded for their work and provided sufficient technical and collegial support through teaching assistants, mentors, and perhaps, ultimately, participation in a distinct college or department dedicated to service-learning classes.

Support from such university centers as the CSL and Center for Faculty Development and the Cross Cultural Center have been integral to the development and continuation of LSP. As such centers face budget cuts, opportunities for innovative pedagogy are imperiled. Promising avenues for implementing service learning, however, remain. We believe that requiring participation in service learning through general education, major requirements, or a mandated first-year seminar would do much to enhance student engagement, critical thinking, and leadership among undergraduates. Requiring participation in at least one course related to intimate violence as a requirement for graduation would likely reduce rates of intimate violence both perpetrated and experienced by college students. Despite the challenges inherent to implementing and evaluating such programs, we remain convinced that university-based service-learning efforts play an important role in reducing intimate partner abuse.

## Appendix A

### *Course Syllabus for the Love Sex and Power Program, Spring 2006 Psychology 190 Current Issues in Psychology*

*Family Violence Across the Globe: Understanding and Addressing Sex, Love, and Power in Cultural Context*

**Course Description:** Psychology 190 is an integrative survey of current issues and viewpoints in psychology and examines the development of current perspectives and likely future directions. This course will explore psychological research and theory related to intimate violence. Specifically, we will examine the etiology of family/intimate violence and responses to such violence in different cultures around the world. This course also examines "local" manifestations of "global" cultures through an exploration and comparative analysis of violence in indigenous, refugee, and immigrant communities in the United States. Using a community psychology paradigm, we will examine the ways in which cultural values, beliefs, and practices play a key role in both risk and protective factors for violence. Students will gain insight into the science of prevention, a key aspect of community psychology, by critically reviewing state-of-the art research pertaining to the development, manifestation, and deterrence of family violence in a variety of cultural contexts. As a community psychology course, this class will involve taking action based on the material you have learned in class. Toward that end, you will have the opportunity to *provide scripted violence prevention workshops* in various settings such as university classes, local K–12 schools, and youth programs.

**Service-Learning Component:** You will be expected to practice at least one team-taught, scripted prevention workshop in the context of a supportive class team and to conduct at least one team-taught, scripted prevention workshop to campus or community members. You will receive constructive feedback from your peers and instructors on the clarity, accuracy, and interpersonal sensitivity of your workshop presentation. You will not be provided with the opportunity to present a workshop to campus or community members outside the class context until you a have successfully conducted a practice workshop in front of class members.

**Student Learning Objectives:**

1. Compare and analyze the beliefs, practices, and institutional structures that mediate and shape the manifestation of intimate violence in different societies.
2. Identify the consequences of ideas and practices related to culturally situated forms of power and control.
3. Critically examine current scholarly research and theories related to the causes and prevention of intimate violence.
4. Identify key local and global resources available in the prevention of intimate violence.
5. Review psychological and interdisciplinary academic research, and demonstrate critical thinking in written reports.
6. Communicate effectively in oral presentations and written reports and master skills related to public speaking and community education.
7. Develop leadership skills and a sense of civic engagement.

**Course Reading:**

The reading for this course includes two books and one reader:

1. *Family Violence in a Cultural Perspective: Defining, Understanding and Combating Abuse* by Kathleen Malley-Morrison & Denise A. Hines will serve as your textbook. The book was published by Sage Publications in 2004 and is available at Spartan Bookstore and Roberts Bookstore.

2. *Ending Domestic Violence: Report from the Global Frontlines* published by Family Violence Prevention Fund (2005) can be downloaded for free at http://endabuse.org/programs/display.php3?DocID=94. To access each chapter from the report that is assigned in class, please click "full article." This report is referred to as "Ending DV" in your greensheet.

3. The *Course Reader* for *Psych 190 Family Violence Across the Globe* will be available at Maple Press (located at 481 E. San Carlos St. b/t 10th & 11th) as of the first day of class.

**Course Requirements: Total possible points = 100 points.**

- 3 Integration Assignments (30 points)
- Practice Presentation of Prevention Workshop (10 points)
- Final Research Project (40 points)
- Participation (20 points)

**Specific detailed handouts will be provided for each assignment.**

**I. Integration Assignments (30%)**

Integration Assignment 1 will involve answering essay questions to demonstrate your understanding of the course material from Unit I: Prevention Psychology.

Integration Assignment 2 will involve answering essay questions to demonstrate your understanding of the course material from Unit 2: Power and Control.

Integration Assignment 3 will involve answering essay questions to demonstrate your understanding of the course material from Unit 3: Cultural Contexts for Violence and Unit 4: Culturally Competent Intervention.

## II. Prevention Workshop Evaluation (10%)

Your practice prevention workshop will be evaluated on three areas: clarity in communication, accuracy of information, and ability to address questions.

## III. Research Project (40%)

Using at least five empirical articles and at least five readings from this class, you will develop a research question related to one type of intimate violence in one of the ethnic/cultural/geographic communities discussed in this course. You will be required to do outside library research on this topic, and write a five-page double-spaced *APA*-style report examining the issue and effective ways to prevent and address the problem. At the end of the semester, each student will create a poster to present his or her research findings to the class and community members. During the semester, I will pass out information regarding each stage of the project. See syllabus for the due date of each of the following components of the assignment:

- Research Question With Reference List (5 points)
- Outline of Paper (10 points)
- Final Paper (15 points) Final Poster Presentation (10 points)

## Appendix B

### *LSP Workshop Script: Intimate Partner Violence*

*Love, Sex, and Power*

Dr. Elena Klaw, Psychology Department, San Jose State University
Sex, Love, and Power: Dating Violence Workshop Script (70–75 min.)
Materials: Video, whiteboard pens or newsprint with tape and markers, tape, chalk, handouts, name tag

### Videos:[3]

- For high school and up: video *What Love Takes* (12 min.), standard dating violence video, touches on sexual violence
- For high school and up coed: video *Dealing With Teen Dating Abuse: Matters of Choice* (18 min.), dating violence video with inconclusive ending about a couple in which abuse occurs. Has an explicit scene of sexual coercion

- For junior high coed (8–9 grades): video *Dangerous Relationships* (30 min.), example of a couple
- For junior high/high school girls (7–11 grades): video *Toxic Relationships* (32 min., 17 sec.), particularly for youth with some prior exposure to dating violence topic, focused on peer activism, touches on sexual violence
- For junior high (6–8 grades): video *The Dating Bill of Rights* (26 min.): nonthreatening video covering dating violence, touches on sexual violence, emphasis communication
- For college-age and adult audience: video *Violence Against Women: Beyond the Statistics* (32 min., 24 sec.), overview of domestic violence

(Note: We have a separate curriculum and video for grades 3–5 on "Healthy Relationships" that addresses family, peer, and teacher relationships.)

## I. Introduction (1–2 min.)

*Tasks:*

1. **Begin with introduction:** Write your name on the board, introduce yourself and tell audience that you are part of the new peer educator program available through the psychology department at SJSU.
2. **Pass out feedback sheets:** Give the feedback sheets to the audience.

## II. View the Videotape (12–33 min. depending on the video shown)

*Task:*

1. **Show video: The standard dating violence video shown will be** *What Love Takes* (12 min.). Other videos will be used based on the workshop audience.

## III. Brainstorming on Healthy Relationships (5–10 min.)

*Tasks:*

1. **Put on the board:** Healthy Relationships . . . Unhealthy Relationships
2. **Brainstorm associated words under each category**
3. **Discuss the difference:**

Healthy relationships are based on trust, caring, and respect.

Unhealthy relationships are based on power, control, harm, fear, and manipulation.

## IV. Discuss Statistics (5 min.)

*Task:*

1. Discuss statistics

   - According to the Centers for Disease Control and Prevention, 25% of women reported being raped or physically assaulted by an intimate partner at some time in their lives. Eight percent of male participants reported such an experience.[4]
   - According to the Centers for Disease Control and Prevention:[5]
     - 1 in 4 adolescents reports experiencing verbal, physical, emotional, or sexual abuse each year from a dating partner
     - 1 in 5 high school girls has been physically or sexually abused by a dating partner
     - 1 in 5 adolescents reports being a victim of emotional abuse
   - Many of the DV homicides in Santa Clara County involved people who started dating as teens (P. Dixon, personal communication, 2002).
   - Note dating violence occurs across ages, ethnic groups, socioeconomic classes, genders, and sexual orientations. However over 90% of adult domestic violence is perpetrated by men, and the serious injuries occurring in violent relationships are more often perpetrated by males.

## V. Discuss Definitions (5–10 min.)

*Task:*

1. Discuss definitions

   - Go through the various types of physical, emotional, sexual violence (*use power and control handout or teen wheel for teen audience*).
   - Discuss aspects of control specific to teens, e.g., keeping tabs through Internet, pagers, cell phones, isolation from friends/parents, preying on someone's insecurities about looks, sexual experience, or popularity by taunting or threatening to spread gossip.
   - Discuss jealousy and possessiveness as an aspect of control that can

be confusing to teens. "No one will ever love you like I do!" can be a form of control and manipulation.

- Note jealousy = insecurity, not love. Real love is based on trust and a desire to enhance the other's well-being, and to see the other person happy.
- Note a good relationship should give you more energy and make you feel good about yourself, not take your energy.

## VI. Explain and Show the Cycle of Violence (2–5 min.)

*Task:*

1. **Explain and show the cycle of violence** (*use The Battering Cycle handout*)

   - Tension-building phase (victim is walking on eggshells, tries to keep things calm)
   - Explosion (violence triggered all of a sudden)
   - Presents and Promises stage (promises to change and apologies given, also called honeymoon stage and hearts and flowers stage)

*State*: The cycle continues in an escalating fashion. For example, while this explosion may be a slap, the next one might be pushing, until eventually the explosion is murder.

## VII. Ask and Discuss Questions

*Tasks:*

1. **Ask the audience: "Why do you think abusers abuse?"**
   **Discuss and cover all of the following points: (5–10min.)**

   - Violence is a learned behavior and it is a conscious choice
   - Male role stresses domination, insecure man uses power and control
   - ~ 60% abused or witnessed abuse in home
   - Thinks it is OK
   - Thinks it won't be punished
   - Thinks the victim won't tell or be believed
   - Uses violence to solve problems

- Believes in traditional gender roles, doesn't respect women as equals
- Substance use escalates (*doesn't cause*) violence
- Violence is used as bullying weaker person (displaces feelings of anger)

2. **Ask the audience: "Why might it be hard to leave an abusive relationship?"**

**Discuss and cover all of the following points: (10 min.)**
**Facilitator:** Challenge victim blaming by asking, "Why is this often the first question that comes to mind?"

- Physical threats of harm to self/others/property/pets, emotional threats (e.g., you will be all alone)
- In domestic violence relationships, 75% of murders occur when partner leaves abuser
- Crazy-making behavior by abuser erodes victim's sense of self (e.g., she starts to believe she's stupid, worthless, and no one else could love her)
- Denial that relationship is abusive, accepts it as normal, hopes that it will get better
- Isolation (physical, social, and cultural)
- Learned helplessness, feels that the situation can not change no matter what they do
- Teens' concerns "wanting to be liked/accepted" by partner and peer
- Discuss how hard it is to leave a relationship because at some point you cared about the person, and you felt happy/special, may still love the abuser but not the abuse
- Loyalty, want to protect the abuser
- Discuss why teens might be confused about abuse: might be their first relationship so they think that is how dating couples act, ideas in culture about women and men's roles stress women as dependent, men are supposed to be in control
- Ideas about romance as being possessive may lead victim to see jealousy as sign of love
- Female socialization makes it hard to resist abusers' claims that "he needs her," "he loves her," and she can "change him"

- Lack of information on rights and safety options
- For gay/lesbian individuals, fear of being outed/disbelieved/ostracized

Specific to Domestic Violence

- For adults, economic threats, especially if abuser is the sole provider
- Cultural beliefs about marriage
- Concern children need 2 parents

3. **Ask the audience: "Why do you think most teens tell no one about abuse?"**

   **Discuss and cover all of the following points: (2–5 min.)**
   - Discuss guilt and shame
   - Desire for independence from parents
   - Discuss fear of abuser
   - Victim believes what abuser says
   - Victim doesn't see it as abuse
   - Fear of not being believed

4. **Discuss: "What can friends do if they know of an abusive relationship?"**

   **Cover all of the following points: (3–5 min.)**

   - Confront abuser, Say: "This isn't cool."
   - Believe the victim
   - Tell victim it was not his or her fault
   - Tell victim he or she doesn't deserve abuse
   - Give victim control back by discussing options, helping to identify support figures
   - Encourage victim to make a safety plan in the event of abuse (e.g., can call someone and use code expression to get picked up, have form of transportation, ID, money, medicines)
   - Encourage victim to get medical treatment, legal help, and seek counseling at appropriate local agency: e.g., Support Network for Battered Women, Next Door Solutions, DA for restraining order preventing abuser from contact

## VIII. Distribute Handouts and Complete Self-Evaluation (3–5 min.)

*Tasks:*

1. **Discuss where participants can turn for help:** If you or anyone is dealing with dating violence, we are passing out handouts providing bay area resources and education programs, plus card with hotline numbers
2. **Pass out resource handouts**
3. **Discuss contact information for future workshops:** Dr. Elena Klaw, Department of Psychology, San Jose State University 408-924-5623, eklaw@email.sjsu.edu, http://www.psych.sjsu.edu/~eklaw
4. Collect audience feedback sheets and thank audience.

## Notes

1. For more information about the La Familia Program for Latino families affected by domestic violence contact the La Familia program coordinator at Support Network for Battered Women at 408-541-6100, ext. 144, or 408-541-6100, ext. 143. The offices of Support Network for Battered Women are located at 1257 Tasman Drive, Suite C, Sunnyvale, CA 94089. Comprehensive information about services provided by Support Network for Battered Women is available on the Web at http://www.snbw.org

2. For more information about the CARE program, contact Patricia Morey, assistant dean of students, University of Illinois, 300 Turner Student Services Building, 610 E. John St., Champaign, IL 61820; pmorey@turner.odos.uiuc.edu; 217-333-3137.

3. With the exception of *What Love Takes*, produced by a local collaborative, all videos listed are distributed by Human Relations Media, 41 Kensico Dr., Mount Kisco, NY 10549; 1-800-431-2050.

4. *Dating Abuse Fact Sheet*, 2006, Centers for Disease Control and Prevention, National Centers for Injury Prevention and Control, available from http://www.cdc.gov/ncipc/dvp/DatingViolence.htm

5. Injury Fact Book: Intimate Partner Violence, 2002, Centers for Disease Control and Prevention, National Centers for Injury Prevention and Control, available from http://www.cdc.gov/ncipc/fact_book/16_Intimate_Partner_Violence.htm

## References

Anderson, L., Stoelb, M. P., Duggan, P., Hieger, B., Kling, K. H., & Payne, J. P. (1998). The effectiveness of two types of rape prevention programs in changing the rape-supportive attitudes of college students. *Journal of College Student Development, 39*, 131–142.

Brener, N. D., McMahon, P. M., Warren, C. W., & Douglas, K. A. (1999). Forced sexual intercourse and associated health risk behaviors among female college students in the United States. *Journal of Consulting and Clinical Psychology, 67*, 252–259.

Burt, M. R. (1998). Rape myths. In M. Odem (Ed.), *Confronting rape and sexual assault: Worlds of women* (pp. 129–144). Wilmington, DE: Scholarly Resources.

Carr, J. L., & VanDeusen, K. M. (2002). The relationship between family of origin and dating violence in college men. *Journal of Interpersonal Violence, 7*, 63–66.

Centers for Disease Control and Prevention. (2003). *Costs of intimate partner violence against women in the United States*. Atlanta, GA: Author. Retrieved from http://www.cdcngov/ncipc/pub-res/ipv_cost/ipv.htm

Centers for Disease Control and Prevention, National Center for Injury Prevention and Control. (2005). *Intimate partner violence: Overview*. Atlanta, GA: Author. Retrieved from http://www.cdc.gov/ncipc/factsheets/ipvoverview.htm

Drieschner, K. & Lange, A. (1999). A review of cognitive factors in the etiology of rape: Theories, empirical studies and implications. *Clinical Psychology Review, 19*(1), 57–77.

Eisen, A., Cimino, A., Aparicio, H., Marstteller, P., & Kushner, H. (2003). Race and science: Using a comprehensive interdisciplinary approach to address complex issues, *College Teaching, 51*(2), 46–51.

Eyler, J., Giles, D. E., Stenson, C., & Gray, C. (2000). At a glance: What we know about the effects of service-learning on students, faculty, institutions and communities, 1993–2000 (3rd ed.). Nashville, TN: Vanderbilt University.

Fisher, B. S., Cullen, F. T., & Turner, M. G. (2000). *The sexual victimization of college women* (National Institute of Justice Publication No.182369). Washington, DC: U.S. Department of Justice.

Fonow, M., Richardson, L., & Wemerus, V. A. (1992). Feminist rape education: Does it work? *Gender and Society, 6*, 108–121.

Foubert, J. D. (2000). The longitudinal effects of a rape-prevention program on fraternity men's attitudes, behavioral intent, and behavior. *Journal of American College Health, 48*(4), 158–163.

Frias-Armenta, M. (2002). Long term effects of child punishment on Mexican women: A structural model. *Child Abuse & Neglect, 26*, 371–386.

Gibson, L. E., & Leitenberg, H. (2000). Child sexual abuse prevention programs: Do they decrease the occurrence of child sexual abuse? *Child Abuse and Neglect, 24*(9), 1115–1125.

Klaw, E. L., Lonsway, K. A., Berg, D. R., Waldo, C. R., Kothari, C., Mazurek, C. J., et al. (2005). Challenging rape culture: Awareness, emotion and action through Campus Acquaintance Rape Education. *Women and Therapy*, *28*(2), 47–63.

Koss, M. P. (1993). Detecting the scope of rape. *Journal of Interpersonal Violence*, *8*(2), 198–222.

Lonsway, K. A. (1996). Preventing acquaintance rape through education: What do we know? *Psychology of Women Quarterly*, *20*, 229–265.

Lonsway, K. A., Klaw, E. L., Berg, D. R., Waldo, C. R., Kothari, C., Mazurek, C. J., et al. (1998). Beyond "No Means No": Outcomes an intensive program to train peer facilitators for campus acquaintance rape education. *Journal of Interpersonal Violence*, *13*(1), 73–92.

Lonsway, K. A., & Kothari, C. (2000). First year campus acquaintance rape education: Evaluating the impact of a mandatory intervention. *Psychology of Women Quarterly*, *24*(3), 220–232.

Markus, G. B., Howard, J. P. F., & King, D. C. (1993). Integrating community service and classroom instruction enhances learning: Results from an experiment. *Educational Evaluation and Policy Analysis*, *15*(4), 410–419.

Melton, G. B. (2002). Chronic neglect of family violence: More than a decade of reports to guide U.S. policy. *Child Abuse & Neglect*, *26*, 569–586.

Smith, P. H., White, J. W., & Holland, J. H. (2003). A longitudinal perspective on dating violence among adolescent and college-age women. *Journal of Public Health*, *93*(7), 1104–1109.

Tjaden, P., & Thoennes, N. (2000). *Extent, nature and consequences of violence against women: Findings from the National Violence Against Women Survey*. Atlanta, GA: National Institute for Justice and the Centers for Disease Control and Prevention. Retrieved from http://www.ncjrs.org/pdffiles1/njj/183781.pdf

Widom, C. S., & Maxfield, M. G. (2001). An update on the cycle of violence (NCJ-Publication No. 184894). Washington, DC: U.S. Department of Justice.

Wolfe, D. A., Wekerle, C., Scott, K., Straatman, A. L., Grasler, C., Reitzel-Jaffe, D. (2003). Dating violence prevention with at-risk youth: A controlled outcome evaluation. *Journal of Counseling and Clinical Psychology*, *71*(2), 279–291.

# SERVICE LEARNING IN A PSYCHOLOGY COURSE

## Women and Violence

*Gloria Cowan*

S ervice learning provides an opportunity to practice psychology in addition to learning about psychology. In addition, service learning in a class on women and violence provides a mechanism for students to realize that they can do something to influence violence against women. An underlying assumption is that taking a course in women and violence, or in fact most women's studies classes, does not directly lead to enhancement of women's lives through reduction of violence. That is, taking a women and violence class does not directly prevent violence. I learned this painfully by discovering that students were raped, assaulted, and stalked even while enrolled in the women and violence courses I have taught. The service-learning experiences, in which my students engage, provide multiple dimensions for personal growth, and have real impact in addressing the issues of violence in the communities in which they serve. As we shall see in examining students' writing later in this chapter, their reflections on their community experiences illustrate the many ways in which service learning enhances their efficacy and their personal development.

## Reasons for Taking a Women and Violence Class

The reasons students enroll in a women and violence class can be both academic and personal. Some students may have a purely intellectual passion to understand violence against women. In my Psychology 341 course, Women and Violence, at California State University, San Bernardino, however, most students have personal motives for enrolling. Many have been victims in their own lives or have family members who are victims. Some take this course to provide some meaning for their lives, ways in which they can reorient themselves and their relationships. Others want to find a way to get involved in social problems so that they can feel better about themselves, or they may want to help others (a common desire of psychology students). And for those who have been helped to cope with violence, taking a service-learning course to become a certified advocate may be a way to pay back by helping others.

## The Non-Service-Learning Course on Women and Violence

At the outset, I need to say that the psychology of women and violence courses I teach, service learning or otherwise, have a feminist underpinning. I regard gendered violence as primarily violence committed by men and boys against women and girls as part of a patriarchal system that holds that women do not have rights to their own bodies and that exists to sustain male power and dominance. Therefore, when I bring in speakers for my women and violence course and choose relevant agencies for service learning, I gravitate toward issues that are related to men's violence against women, such as pornography, and toward agencies that primarily deal with violence toward women by men. This is not to deny that men can also be victims of rape or battering. Rather, I see men's violence against women as part of an embedded system that treats women as chattel. I do not regard women's violence against men as part of this system of male dominance and control. Violence against men is typically perpetrated by men and is gendered by virtue of the masculine ideology that supports violence. Women may incorporate the system of patriarchal values of control though aggression. Further, much female violence is motivated by self-defense.

A description of the courses I have taught on women and violence that did not use service-learning pedagogy illustrates the differences between a standard academic course and a service-learning course.[1] Typically, the courses covered areas of sexual harassment, male partner violence, child sexual abuse, rape or sexual assault, pornography, and general prevention issues. Most students who elect to take a women and violence class are already antiviolent in their beliefs and attitudes and are unlikely to be perpetrators. This is not to say that the myths that support violence against women are not present in those who take the course, but they can be demystified in the classroom setting. Because victim-blaming myths sustain and promote violence against women, disavowal of these myths can indirectly contribute to reduction of violence against women.

I have used two texts: one covering scientific knowledge in the area of violence against women, *No Safe Haven: Male Violence Against Women at Home, at Work, and in the Community* (Koss et al., 1994), and another that contains timeless essays that present unique views of violence against women and includes suggestions for changing the rape culture, *Transforming a Rape Culture* (Buchwald, Fletcher, & Roth, 1993). The Buchwald text balances theoretical and research knowledge with the impetus for social change. Students have remarked frequently how valuable they find the texts.

Students were asked to keep a journal covering the readings, the material presented in class, and their own thoughts and ideas about women and violence. Students were told that they could include personal information, but it was not necessary. Primarily, the journal was a vehicle for students to demonstrate what they were learning throughout the course and consequently was an educational rather than emotionally expressive journal. In addition to the journal—collected and responded to at four points during the course—students wrote an integrative summary of the material of the course, and were asked to point out commonalities and differences in different forms of violence against women with ideas about prevention.

I brought in a number of speakers from the community in order to provide an education on violence against women that was not part of mainstream academic work. This included a campuswide talk by Paul Kivel, a key member of a men against violence group in San Francisco. Kivel educates male students about the roots of male violence in gendered expectations for men and boys. We have had speakers from a domestic violence shelter, a deputy district attorney in charge of prosecuting domestic violence cases, a therapist who works with batterers, an expert witness on domestic violence, the director of a victim-witness program, a therapist who deals with violence victims, speakers from a local rape crisis center, a counselor on campus talking about harassment, and members of a community group (Enough is Enough) that is explicitly antipornography.

On one occasion, I invited a woman from San Diego who had been raped and had chosen not to be anonymous or remain passive. She was a perfect model for students to understand that victims are not to blame and that it is possible to think of violence against oneself or others without shame and self-recrimination. During this same quarter, a student in the class was raped in a Wal-Mart shopping center. The speaker not only offered to accompany the student to court to face her assailant, but also (and more important) served as a model of a victim who refused to capitulate. Because of the speaker, the student victim was able to confront the assailant in court. Many other women who took this course were victims. Some had been victims previously, and others were victimized during the course of the class. For example, in one tragic quarter, two were raped during the 10 weeks of one course, and another student was stalked in her apartment near campus.

It is not that these classes were unsuccessful that made me interested in service learning. Instead, it was that service learning would be a way for students to get involved in the antiviolence community, rather than having that community come to speak to them. I also hoped that the service-learning component would give students an avenue to do something themselves. Thus, after teaching this very rewarding though personally intense course, I proposed a modification of the course as a service-learning course to the curriculum committees on campus. The proposal was accepted.

## Providing Service Learning to Students of Women and Violence

How do we provide service-learning opportunities that enrich both the student and the service targets? The way that has proven helpful to me in the area of women and violence is to have the student enroll in training programs that prepare volunteers and advocates in nonprofit agencies. The agencies, often supported by state and federal funding, offer training programs for volunteers. The programs involve at least a 30-hour commitment for classes. At the end of the training, students are given a certificate making them eligible for volunteering in a state-funded agency. Nonprofit agencies, such as sexual assault and rape crisis centers and shelter organizations, are greatly in need of well-trained volunteers. These agencies experience much turnover as volunteers experience burn out, move, or find themselves otherwise unable to continue. Volunteers are the arms and legs of the agencies, the angels of the agencies, as well as the foot soldiers. Without the volunteers, the administrative functions would be empty gestures.

On some occasions, for example, sexual violence centers have a number of victims taken to the hospital; almost all need a volunteer advocate to accompany them. Therefore, nonprofit agencies that deal with gendered violence must rely on a continuous supply of volunteers. This is the benefit of the type of service learning that places students in training programs; it provides the bank of future volunteers for the agency.

Two students who obtained training in a shelter for domestic violence were able to help the shelter with its fund-raising activities. For this agency, as for many others, funding is the constant wolf at the door. A secondary gain to the agency is educating the public through the training program. Although some trainees may not pursue volunteering as they have committed themselves to doing, they may still take with them important knowledge about the specific areas important to the agency focus and an increased awareness of the seriousness and consequences of violence against women. At the very least, they should have learned not to blame victims for the violence committed against them.

## Student Benefits and Learning via Training

The benefits to the students are many. From a purely functional approach, the students are getting training that they can acknowledge via the certification on their résumé when looking for a job or applying to a graduate program in areas such as social work and psychology. Beyond the obvious benefits of enhancing one's résumé for future endeavors, the opportunity to learn how to be an effective volunteer with women who have been victimized is important. The knowledge and skills obtained in these 30-hour, state-mandated programs go beyond academic information. Volunteers may actually learn how to communicate effectively and do short-term counseling. They learn to be helping people. They learn about the systems surrounding victimization by hearing from community members who work in these systems. For example, in the shelter training program students enrolled in, they were able to observe a domestic violence judge in action in the courtroom. They could learn firsthand all the details about obtaining restraining orders. For sexual assault, they would accompany a trained volunteer to the hospital to observe how to respond to a rape victim in the hospital setting immediately following an attack. In other words, they were learning the practical behaviors and knowledge required of volunteers.

In addition to these practical gains, students also obtain grounding in myth-free beliefs and facts about rape. They have had the myths dissected as in any rape-education program. The benefit here is that hopefully they have learned to be less judgmental of victims and not to blame them for their victimization. Despite what they have learned in their women's studies or psychology of women classes, many students still believe that women lie about rape, that women can "just leave" their abuser, that it takes "two to tango," and that women are at fault for behaving seductively toward men. They may learn about many issues related to violence against women in their training course, including culture and violence against women. After meeting with domestic violence victims and sexual assault (rape) victims, it is more difficult to hold on to these victim-blaming beliefs.

Lastly, students learn about themselves and the importance of staying away from demeaning and violent relationships. Some have told me that they learned to give up abusive partners because of the training they received. In summary, getting involved in training produces a commitment to do even little things. Getting involved in training (a) aligns training with antiviolence values, (b) helps trainees see how it really is to be victimized instead of being the stereotyped thrilling encounter, (c) demystifies and reduces stereotypes of victims, and (d) helps the trainee feel good about himself or herself by learning skills that can be helpful to others.

## Academic Component

As one might expect, the coverage for the academic component depends on the instructor's goals. A perfect coordination with the training program is not likely because training programs have their own unique tasks and areas to cover. In the training programs, the material is likely to be practical, and even when conceptual, is not necessarily based on empirical research. Occasionally, coverage of the material is more folklore than fact. As a researcher and teacher, I strongly believe that material in the classroom should cover knowledge gained through research. For the service-learning course, I chose a primary text that is research oriented: *Hurting the One You Love* (Frieze, 2005). Large gains in knowledge have occurred in the area of women and violence. The students should be exposed to some compilation of new knowledge gained empirically.

In my course, I have coverage of conceptual issues, empirical issues, ideas about changing society, and in the training, exposure to practical issues. Because the training programs are extensive and require a large number of hours, for grading purposes I choose to use a journal format. This format allows students to integrate information from the books, the class, the training, and even the news into their journal. The journal is graded according to how much of the material covered in the academic part is discussed. For example, I grade based on whether they have paid attention to the assigned material and have thought about it. I regard the material learned in training as material they can discuss in their journals. This material in the journals is evaluated along with any other awareness expressed in their entries.

## The Service-Learning Course

When the women and violence course was finally taught completely in a service-learning format, 18 students enrolled in the course. The class enrollment was smaller than average because finding time for the service-learning component was a challenge for working students; however, the size of the class clearly contributed to its success. I deliberately did not overload my part of the course with work, considering they were enrolled in a 30-hour training program. For the academic part of the course, I found a new, short text (Frieze, 2005) and continued using the readings book. Throughout the class, students got to know each other, especially because they were required to make presentations from the readings book to the class. Students took their assignments seriously and, for the most part, attempted to grasp the full meaning and impact of the essays they presented. My requirements for the course again included a journal integrating material learned in their service-learning program with coverage of material learned in class, and their own thoughts and ideas. Two journals were graded. In addition, students presented two or three readings to the class. Students in this class had a special rapport, probably because the class was small and they presented essays to the class as a whole. For some reason, perhaps because of the small and intimate nature of the setting, students in this class decided to try to enrich their presentations as much as possible. The way they enriched their presentations was to integrate the essay into their own thinking and enthusiastically convey the information to the rest of the class. It was not that they brought in additional material, but that they presented the information in an informed and attractive way. The presenters connected with the rest of the class and wanted them to share their enthusiasm.

## A Problem of Coordination of the Course With the Training

Teaching a service-learning course that relies on training offerings in the community has one major problem. The nonprofit agencies have to be offering training in the quarters or semesters in which the course is offered. It is important that the trainees be from the agency's community. If the university student body is primarily commuters, as ours is, students will have to take a training program in their own community. The faculty member does not have control over when the training will be offered, and also doesn't have control over the training program itself. An example of a problem I faced was that the sexual assault agency in the university community backed off from offering training during the quarter the course was scheduled. Most of the local students had to select a volunteer training program at a battered women's shelter, although their initial preference might have been for sexual assault training. Some students found training programs in their own communities. Several students made a commitment to take the training for sexual assault when it was offered in the subsequent summer. One student contracted with me to do a special project. She had already worked in an agency and, as a teacher's assistant, wanted to take on a relationship with a mother of a child in her class whom she thought was being abused. Her project was to gain the trust of the mother so that she could enable the mother (and child) to get help.

## Evaluation

My evaluation of the course came from examining the 10 students (of 18) who had written unsolicited remarks in their last journal about the positive reactions to the course. The student comments focused on a two-step process—changing themselves and changing the world. The reactions included comments from students who had themselves been abused. They, and others as well, viewed the course as a personal learning experience. Clearly, some of the comments indicated motivation to be part of the process of social change at both individual and societal levels. Many of them stated that the course had a special significance for them and changed their thinking. The following example illustrates both personal and social change:

> I feel as though this quarter has been a very personal journey for me, and though I may have shared it with 20 or so other people, it was my own experiences that made it so extraordinary. Not only did I gain perspective on myself, my past and present relationships, and the relationships of my friends and children, I gained perspective on the functioning of society as a whole. There are more unanswered questions than answered ones, but this fuels the drive for change, I suppose. It sounds crazy, but this may be one of the few classes I have taken where I can take the knowledge gained in the classroom setting and actually apply it to real life. Overall, I just wanted to thank you for letting me join your class, because it was an amazing growth experience for me. I'm truly grateful for everything I've learned and the fire that has been ignited inside of me. There are so many important things that we have discussed, and it was great that the service course was speaking about the same issues, because the major points were driven home in such a consistent and powerful way. I am so glad you offer this course, and I hope you continue to teach it in the future, because it is vitally important to the growth of our society. Change starts within an individual, and I know this class changed me.

Here is an example of purely personal change:

> and sometimes you need to cry and get angry to make yourself feel better. So I did do a lot of crying and a lot of screaming and then I went through the phases. Now I'm at the point where I know that it wasn't my fault, and that he's an evil bastard for the crap he did to me. But it has made me a stronger person and it has taught me a lot about myself. So I am actually getting something else besides a grade from a class that I am taking. If it wasn't for this class that I am taking with you then I might not have been able to move on. So in a weird way I want to say thank you. So thanks. You might not ever know but it means a lot to me that I can sleep now through the night without freaking out. Thanks.

This comment shows personal change leading to wanting to help others:

> I view this as the biggest coincidence ever, that I got into this class at the very moment that I was going through all these problems in my life. I

learned so much about myself as well as how to stand up for myself. I went though so much this quarter it was not a good experience yet it helped me a lot to learn what I can do to help others avoid the kind of relationship I was in. We do not just wash our hands of these women when we get frustrated because they will not leave the abuser. We can make sure that we give these women the information so when they finally decide that they are ready to do something about it, they know how and that there is help available and people who care.

This is an example of working to change society and help others:

Before I took this class, I was aware of and empathic to the issue of domestic violence. I had experienced it, read about it, and even decided to write my thesis on an aspect of it. Through the last 10 weeks, this issue has consumed me. It is constantly on my mind and in my conversations. My friends think I'm obsessed. I think they may be right. I am so aware of the amount of abuse that occurs on a day-to-day basis, it is almost overwhelming. It is also empowering, though, to know that I have gained the knowledge and understanding of the issue to rationally explain it to others and offer some insight, when asked. I have already begun volunteering at _____ by helping them plan a fundraiser. I realized upon talking to them that the types of volunteers they need aren't the ones you would automatically expect, there is a lot to be done behind the scenes with little staff and no money to do it with. The appreciation they have shown to me, just because I show up, is truly touching. Taking this course has awoken a part of me I didn't know existed, the activist. I am ready to get up and fight for change because I have been made aware of all the ways that women are treated as subordinates in this world. I was aware of the injustices before, but now I want to do something about it. I also thought that taking the service part of the class outside of a traditional classroom really helped add to the experience. Rather than dealing with a small sample of people, all with relatively similar goals (a degree) we were dealing with people from all different perspectives—those who were forced to be there, those who were there to help clients in the field, and us students. This cross-section of people helped me ascertain the realness of what we were doing and why we were doing it. I really gained a lot from the experience and I am proud to have earned my certification.

This example illustrates changing oneself though knowledge and changing others:

This class has been extremely valuable and informative. Before coming to this class, I thought that I was fairly knowledgeable, compassionate, and educated about violence committed against women. But what I found during the course of the class is that I am not very knowledgeable, [or] educated and at times may not have been very compassionate. For example, I discovered that I had believed many of the rape myths and was at times not understanding of women who stayed in abusive relationships. I also found that I have been a part of the problem that plagues our rape culture and helps perpetuate the violence that is committed against women. Although I have discovered this about myself, I don't believe that these beliefs were intentional. I believe that they were all born out of ignorance and lack of education or training. After making this horrible realization, I want to be a part of the solution instead of being a part of the problem. I realize that the most powerful thing I can do to end the violence against women is to change myself and learn as much as I can to help inform others, who are also misguided and ignorant.

One student summarized the feelings of many of the students in this course:

I am saddened to say that this is the end of the quarter. I am happy to state that this has truly been the most motivating class I have ever been in! In all of my training, I believe this to be the most informative. . . . [t]omorrow depends on what we learn TODAY.

These comments I have quoted indicate that taking a course like this generates strong emotions and self-relevant statements. Regarding changing ourselves, this course is very important. If we don't change ourselves, we can't change the world. We need, as these students indicated, to change our basic assumptions and beliefs. Further, we need to speak out, act when we can, teach our children and students the truth, and listen to the truth. We need to support other women. We need to understand that the truth heals; reality is ugly, but blinders are worse. Then, when we have changed ourselves, we need to identify ways to change the world toward a deinstitutionalization of violence against women, even if it's only tiny steps. As Gloria Steinem (1992) argued, we need to engage in small outrageous acts. Although treatment is not seen as important as prevention, there are many women in this world (one-third abused worldwide) who need treatment and cannot wait for prevention.

Would students feel the same way if the class was not service learning? I can't answer that question; however, my response would be that the service-learning component provides the opportunity for students to actually be part of the solution. It seems that getting all the information about the extent, depth, and implications of violence against women would leave students feeling helpless about doing anything about it. The agencies that provide the training are the ones that provide the opportunities to help in many different ways. For example, the rape crisis center for which I have served as a board member for many years now has a grant for an antirape campaign, MyStrength,[2] in a local high school. Volunteers in that organization can be part of the educational aspects of preventing rape.

Service learning or not, students are not just intellectually curious or blank tablets. They come to this course with many personal emotions. Most have been victimized or have known family members who were victimized. Sometimes it does not surface at all or it surfaces late in the course. For example, in my psychology of women class a large percentage of women students who chose to comment on a battering article in the readings had, by the end of the quarter, reported being victims themselves—frequently of severe abuse, of being raped, were sexually abused as children, and/or had children who were sexually abused by others.

I believe that one minor reason students regarded the service-learning women and violence course as special was that I communicated the appreciation of them. I enjoyed their presentations and attempted to be supportive, knowing that they were spending a large amount of time on this course. I tried not to overburden them with academic research, balancing knowledge in the field with applied issues. From my perspective, it is important to be open to the emotional issues students bring and to validate them when they surface without being intrusive. It is important to respect the depth of their pain. I believe there's a balance in this type of course between an intellectual focus and an emotional focus. The professor should be available, warm, and empathic, but should not do therapy with the student, even when the professor is a therapist. As professors, we are not saviors, but we also are not cold intellectuals when we teach this kind of course. Students want to help. Of course, the ultimate idea is to get students to foster social change and prevention, as well as work with all elements of the community—legal, medical, police, family, schools, and religion—to make violence against women intolerable. Still, as work progresses on changing the culture, there is a need for individuals who have all this knowledge to be able to do something concrete that ameliorates the suffering of those who are victims of male violence.

## Notes

1. For one quarter, I taught the course with both service learning and non-service-learning students in the class. For this term, 25% of the students (13 of 48) chose service learning. The choices reflected the fact that they did not know of the service learning option until just prior to the quarter in which the course was taught. Most of our students have jobs outside the university, and in order to participate in service learning they have to have the time available when the agencies are doing the 30-hour training. I strongly recommend against offering a course under two conditions: service learning and non-service learning. The assignments are different, the requirements are different, and even the class hours are different. Housing the different students in one course creates an "us versus them" mentality, and it prevents cohesiveness that comes with having similar experiences.

2. MyStrength is a project of the California Department of Health Services and the California Coalition Against Sexual Assault. See http://MyStrength.org for more information.

## References

Buchwald, E., Fletcher, P. R., & Roth, M. (1993). *Transforming a rape culture.* Minneapolis, MN: Milkweek Editions.

Chrisler, J., Golden, C., & Rozee, P. (Eds.). (2004). *Lectures on the psychology of women* (3rd ed.). New York: McGraw-Hill.

Frieze, I. H. (2005). *Hurting the one you love: Violence in relationships.* Belmont, CA: Thomson Wadsworth.

Koss, M. P., Goodman, L. A., Browne, A., Fitzgerald, L. F., Keita, G. P., & Russo, N. F. (1994). No safe haven: Male violence against women at home, at work, and in the community. Washington, DC: American Psychological Association.

Steinem, G. (1992). *Revolution from within: A book of self-esteem.* Boston: Little, Brown.

# SECTION FIVE

# SERVICE LEARNING AND RESEARCH

# 12

# EMPOWERING OLDER WOMEN THROUGH SERVICE-LEARNING RESEARCH

*Luciana Laganà*

S ervice learning (SL) is a form of hands-on community intervention specifically designed to increase students' educational outcomes and civic engagement (Bringle, 2005). SL faculty and students can work toward effecting positive changes through participatory research conducted in community facilities, hospitals, and the workplace (Senn, 2005), among other social settings, to positively transform services and communities. Recently, SL has been increasingly used to provide students with real-life experience concerning older adults and aging (Karasik, Maddox, & Wallingford, 2004). Professors have been successful in adding SL components to their Psychology of Aging classes, as documented by Collins, Skultety, and Whitbourne (2001), significantly enhancing the class experience for everyone involved in SL endeavors. Similarly, as reported by Blieszner and Artale (2001), exposure to SL experiences by undergraduate gerontology students has enhanced their understanding of course concepts and myths regarding aging, as well as reinforced their career choices as future gerontology professionals. Furthermore, students' attitudes toward older workers often improve after involvement in SL work (Hanks & Icenogle, 2001). The interested reader is referred to an article by Hegeman, Horowitz, Pillemer, Schultz, and Tepper (2002) for an overview of the rationale and history of SL in elder care, and for a description of geriatric SL programs that have been implemented in the last decade.

Americans over the age of 65 of racial and ethnic minority backgrounds represent a rapidly growing segment of the U.S. population, currently totaling over 13% (U.S. Census Bureau, 2003). Statistics on Los Angeles County (where the author of this chapter conducts SL research) indicate that 9.7% of the population in this southwest region of the United States is composed of older adults, 59% of these being women (U.S. Census Bureau, 2000). The latter represent the majority of many older ethnic minorities (National Center for Health Statistics, 1996). Overall, women make up the largest portion of older populations, and their number is expected to grow fast in the next decades (Laditka, 2002). Thus, it is critical to include them in research efforts and to encourage the recruitment of ethnically diverse older women in particular. To contribute to addressing this research need, the present chapter proposes potential topics for SL endeavors targeting elderly women. This is followed by a discussion of some methodological and assessment issues that should be taken into account when developing and implementing SL research.

Including older women from various ethnic backgrounds in SL research is paramount. In doing so, it should be kept in mind that the communities in which they live are complex and understudied entities, which must be carefully explored and accepted, instead of asked to adapt to a university culture (Gamson, 1997). Therefore, it is important to send our students to study and service the communities where the target population in question resides. However, most scholarly studies still ask research participants/SL clients to go to academic facilities in order to participate in research endeavors; undeniably, this could not be possible for most of the SL projects proposed herein. Ethnically diverse older women are often neglected in research because, at least partially, of recruitment problems frequently encountered when trying to involve elderly minorities in research (Heller, Rody, & Thompson, 1994). Some of the reasons for such difficulties include problems in transportation to research facilities (Kail & Mindel, 1989) and unavailability of ethnically matched researchers (Ballard, Harrell, Nash, & Raiford, 1993). Moreover, most minority elderly do not volunteer for research advertised in the media, as documented by Arean and Miranda (1995). Therefore, SL projects that send our students out into the community, in order to locate often isolated seniors and include them in research, could also serve the academic purpose of filling a gap in the geriatric literature.

## Theoretical Underpinning

The theoretical framework of each SL project proposed below would depend upon professors' individual views of the psychosocial issues relevant to each study and their personal preferences for a particular theory. A potential theoretical base is a participatory community research approach, in which SL clients (in this case, older women) are empowered to shape the research agenda. Such an approach often achieves higher sociopolitical awareness (Davis, Jason, Keys, Suarez, & Taylor, 2004). Faculty could develop SL research based on the feedback provided during individual interviews and/or focus groups by older women, and should verify that the latter have clearly articulated their needs and concerns. It is important that researchers fully understand SL clients' point of view, beyond merely taking notes while already set on the choice of a particular research design or assessment procedure. The way to conduct this research should be truly informed by the senior clients, and professors should aim at empowering them at all levels of the research process. This could be achieved by infusing their clients' ideas and needs throughout each step of the research development and implementation.

A participatory research method, as pointed out by Bloodworth et al. (2004), differs from more traditional research approaches that put the researcher in charge of coming up with the research ideas, identifying the research methodology to be used, as well as selecting the procedures to collect and interpret the research outcomes. SL professors need to be open minded if they intend to truly empower older women by allowing the latter to shape the research agenda. This creative process could produce high-quality research findings that tap into psychosocial domains often ignored in mainstream academic research. Moreover, empowering elderly women who participate in SL studies by including them in the design of such projects could offer students excellent role models of the application of feminist and phenomenological principles of research; a discussion of such issues is beyond the scope of this chapter.

## Potential Research Topics for SL Projects Targeting Older Women

The following suggestions regarding prospective topics of SL research were derived from a review of the current literature on older women related to issues of empowerment; it should be noted that the studies in question (with the exception of the last one) did not incorporate SL in their research format. However, as discussed below, professors could target these sensitive issues by addressing the proposed topics in carefully designed SL studies.

SL research could focus on addressing health disparities (Ottenritter, 2004). Sadly, older women are often deprived of the power of choice in their medical treatment, and this should not be tolerated when this treatment could be harmful and avoided by favoring less damaging procedures. For instance, research shows that, although controversial in its use, electroconvulsive therapy is an increasingly popular treatment of older women with depression. Not surprisingly, a qualitative study on these patients' perception of such a medical treatment found that the central theme of their interviews reflected a perceived shifting of power from themselves to others (O'Connor & Orr, 2005). SL research could target this delicate topic, carefully considering the authority balance in question, in particular the power held by medical doctors, focusing on identifying older women's medical needs as well as facilitating their communication with medical professionals, especially in regard to the potential consequences of each treatment option.

Indeed, many elderly women are faced with the necessity to negotiate having their health needs met. This can be a challenging process that, according to Kinch and Jakubec (2004), often requires mutual support. Interviews by Kinch and Jakubec with groups of older women that included immigrants and multicultural elders found that access to service, poverty, and power were all crucial issues related to these women's health care experiences. Thanks to the support received from the group, many older women became inspired regarding consciousness-raising, reflection, and activism. Group reflection was particularly conducive to better understanding of how "multiple margins" (being a woman, a member of a visible minority, and elderly) can impair access to health care. SL research on this topic could focus on facilitating empowerment groups; its results could contribute to better management of older women's own health care, which is a significant issue given the higher probability of becoming physically ill and requiring medical attention later in life.

Geriatric clinicians could help elderly women in many circumstances, for example, when the latter experience intimate partner violence. Unfortunately, disclosing such violence is often perceived as a violation of personal privacy about domestic affairs and viewed as inappropriate by older women (especially those from ethnic minority backgrounds); yet, it is critical to assist abused elders in this process. Sadly, when disclosure does happen, many abuse survivors feel unsupported and discounted by their medical care providers (Zink, Regan, Jacobson, & Pabst, 2004). Zink et al. acquired such information by interviewing women reportedly involved in abusive relationships since age 55. Many of those interviewed stated that they did not disclose the abuse to their health care providers because of a perceived lack of both societal understanding and available resources for older women's intimate partner violence. Zink, Regan, Jacobson, and Pabst (2003), investigating this delicate topic further by conducting interviews, identified several reasons why older women remain in abusive relationships. These included their lacking job skills or education, receiving little assistance from social institutions, and/or having health problems that limited their options. Professors could address these problematic issues through SL studies. Such a fertile, potential SL area of research could focus on empowering older women who are being abused by their partner, and/or on sensitizing clinicians to the realities of this neglected problem, including the need to identify signs of potential abuse (understanding that disclosure by the abused women may not happen), establishing an atmosphere of trust and privacy for these women, and providing appropriate referrals to make sure that the abuse survivors are safe and can receive high-quality care.

On a somewhat lighter note, having support during stressful times and companionship in daily life is essential; however, many older women do not have friends available to fulfill these important functions. SL research initiatives could follow the example of Stevens (2001), who developed a successful educational program on friendship enrichment. Its main goal was empowerment (in line with the focus of this chapter), as well as reduction of loneliness. Data analyses showed that the program facilitated both the clarification of older women's needs for friendship and the analysis of their existing social network; it also supported them in setting goals of friendship and in developing strategies aimed at achieving such goals.

A prospective SL support group could follow the example of Blatter and Jacobsen, who, in 1993, described a six-session peer support group program, Expanding Horizons, which was facilitated by a psychotherapist. The goal was to reduce the potential negative impact of divorce on older women. The focus of the sessions included setting goals and grief-stage identification, building self-esteem, coping with stress, sharing experiences in small groups (if preferred), and rechecking goal setting as a function of the progression of the group sessions. SL students, once appropriately trained for this clinical endeavor, could act as facilitators of similar groups and target critical topics brought up by older women during individual interviews and/or focus groups.

Physical activity interventions for the research population in question could facilitate building an exercise identity and decreasing conflicts concerning feeling guilty about exercising. However, mainly because of the traditional way in which many older women were socialized, it is often hard for these women to allow themselves to find time to exercise without feeling guilty about conflicting roles and identities. Nonetheless, inactive older women can indeed improve their sense of exercise identity via participating in a 10-week community exercise intervention. This was ascertained through semistructured, repeated interviews; the research participants reported that exercise increased their sense of control, achievement, and cognitions (Hardcastle & Taylor, 2005). Interestingly, to assess the leisure perceptions of older women, a study involving several focus groups found that some of them described feeling guilty when idle (Vaughan & Siegenthaler, 1998), making the topic of guilt in older age a neglected area to explore further. These women resided in retirement communities, yet the pressure of being socialized as having to take care of others and/or engage in multiple tasks on a regular basis might have been holding them back from enjoying leisure activities even after retirement. SL research could shed more light on the guilt experienced by older women when exercising or engaging in enjoyable activities, possibly facilitating a decrease in guilt and a corresponding increase in life satisfaction through appropriate interventions.

As an example of ongoing SL research, the author has been implementing a community-based intervention to teach older adults (mainly older women) how to use computers and the Internet. This project is funded by the National Institute of Mental Health; its pilot findings are presented in Laganà (in press-a). Very briefly, this research takes place within the context of the author's undergraduate general education SL course Introduction to Gerontology. This class provides an overview of the field of gerontology and emphasizes life-cycle changes and adult developmental processes, critically examining the applications of theoretical and empirical research for the practice of geriatric psychology from a multidisciplinary perspective. It focuses especially on race, ethnicity, gender, disability, sexual orientation, and other diversity issues as critical variables. Moreover, students (i.e., multicultural individuals of all ages) are asked to teach ethnically diverse, community-dwelling older adults how to use computers and the Internet in a randomized controlled study. This research work counts for one-third of the final class grade. The author has created a manual, carefully followed by all students/computer trainers, in order to standardize the SL training procedure.

As part of their class assignments, students receive a diary outline in the course syllabus. They are asked to address the three points of this outline soon after each encounter with their SL clients. In particular, to evaluate the impact of the SL experience, students are required to write one diary/reflective essay per senior participant, in which they discuss how and to what extent their SL work has (a) had an impact on their views of older adults, (b) changed them at a personal and social level, and (c) reflected topics discussed in class and addressed in the textbook. This format makes it relatively easy for students to express their thoughts and feelings associated with the SL experience. Faculty could adopt a similar diary structure in new SL studies and publish articles/book chapters on the feedback provided by students in such diaries, as well as on the impact of the research projects on students' and SL clients' outcomes.

## Methodological Issues

Upper-division undergraduate classes and graduate classes could involve students in advanced SL applications targeting some of the complex issues discussed above. Foundational knowledge should be imparted by the professor in class, prior to starting SL work. The training should focus on providing students with in-depth understanding of important topics, such as an appreciation of diversity, for students to become sensitive to all kinds of minority issues. As discussed later on, it is always best to dedicate ample class time (and time outside of class if at all possible) to offer students clinical and other relevant training prior to engaging them in mental-health-related SL endeavors, even if they have already taken classes that should have prepared them for this work.

Once professors have decided to target older women in their SL research effort, they need to identify the critical characteristics of the research questions/challenges to address in their projects by conducting pilot research work prior to incorporating SL research components into the class curriculum. It is recommended that professors and/or their experienced research assistants conduct in-depth, one-on-one interviews and/or focus groups to clarify their SL clients' needs, which might be different from what was originally anticipated by the professors or the administrators of the community facilities involved in the project.

Faculty need to be prepared to make changes to their research design before investing time and resources into SL projects that do not meet the actual needs of older adults. This author had preliminarily designed the Internet SL research as a group intervention, based on the format typically used in the existing relevant literature and on the input provided by those in charge of a retirement home facility for cognitively high-functioning seniors. This location was chosen as the first site of the study. Such a group format sounded ideal, since it would have maximized the feasibility of the project, making it viable on a large scale without having to meet the demands of one-on-one computer/Internet instruction. It would have allowed the SL research team to train older adults in a less costly manner in terms of both resources and time. However, upon conducting a pilot group intervention with nine older adults at the facility in question, the results were very clear. The second day of training, only two out of the nine seniors who had joined the training session the first time returned, and the next day of training only one did, an older woman who had made a positive personal connection with her trainer. When asked why they dropped out so quickly, seniors (who had originally signed up for the group training) reported that they were no longer interested in the project, for reasons that included being embarrassed to make mistakes in front of other residents, not being able to focus when others were present, or just not liking the group format. Based on this finding, one-on-one training was selected as the intervention modality for the SL study in question.

Once the research outcomes for students and older women are identified, professors need to work on designing their SL research projects, a task that can often be problematic, for reasons summarized below. Unfortunately, the methodological challenges associated with conducting SL studies are deterring many colleagues from using SL research strategies in their courses. However, it is possible and indeed feasible to assess and manipulate student outcomes (and community client ones) in SL endeavors. Multiple methods can be successfully used, as briefly discussed in the next paragraphs.

## Implementation of SL Research

Ways to minimize the possible methodological challenges inherent in the implementation of SL studies are described in a book chapter proposing an original SL research model (Laganà & Rubin, 2002) to cover basic yet critical SL research issues. Its steps for the implementation of SL research are as follows:

1. Define preliminary research objectives and operationalize the research variables of interest.
2. Plan community collaboration and select a research sample.
3. Design the course and its SL research component.
4. Guide students to conduct the community intervention, reflect on their experience, and create a "deliverable" (i.e., a product that is donated to community partners for their future application).
5. Perform baseline and intervention assessment and evaluation.

Following this model could help plan and implement high-quality SL research. Because of space limitations, practical examples of these five steps are not provided herein. The interested reader is referred to Laganà and Rubin (2002) and to an article on how to follow the model's steps when implementing SL projects targeting older adults' quality of life (Laganà, 2003). The model could also serve as a basic template for faculty who are in the initial process of planning SL research that includes a formal assessment component targeting students, SL clients, and/or staff at the community facilities serviced. When adopting this model, professors should plan on carefully monitoring whether the objectives and outcomes of their SL research have been reached, and should establish a corresponding timeline of multiple assessments.

Discrete objectives for the aforementioned SL projects need to cover outcomes for older women/SL clients as well as for students, since they will both enrich each others' lives through SL participation. Concrete research outcomes for older women could include increasing their knowledge of medical care options, or the number of hours they engage in exercise or leisure activities, as a function of well-planned SL interventions. For a discussion of civic engagement student outcomes, see Laganà (in press-b). Ideally, whenever feasible, SL client outcomes should correspond to as many needs as possible that were identified by the clients as their main concerns, with the clear understanding (by all parties involved) that a single SL endeavor is not likely to address all the needs of SL clients. This is important, in order for faculty, students, clients, and facility administrators not to develop unrealistic expectations that are unfeasible.

## SL Student Training

It is critical to design a formal SL training protocol, in order to ensure that all students will adhere in a uniform way to the planned assessment and, whenever applicable, intervention procedures. This training is necessary for students to conduct themselves in an approachable yet professional manner with their SL clients. For instance, in the author's SL projects, students are trained extensively, starting at the beginning of the semester, as part of the class syllabus. It is useful to schedule weekly mentoring group meetings and individual appointments with students whenever needed, to make certain that all of them are well trained. This task takes some additional time, but it is worth doing if we want to conduct high-quality SL research. As part of the training, professors could discuss several articles and book chapters relevant to their SL project. All students need to be trained, not only in interviewing and assessment skills, but also in active listening. Additionally, the training must focus on how to cover all assessment and intervention materials within the estimated amount of time, and to concurrently establish a warm rapport with the older women recruited. Students need to stop the assessment/intervention if fatigue becomes an issue, and should resume it whenever feasible.

For example, the author's study (Laganà & Sosa, 2004), funded by the National Institute of Health, was an SL clinical assessment project conducted over a period of three years, during six semesters. Its main objective was to identify the psychosocial and medical needs of ethnically diverse, cognitively high-functioning older women residing in Los Angeles County. Several lessons learned at the beginning of this research informed the content of subsequent student training. After collecting pilot data, it became evident that many students needed supplementary information on what to expect during interaction with their research participants, mainly because of their having little or no experience with this population. To address this issue, they were given extra guidance and relevant reading assignments to identify and dispel possible preconceptions and biases toward older women. Several students in the first semester of the project repeatedly commented on how important it was to build good rapport with potential participants in order to facilitate their retention throughout the lengthy assessment procedures. Considering this feedback, students in the following semesters were strongly encouraged to clearly communicate to SL clients their importance to the study, and to exhibit a professional interest in, and respect for, the delicate psychosocial and medical issues disclosed by participants during the administration of the clinical assessment protocol.

## Assessment Issues

Professors should carefully consider how to evaluate whether the anticipated outcomes of their SL research are achieved. The use of appropriate qualitative and quantitative assessment tools will track changes in both SL students and clients. The specific content of the measures used is going to depend upon the nature of the individual project, especially on the particular variables to be assessed. Generally speaking, it is best to employ well-established standardized measures, as opposed to creating new ones, to maximize the generalizability of the research findings. However, in reality some SL projects are going to ask questions that are not covered by existing assessment tools. In these cases, professors need to come up with new measures or modify existing ones to fit the aims of their research. This is definitely time consuming and, understandably, can deter many professors from implementing novel SL studies.

Ideally, assessment tools are tailored to the unique characteristics of the individuals who will be assessed, including the staff at the SL facilities if applicable; yet again, this is not always a feasible option. For instance, in terms of norms, it is often difficult to find measures with established norms on older adults, especially multicultural older women. SL research on the latter will have the added benefit of collecting data that will establish assessment tools' norms for this neglected population. The research team should pay particular attention to recruiting SL clients from several ethnic backgrounds to optimize the diversity of the final research sample, or focus on a specific ethnic group for the development of ethnicity-specific norms.

Once the assessment tools are created, refined, and/or modified to fit the scope of a specific SL project, learning objectives and outcomes can be assessed multiple times, depending on the nature and design of the study. Prior to implementing SL interventions, baseline assessment of the problem/situation to be targeted will provide a picture of the original circumstances. The postintervention findings are very rewarding for all people involved in the study. It is a great satisfaction to realize that the extensive effort put into developing and implementing the SL research results in an enhanced quality of life for SL older clients, as well as in increased awareness, civic responsibility, and many other satisfactory experiences for our students.

As already mentioned, SL projects should also ask students (and, if feasible, SL clients) to keep diaries, and postintervention interviews with the clients should be planned, in order to collect their feedback on the research in question. To assess changes in the students at a qualitative level, a content analysis of their diaries is usually implemented. Marchel (2004) has proposed a rubric that could be used to monitor students' quality of reflection and changes in their sociocultural awareness as a function of becoming involved in SL research.

It is important to match the types of assessment tools used with the characteristics of those who will be assessed by them, to be able to operationalize the planned outcomes without making the assessment procedures excessively cumbersome for the SL clients. For instance, in the case of older adults, asking them to keep a diary may be too much, and could have the counterproductive result of their choosing to drop out of the study. Conversely, students often report that keeping a diary is a useful and productive way to monitor their own reactions to interacting with older adults (Laganà, in press-a).

## SL Student Learning Outcomes

In the prospective SL projects proposed above, pre- and postintervention assessment can be conducted on student variables of particular interest, such as self-esteem, understanding of diversity, civic engagement, and other meaningful issues. Bringle, Hudson, and Phillips (2004) offered assistance to faculty by compiling numerous scales that could be used to assess SL students' experiences, covering variables related to their moral development, critical thinking, and attitudes. In a similar vein, Dunn, Halonen, & Mehrotra (2004) targeted the challenging tasks of appropriately assessing student outcomes and measuring their achievements in a book on assessment options, which also offers a compilation of articles on assessment from psychological literature. This book could be useful to professors interested in conducting research on how their SL projects affect their students.

Depending on the nature and scope of each SL study, students will engage in many creative activities, such as implementing workshops for health care facilities personnel, providing empowerment training to older women, and/or facilitating the implementation of peer support groups for these SL clients. Faculty who decide to pioneer such initiatives can set student learning outcomes of various kinds. For instance, they may target enhancing students' commitment to service, community awareness, involvement with community, self-awareness, sensitivity to diversity, and communication skills (Driscoll et al., 1998). In regard to the SL research projects proposed earlier, their appropriate implementation could achieve several student objectives, such as gaining positive experience, learning issues related to citizenship/civic engagement participation, acquiring a variety of skills (including those applicable to their specific academic fields), experiencing critical personal changes, understanding ethics concepts, and learning about diversity. This outcome prediction is backed up by some of the latest research on what students gain from becoming involved in SL endeavors. In particular, the aforementioned objectives were identified in a study by Marty and Rienzi (2005), in which the authors' qualitative assessment of reflection papers/diaries (written by students at the conclusion of their community-based projects) identified the most common outcomes of SL participation. Although their research participants were psychology students, these objectives could easily apply to students from many other majors.

Several interesting changes can take place on a personal level for SL students as a result of their interactions with older adults. In the case of the author's Internet study in progress (Laganà, in press-a), reading students' diaries revealed many of these changes, like having an enhanced appreciation for life: "I take for granted some of the abilities I have today that my research participant no longer has. . . . he goes through life losing more and more of these abilities and still manages to smile and do the best he can."

Students have become more patient when dealing with older adults: "[during training] I have to remind myself that [a 96-year-old woman] has it much more difficult than me and secondly, has earned every right to be the way [she] is . . . to be moody and difficult . . . or hyper and chatty."

A trainer feels more respected by the older trainee who now views the student as a competent person: "[During the final training session], he speaks to me as though I am a normal person, not a child."

Other changes in SL students may involve finding similarities between self and the older trainee: "when I look at younger children . . . [I] think about the times I had and what it felt like to be a 10-year-old child. When I look in [my trainee's] eyes, I see that [he] too flashbacks and thinks about what it feels to be 22 again." And they are acquiring enhanced empathy toward seniors: "elderly people are not respected much or looked well upon by the community, so I don't blame her [a 75-year-old trainee] for the way she tries to get respect and attention from everyone." Several of these changes may also occur as a consequence of learning about older adults through attending lectures and participating in class discussions; the actual SL experience often clarifies and solidifies what is learned in class.

Definitely, faculty can foster the chosen SL student objectives by augmenting the learning that will occur in the field with relevant knowledge provided through class lectures and activities. It should be noted that the prospective studies described earlier could target SL client populations other than those described, depending upon the professors' and students' interests. It is possible for some students, once they complete SL research on such important social issues, to become so enthusiastic that they may choose to engage in activist activities to enhance social justice (Elias, Roschelle, & Turpin, 2000).

Not surprisingly, students' feedback positively contributes to the development of SL research. They spend many hours conducting SL projects and therefore are in the position to provide insiders' feedback on the research practices implemented. If the study is still in a developmental stage, they can offer input on research strategies that could be adopted to optimize results (Bloodworth et al., 2004). The diversity of students, in terms of their gender, age, ethnicity, socioeconomic status, sexual orientation, disability status and other factors, certainly contributes to gathering a vast array of comments that provide differing viewpoints, which should be taken into account as the SL research is developed, implemented, or revised. Giving weight to nonfaculty perspectives is one way to empower our students as they conduct SL research.

## Community Impact Measures

The community populations studied could be assessed on pertinent outcome variables before and after students conduct their SL interventions, to monitor the impact of the latter. The older women targeted in the research proposed earlier are likely to benefit directly from students' actions in a variety of ways specific to each SL project; for example, they could learn how to better manage their health care needs or put an end to their intimate partner violence. The use of standardized measures is recommended, to avoid having to develop new ones and facing related methodological limitations because of using unstandardized research tools, as further discussed in Laganà (2003). The choice of each specific measure is going to depend on several factors, such as the characteristics of the SL clients, the nature of the project, its discipline focus, and many other considerations. In the case of the Internet study (Laganà, in press-a), the author is quantifying older adults' computer self-efficacy and attitudes, as well as depression and self-esteem. The research protocol calls for the administration of pre- and postintervention assessment batteries (the latter is administered twice, immediately after training and three months later). No measure was available to assess older adults' computer attitudes, so the author created one, and is currently testing its reliability.

It is also crucial to consider who will be administering the SL research measures and under what circumstances. Students can be trained to ask older women detailed questions of a psychosocial nature by using quantitative tools and/or interview protocols (with question formats ranging from open ended to highly structured). This process provides valuable insight into SL clients' needs and concerns. Incidentally, to interview students in order to assess SL student outcomes can be problematic, since professors have to dedicate extra time to this task, either by performing it themselves or assigning it to research assistants/associates. Therefore, it may be more feasible to assess students' outcomes via administration of paper-and-pencil standardized measures, or original ones if no tools are available on important variables.

It is exciting to see the impact of SL interventions from the point of view of our students through reading their diaries. In the case of the Internet project (Laganà, in press-a), a preliminary review of such diaries provided interesting information on how older adults handle being faced with the challenging task of learning how to use computers and the Internet. Some of the students' reflections covered topics such as seniors' expectations and feelings about the Internet prior to training, "[the trainee] thought that people go on [the Internet] to talk with each other only," "he feels that the new technology only benefits the younger generations"; older adults' wish to have had access to this technology earlier, "[my research participant] wishes she had everything there is now [technologically] when she was younger"; the excitement of seniors upon learning the new technology, "when he learned to copy and paste [text] he was amazed, and that was only the beginning!";

and the students' admiration for older adults' perseverance at computer/Internet tasks, "[at 96] instead of worrying [during difficult parts of the training] . . . he tries the best he can. . . . I will continue to recognize this strength in all older adults." It is definitely rewarding to realize how much students learn, at multiple levels, during their SL experiences. Hopefully, the implementation of such projects will have a long-term, positive impact on the SL students and clients, well beyond the point of the last assessment session.

## Conclusion

Students could excel at empowering older women in a variety of ways through their involvement in high-quality SL research. They are also encouraged to search the Web in order to offer faculty additional ideas on potential topics to be targeted in research with this underserved population. Indeed, they could explore sub-areas in which they are particularly interested in contributing to the lives of seniors, and tackle them from different angles, depending on their particular talents and abilities. Students have much to learn from older adults as well, and are likely to do so as they conduct their SL projects.

It is evident that the proposed research on older women is only a small step toward facilitating the improvement of their quality of life. It is particularly important to avoid reinforcing students' possible tendency to blame victims of social problems for their own condition (Hollis, 2004). Indeed, factors including finances, race/ethnicity, sexual orientation, and other sensitive issues have a lot to do with the conditions in which older women live, and targeting their empowerment should not neglect considering these critical factors. The empowerment process occurs through many channels, and SL research should focus on empowering both students and their SL clients as much as possible. In this regard, an area of study that has been particularly neglected in the literature is participatory research on self-help groups. Conduction of this research could place older women in a shared situation within peer-governed groups, allowing them to develop meaningful relationships inside the group, and potentially freeing them, at least partially, from ever-present professional control (Humphreys, Isenberg, Loomis, & Maton, 2004).

A possible challenge is the realization by faculty that an unfamiliar research design is called for, once SL students, clients, facility administrators, and other relevant parties provide their input on the project to be implemented. At times, the answer is an interdisciplinary research approach, requiring the collaboration of several departments, or the faculty's acquisition of new methodology skills (for instance, those needed to conduct qualitative SL research). Flexibility is key, together with openness to unexpected changes in research procedures and methods, as pilot research assesses the feasibility of implementing the envisioned project on a larger scale. Letting go of control for researchers (including junior ones) is not always an easy task, but it could lead to profound positive changes in all people involved in SL research, including the professors themselves.

# References

Arean, P. A., & Miranda, J. (1995). *The prevalence and implications of mental disorders in disadvantaged and elderly medical patients.* Paper presented at the Eighth International Conference on Mental Health Services Research, Bethesda, MD.

Ballard, E. L., Harrell, L. E., Nash, F., & Raiford, K. (1993). Recruitment of Black elderly for clinical research studies of dementia: The CERAD experience. *The Gerontologist, 33,* 561–565.

Blatter, C. W., & Jacobsen, J. J. (1993). Older women coping with divorce: Peer support groups. *Women and Therapy, 14*(1/2), 141–155.

Blieszner, R., & Artale, L. M. (2001). Benefits of intergenerational service-learning to human services majors. *Educational Gerontology, 27*(1), 71–87.

Bloodworth, M., Kapungu, C., Majer, J., McDonald, K., Sharma, A., Viola, J., & Wilson, B. (2004). Student reflections on community research practices and their implications. In L. A. Jason, C. B. Keys, B. Y. Suarez, R. R. Taylor, & M. I. Davis (Eds.), *Participatory community research: Theories and methods in action* (pp. 227–238). Washington, DC: American Psychological Association.

Bringle, R. G. (2005). Designing interventions to promote civic engagement. In A. M. Omoto (Ed.), *Processes of community change and social action* (pp. 167–187). Mahwah, NJ: Erlbaum.

Bringle, R. G., Hudson, M., & Phillips, M. A. (2004). *The measure of service learning: Research scales to assess student experiences.* Washington, DC: American Psychological Association.

Collins, K. J., Skultety, K. M., & Whitbourne, S. K. (2001). Formative reflections on service learning in a course on the psychology of aging. *Educational Gerontology, 27*(1), 105–115.

Driscoll, A., Gelmon, S., Grosvold, K., Holland, B., Kerrigan, S., Longley, M., et al.

(1998). *Assessing the impact of service learning: A workbook of strategies and methods.* Portland, OR: Portland State University, Center for Academic Excellence.

Dunn, D. S., Halonen, J. S., & Mehrotra, C. M. (2004). *Measuring up: Educational assessment challenges and practices for psychology.* Washington, DC: American Psychological Association.

Elias, R., Roschelle, A. R., & Turpin, J. (2000). Who learns from service learning? *American Behavioral Scientist, 43*(5), 839–847.

Gamson, Z. F. (1997). Higher education and rebuilding civic life. *Change, 20*(1), 10–13.

Hanks, R. S., & Icenogle, M. (2001). Preparing for an age-diverse workforce: Intergenerational service-learning in social gerontology and business curricula. *Educational Gerontology, 27*(1), 49–70.

Hardcastle, S., & Taylor, A. H. (2005). Finding an exercise identity on an older body: "It's redefining yourself and working out who you are." *Psychology of Sport and Exercise, 6*(2), 173–188.

Hegeman, C. R., Horowitz, B., Pillemer, K., Schultz, L., & Tepper, L. (2002). Service learning in elder care: Ten years of growth and assessment. *Journal of Gerontological Social Work, 39*(1/2), 177–194.

Heller, K., Rody, C. A., & Thompson, M. G. (1994). Recruitment challenges in studying late-life depression: Do community samples adequately represent older adults? *Psychology and Aging, 9,* 121–125.

Hollis, S. A. (2004). Blaming me, blaming you: Assessing service learning and participants' tendency to blame the victim. *Sociological Spectrum, 24*(5), 575–600.

Humphreys, K., Isenberg, D. H., Loomis, C., & Maton, K. I. (2004). Self-help research: Issues of power sharing. In L. A. Jason, C. B. Keys, B. Y. Suarez, R. R. Taylor, & M. I. Davis, *Participatory community research: Theories and methods in action* (pp. 123–137). Washington, DC: American Psychological Association.

Jason, L. A., Keys, C. B., Suarez, B.Y., Taylor, R. R., & Davis, M. I. (2004). *Participatory community research: Theories and methods in action.* Washington, DC: American Psychological Association.

Kail, B. L., & Mindel, C. H. (1989). Issues in research on the older woman of color. *Journal of Drug Issues, 19,* 191–206.

Karasik, R. J., Maddox, M., & Wallingford, M. (2004). Intergenerational service-learning across levels and disciplines: "One size (does not) fit all." *Gerontology and Geriatrics Education, 25*(1), 1–17.

Kinch, J. L., & Jakubec, S. (2004). Out of the multiple margins: Older women managing their health care. *Canadian Journal of Nursing Research, 36*(4), 90–108.

Laditka, S. B. (2002). *Health expectations for older women: International perspectives.* New York: Haworth Press.

Laganà, L. (2003). Using service-learning research to enhance the elderly's quality of life. *Educational Gerontology, 29*(8), 685–701.

Laganà, L. (in press-a). Changes in older adults' computer attitudes and self-efficacy upon receiving computer and Internet training: A pilot study. *Educational Gerontology.*

Laganà, L. (in press-b). Using the research process to enhance civic engagement. In S. Jones & J. Perry. (Eds.), *Quick hits for educating citizens.* Indianapolis: Indiana University Press.

Laganà, L., & Rubin, M. (2002). Methodological challenges and potential solutions for the incorporation of sound community-based research into service-learning. In S. H. Billig & A. Furco. (Eds.), *Advances in service-learning research: Vol. 1. Service learning: The essence of the pedagogy* (pp. 161–182). Greenwich, CT: Information Age Publishing.

Laganà, L., & Sosa, G. (2004). Depression among ethnically diverse older women: The role of demographic and cognitive factors. *Educational Gerontology, 30*(10), 801–820.

Marchel, C. A. (2004). Evaluating reflection and sociocultural awareness in service learning classes. *Teaching of Psychology, 31*(2), 120–123.

Marty, J. R., & Rienzi, B. (2005, April). *Assessment of students' experiences in service-related psychology programs.* Poster presented at the 85th Conference of the Western Psychological Association, Portland, OR.

National Center for Health Statistics (1996). *Health, United States, 1995.* Hyattsville, MD: U.S. Public Health Service.

O'Connor, D., & Orr, A. (2005). Dimensions of power: Older women's experiences with electroconvulsive therapy (ECT). *Journal of Women and Aging, 17*(1/2), 19–36.

Ottenritter, N. W. (2004). Service learning, social justice, and campus health. *Journal of American College Health, 52*(4), 189–191.

Senn, C. Y. (2005). You can change the world: Action, participatory, and activist research. In L. M. Coutts, J. A. Gruman, & F. W. Schneider. (Eds.), *Applied social psychology: Understanding and addressing social and practical problems* (pp. 355–374). Thousand Oaks, CA: Sage.

Stevens, N. (2001). Combating loneliness: A friendship enrichment program for older women. *Ageing and Society, 21*(2), 183–202.

U.S. Census Bureau. (2000). *State and county quickfacts.* Data derived from Population Estimates, 2000 Census of Population and Housing. Retrieved from http://www.census.gov/main/www/cen2000.html

U.S. Census Bureau. (2003). *Statistical Information.* Los Angeles Department of City Planning/Demographic Research Unit. Retrieved from http://www.lacity.org/pln/DRU/HomeDRU.htm

Vaughan, J., & Siegenthaler, K. L. (1998). Older women in retirement communities: Perceptions of recreation and leisure. *Leisure Sciences, 20*(1), 53–66.

Zink, T., Regan, S., Jacobson, C. J., Jr., & Pabst, S. (2003). Cohort, period, and aging effects: A qualitative study of older women's reasons for remaining in abusive relationships. *Violence Against Women, 9*(12), 1429–1441.

Zink, T., Regan, S., Jacobson, C. J., Jr., & Pabst, S. (2004). Hidden victims: The healthcare needs and experiences of older women in abusive relationships. *Journal of Women's Health, 13*(8), 898–908.

# 13

# DNA AS A TOOL FOR SOCIAL JUSTICE

## Service Learning and Paternity Testing in Tanzania, Africa

*Ruth Ballard*

## Nuruana's Story

On a sunny morning in August of 2002, I was sitting in a two-room mud hut in the village of Orkesumet, Tanzania, with two students from my research lab at California State University, Sacramento (CSUS), an interpreter, a local woman named Nuruana Ingi Mayo, and Nuruana's two young sons. Chickens squabbled over scarce corn seed in the yard and occasionally appeared and disappeared through the cloth-covered doorway as the seven of us crowded together on the two single beds that occupied most of the tiny front room. The only light came through a single window over one of the beds, and the bucket of murky liquid in the corner was the sole source of the Mayo family's drinking, cooking, and cleaning water for the day.

The father of the boys, we were told, had abandoned the family and had not sent money home for many months. In fact, he had acquired a new girlfriend in the city, and it was becoming increasingly clear that he had no intention of ever helping to support his family again. As a result, Nuruana had taken a job (at US$35 per month), and she would need to leave us soon to go to work. The boys, she said, would have to fend for themselves while she was away.

Nuruana's story was one we had heard repeatedly from Tanzanian women all along our route from Arusha to Orkesumet that summer (see Figure 13.1), and my students and I listened in respectful silence. We had heard the story in many other tiny mud huts, beside communal water holes, and in roadside shops. A woman who sold us warm sodas in Nabarrera told us she was raising five children on her own. Her two daughters helped in the store, but her three sons ran wild through the village and often got into trouble. An evangelist we met along the road said he was raising several orphans who had been abandoned by their fathers and, eventually, in desperation, by their starving mothers. Some of the mothers had disappeared to work as prostitutes at the Tanzanite mines or in Arusha and had died of tuberculosis there (the disease that kills many Tanzanians who are infected with HIV).

Nuruana was luckier than most; she had found a job and was able to afford the rent on her small hut. She owned a donkey, too, which allowed her to gather water in large buckets and store it for several days so that she didn't have to make the long trek to the water hole every morning with the other women. Instead, she rationed her family to a bucket a day, and her boys watched over the water supply and the domestic animals (several chickens, the donkey, and two goats) while she was at work. However, she worried constantly about the health of one of her boys, Maoni, who was suffering from a bad eye infection and seemed particularly prone to repeated bouts of malaria. I was relieved when the chloramphenicol eye drops I had purchased in Arusha a few weeks before appeared to help him.

## The DNA-HIT Program

In that dry summer of 2002, my students and I had not come to Tanzania expecting to hear Nuruana's story or with the intention of helping Tanzanian women with their plight. Instead, we had come on a much different mission: to help scientists at the Muhimbili University College of Health Sciences (MUCHS) in Dar es Salaam develop a research laboratory in DNA forensics. Forensics is the use of science and technology to investigate crimes, and my area of expertise is the use of DNA to establish human identity and thereby link criminals to crimes through the analysis of biological evidence (e.g., blood, semen, hair, etc.). In developed nations like the United States, the technology for achieving this had taken giant leaps forward in the late 1990s, and U.S. forensic biologists could now unequivocally identify a human being

## FIGURE 13.1
### Map of the Republic of Tanzania, Showing the Route of Dr. Ballard and Her Research Students in 2002.

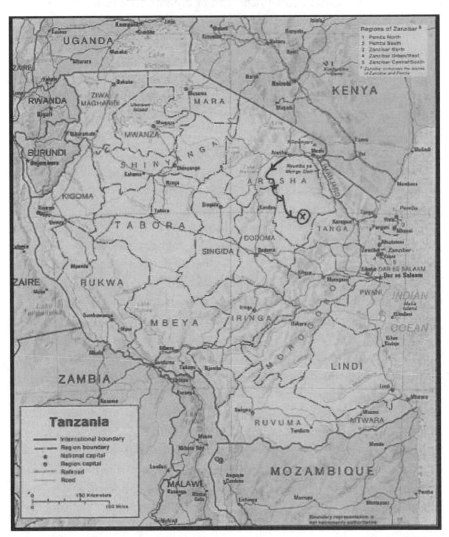

The village of Orkesumet is marked with an "X." Adapted from http://www.farmershelping farmers.ca/tanzania.php.

solely on the basis of trace amounts of biological evidence. The governments of third world countries, like Tanzania, were understandably anxious to acquire this ability as well, and I began an international collaboration to help Tanzanian scientists establish a laboratory for this purpose in 2001.

The idea for the collaboration had first occurred to me when I was visiting the country as a tourist in January of that year, and had taken root during conversations with scientists at MUCHS the following summer and fall. During these conversations, I christened the emerging program DNA-HIT (DNA Human Identification Testing), Tanzania. By the summer of 2002, we were in the process of applying for ethical clearance for the project from Tanzania's Commission for Science and Technology (COSTECH)—an organization that moves at glacial speed—and scouting out some of the areas where we eventually planned to recruit local volunteers to provide us with samples of their DNA.

Fortunately for forensic biologists, there are regions of the human genome that tend to accumulate mutations, or changes, that can be easily detected by modern technology and can be used to distinguish individual humans from one another. These sites are called *markers* and often have no effect on the appearance or behavior of an individual because they occur in regions of the genome that do not code for proteins. Biologists are not quite sure why such "noncoding" regions of the genome exist, but have found them very useful for a variety of purposes, including the mapping and sequencing of the human genome.

By the mid-1990s, forensic biologists had exploited 13 different DNA markers, spread across the 24 chromosomes that make up the human genome, for use in human identification. However, before they could begin using them, they had to determine the frequency of each form of the marker in the human population. Similar studies had been performed on the human ABO blood group proteins in the 1960s when that system was first developed as a crude precursor to DNA typing. These studies are necessary because markers are only useful if there are different forms in the population and no one form of the marker is predominant. For example, the ABO blood system is useless as a way of distinguishing the native peoples of South America from one another because nearly 100% of the population is Type O. However, peoples of Western European ancestry proved more diverse; about 46% are Type O, 40% are Type A, 10% are Type B, and 4% are Type AB. Thus, the system could be used (albeit at a very low level of discrimination) among

U.S. Caucasians and was applied most notably to *exclude* suspects as the source of blood sample in violent crimes and to absolve falsely accused fathers of paternity and child support obligations.

Thus, when DNA was introduced as a possible tool in forensics, hundreds of individuals from different ethnic groups in the United States and other developed nations were tested to determine the frequencies of the human identification markers in those populations. Fortunately, the markers were found to be highly diverse in all of the populations tested, although their frequencies differed across various ethnicities. Therefore, although the markers were clearly excellent choices for performing human identification testing, their frequencies needed to be determined anew in each population in which the testing was to be performed.

Our first task in Tanzania, then, was to gather samples from as many tribes throughout the country as was reasonably feasible and create a DNA marker frequency database that would form the basis for performing all future DNA forensics casework in the country. It was the reconnoitering for this phase of the project that we were engaged in during our trip to Tanzania in 2002, and that led us, on that hot August day, to Nuruana's hut, 100 miles from the nearest flush toilet or refrigerator.

## Broadening the Mission

However, as my students and I traveled the rural countryside of Tanzania in 2002 and heard Nuruana's story repeated again and again, it became increasingly clear that our original mission needed to be broadened. As a geneticist doing DNA forensics research, I was well aware that the same DNA markers that had been developed for use in forensics were also useful for proving paternity and providing a scientific basis for enforcing child support. Why couldn't our work contribute to developing a laboratory that handled criminal cases as well as civil ones? Why couldn't we help provide a resource for Tanzanian women that would allow them to prove the paternity of their children and then demand reasonable compensation from the husbands or boyfriends who had abandoned them? It was a system that was working beautifully in developed nations, was fair and unbiased, and stood to benefit the most vulnerable members of the Tanzanian population: its poor women and children.

As we contemplated this idea, we also began to learn more about how

Tanzanian's problem interfaced with those of other nations in sub-Saharan Africa, particularly South Africa, where apartheid had been systematically dismantling the extended African family for decades. This entire region of the world, we learned, was in the midst of a rapid transition to urbanization that was taking a tragic toll on rural women and children everywhere. In 1988, only 18% of the Tanzanian mainland population lived in urban areas.[1] By 2005, this number had risen to 32%, and the United Nations Department of Economic and Social Affairs projects that 63% of the population will be living in urban areas by the year 2030.[2]

Although some of this growth involves whole families relocating, the majority involves the relocation of men only, many of whom initially promise to find jobs and send the money home but later renege on their promises. Some are unable to find jobs that pay enough to allow them to support a family, while others, like Nuruana's husband, simply build new lives in the city and abandon their existing parental and spousal obligations. Whereas in traditional, intact rural communities, straying men are "kept in line" by the members of their extended family (particularly their mothers and sisters), men who move to the city are no longer subject to this pressure. Similar to the situation that has plagued South Africa in recent decades and is poignantly detailed in Jim Wooten's *We Are All the Same: A Story of a Boy's Courage and a Mother's Love* (2004), urbanization is shattering the family unit in rural Tanzania and creating an epidemic of single mothers mired in poverty. Eventually, as happened among the Zulus in South Africa, second- and third-generation Tanzanian mothers from broken homes may eventually become devoid of even the concept of an intact family unit, and routinely have multiple children from different fathers, none of whom will be involved in their upbringing.

## Incorporating Service Learning

### Student Roles

After we returned from our 2002 pilot trip to Tanzania, I began to develop an idea and a syllabus for a service-learning course that would engage students in the DNA-HIT, Tanzania, project as research assistants the following summer. The students would accompany me on a "saliva safari" through rural Tanzania, gathering saliva samples (the easiest and safest source of donor DNA) from members of reproductively isolated tribes like the Masai and Meru. Later, they would process the samples at MUCHS in Dar es Salaam, extracting and quantifying the DNA, and training the MUCHS scientists, technicians, and students in these techniques. The students would live and work in Tanzania for two months, and I would arrange for the rental of a safe, "Western-style" home near or in the city of Dar es Salaam for the duration of our stay.

The scientific goal of the project was to gather enough samples from the Masai and Meru tribes to determine the frequencies of the 13 human DNA identification markers in these two groups. Toward the end of the summer, the students and I would also gather samples from employees, faculty, and students at MUCHS to achieve a representative sampling of the more than 60 indigenous tribes that are now freely intermarrying in the country and who, unlike the Masai and Meru, often live and work in urban areas. In addition to determining the frequencies of the human identification markers, our research would allow us to examine the substructure of the Tanzanian population, evaluate how much genetic intermixing has taken place among the country's tribes since the advent of colonialism some two hundred years ago, and perhaps even solve the mystery of the origin of the Masai, who are thought to be relatively new to the region.

As part of the project, we would also validate Oragene, a new DNA sampling kit developed by Genotek, a Canadian biotechnology company. The kit had been designed to allow the collection and preservation of saliva samples under conditions, as in rural regions of Tanzania, where immediate refrigeration of the samples was not possible. Although saliva is far safer and less invasive to collect than blood, it also contains a large amount of bacteria, which can destroy the human cheek cell DNA present in the saliva if the samples are not protected immediately following donation. Oragene vials contain an aseptic buffer that is mixed with the saliva after it is collected and protects it until it can be processed. Although scientists at Genotek had tested their product in-house and were confident of its efficacy, no large field study had yet been performed to validate the kits, so I partnered with the company to perform this trial in Tanzania. Genotek provided the kits to our research team at no cost, and we promised to use them, carefully monitor their performance, and disseminate our results.

By January, I had arranged for the rental of a house located in a safe compound 20 kilometers north of Dar es Salaam on Americana Road, which fronts the Indian Ocean and dead-ends in several Western-style resorts. The house, it turned out, was owned by a wealthy Tanzanian businessman who lived with two of his three wives in two separate houses on the compound property. We were to rent the third house in the compound, placing us in the middle of a domestic war that would prove highly entertaining as well as informative to my students.

## Learning Goals

As a central part of developing the course and designing its syllabus, I thought carefully about what I hoped my students would learn. As a result, my original (2003) syllabus contained a series of clearly defined learning goals and outcomes. However, after the 2003 trip, I became somewhat skeptical of setting rigid learning goals for international service-learning courses in third world countries like Tanzania because the students were so clearly being exposed to life-changing new experiences, which were largely beyond my control and made up most of the content of their reflective journals (Ballard, 2005). Although I'm quite certain that the 2003 students did learn how to perform a random DNA sampling effort, the importance of informed consent and how to obtain and document it from nonliterate peoples, how to collect and store saliva samples in the field, and most of the other highly specific learning goals I had defined for them, it was still difficult to formally assess whether or not they had fully accomplished all the goals of the course. The students were much more captivated by the human dynamics of the polygamous household in which they were living, the unhygienic conditions at the MUCHS laboratory, the appalling health problems they observed among the Masai, and the content of the Nigerian soap operas on Tanzanian television, which advocated witch doctoring to solve domestic problems and cure glaucoma.

Thus, the current syllabus for the course (see the appendix, BIO 199, Sessions 1–3, 2005, at the end of this chapter) reflects a more fluid and flexible approach to learning goals but does not abandon them entirely. Rather, students are encouraged to help define them as the experience unfolds, while keeping in mind the overall goal of the DNA-HIT project and their dual role as student researchers and service-learning volunteers. In addition to learning goals, the syllabus also lists the dates of the two mandatory pretrip meetings, details how student performance will be evaluated, and provides an in-depth discussion of service learning as pedagogy and my rationale for using it as a framework for the course.

## Funding

Students are currently chosen from among the existing students in my DNA forensics research laboratory, based on their interest in the project and their ability to cover the cost of their own airfare to and from Tanzania (about $900 for students under the age of 30). The costs of the students' transportation, housing, food, and other expenses within the country are covered by grants and private donations. In addition, students are encouraged to apply for CSUS Project Activity Grants to cover their airfare, and three of the nine students who have participated in the program to date have been successful in receiving this support.

## Safety

Issues of student safety are addressed at two different levels. At the first pre-trip meeting, students are given information about the country of Tanzania and are directed to the U.S. State Department Web site, http://www.state.gov, which is quite comprehensive and provides up-to-date information, suggestions, and warnings for international travelers planning trips to various countries. Students are also given the forms they need to apply for a U.S. passport and a Tanzanian visa, as well as a list of vaccinations that are recommended for U.S. citizens traveling to Tanzania. They are also apprised of the fact that they will be required to show proof of malaria medication prior to travel.

In the second meeting, students are required to fill out a series of forms provided by the CSUS Office of Global Education. These forms include (among many others) a written permission slip enabling me (as trip leader) to seek medical treatment on their behalf in the event that they are incapacitated while traveling, and an information sheet detailing the level of medical insurance they will need to purchase prior to the trip. An emergency contact form is also included in the packet, as well as a form that all students must sign that limits the liability of the university in case of the injury or death of a student while traveling.

In addition, the second meeting is used to develop an emergency plan for all of us in case of separation during the trip. Students are given the address and telephone number for the American Embassy in Dar es Salaam, a map of the city of Dar es Salaam, and a map of the country of Tanzania that details the planned route of our travels. Finally, we discuss how to carry money and valuables safely, and some of the key Swahili words and phrases students should know and memorize.

## Reflection

One of the critical components of a service-learning experience is student reflection. For the DNA-HIT program, I have students keep a personal journal and log of events, which they share with the rest of the students in weekly group meetings. Students are free to write whatever they like in their journals, as long as what they write relates to the trip, is important or pertinent to them, and is appropriate to discuss with their peers. Then, at the weekly meetings, topics for discussion and further reflection naturally emerge, as students go over the week's events and share their individual observations and reactions. Thus, students first reflect at a personal level through journaling and then at a group level through sharing their journals. I am the leader of the group meetings, and students understand that the quality and thoroughness of their reflection at both levels will be used as part of my evaluation of their performance in the class and their final grade in the course. However, I always try to make the meetings comfortable and casual as well.

I also have students reflect on the nature of the DNA-HIT program itself, and what challenges they think the program will encounter in trying to bring DNA-based forensic and paternity testing to a poor, third world country. In 2003, two of the students wrote extensively about the conditions in the biochemistry laboratory at MUCHS, including the lack of basic hygiene on the part of Tanzanian technicians and scientists working at the lab. One student had witnessed a technician spinning some samples in a clinical centrifuge, then opening the centrifuge while it was still running, and stopping the machine manually by putting pressure, with his ungloved finger, on the center of the rotor axis. The student then noticed that the samples in the centrifuge were open glass tubes of blood, and asked the technician what type of test he was performing. "HIV testing," was the nonchalant answer, and the technician then removed the samples (again with ungloved hands) and carried them to his bench for further processing.

Another student pointed out that completing the population database work and training the scientists at MUCHS on how to run human DNA identification tests were just the beginning. "The legal system in Tanzania is so corrupt," he wrote, "I don't know if anyone without money will ever be able to get any justice." His comment was based partly on some of the conversations we had had with rural Tanzanian women who had tried to gain some financial support for their children by complaining to local government officials. While the officials feigned patience with them, and even sometimes arranged meetings with the men in question, the women never received any money because their husbands or boyfriends could simply bribe the officials to leave them alone. We had paid similar "unofficial fees" to gain access to certain populations for obtaining DNA samples (in spite of the fact that we had all the proper permits in hand as well as letters of introduction from COSTECH and scientists at MUCHS), so the women's stories seemed entirely plausible as well as somewhat discouraging.

In 2004, a student questioned whether paternity testing could ever be made affordable to the average Tanzanian. In the United States, the typical cost of a paternity test (which includes analyzing the DNA profiles of three samples: the mother, the child, and an alleged father) is about $500. Currently, a typical Tanzanian mother could order such a test from a European or American company, provided she could get a saliva, blood, or hair sample from the father of her children. However, as the statistics summarized in Table 13.1 indicate, she could never afford it.

Fortunately, I was able to counter the students' concern with some

### TABLE 13.1
### Statistics Comparing Affordability of Paternity Testing in Tanzania and the United States

|  | *United States* | *Tanzania* |
|---|---|---|
| Percentage single mothers, head of household | 7.6[a] | 15[a] |
| Average # children per family | 2.0[b] | 5.5[b] |
| Gross national income (GNI) per capita | 43,740 ($US)[a] | $730 ($US)[c] |
| Average cost of standard 3-sample paternity test | 495 ($US) | 495 ($US) + shipping |

*Note.* [a]From U.S. Population Census, 2000; [b]From "Abortion Policies: A Global Review," by the United Nations Departmentof Economic and Social Affairs, Population Division, 2001; [c]From http://www.siteresources.worldbank.org/DATASTATISTICS/Resources/GNIPC.pdf.

additional statistics that came from my year working as a consultant for a paternity-testing laboratory in Sacramento and from running the tests in my own research laboratory at CSUS. The markup that laboratories make for private paternity-testing cases is almost 400%; in other words, although laboratories typically charge $495 for a paternity test, the test can actually be performed for about $120. In fact, paternity-testing laboratories often charge the U.S. welfare system far less than a private party because they have to compete with other labs for contracts with the welfare system, which provides them the bulk of their casework. Therefore, U.S. paternity-testing laboratories tend to keep their labs operating on the basis of welfare casework but make their profit on private cases. It is thus reasonable to assume that the cost of a paternity test in Tanzania, particularly if the Tanzanian government or nongovernmental organizations are willing to bear part of the cost for indigent citizens, could be brought down to at least $120, and perhaps even further. Currently, the DNA-HIT program is lobbying with the Tanzanian government to charge mothers only $40 for the test and furnish the rest from other sources.

## Outcomes and Assessment

Since its inception in 2002–2003, DNA-HIT, Tanzania has involved nine service-learning students. The size of the program has obviously been limited by the expense and safety issues involved in taking students overseas, the intensive, hands-on nature of the experience, the unusually large number of hours required from the students, and the necessity of running the program during the summer and/or during other breaks in the university's annual calendar. Assessing the impact of the program on student-learning outcomes in any quantitatively meaningful way is therefore clearly impossible; however, a qualitative assessment has been performed every year and has developed into the assessment plan outlined in Table 13.2.

Students are interviewed once before and twice after their trips to Tanzania (at intervals of two weeks posttrip and six months posttrip) by two independent volunteers who are not involved in the DNA-HIT program. Students are asked a series of questions concerning their knowledge of specific scientific approaches and techniques as well as their knowledge and attitudes about social issues of concern in Africa, and their answers before and after the trip are compared. I also perform a series of follow-up, informal interviews with students (either by telephone or e-mail) on an annual basis. My

**TABLE 13.2**

**Assessment Plan for Service-Learning Component of DNA-HIT, Tanzania**

| Assessment Tool | Timeline for Administration | Administrator |
|---|---|---|
| Pretrip interview (formal) | 1–2 months prior to service-learning experience | Third party (two-person interview team) |
| Posttrip interview 1 (formal) | 2 weeks post-service-learning experience | Third party (two-person interview team) |
| Posttrip interview 2 (formal) | 6 months post-service-learning experience | Third party (two-person interview team) |
| Posttrip interview 3 (informal) | 1 year post-service-learning experience | Myself |
| Continuing posttrip interviews (informal) | Annually, starting at 2 years post-service-learning experience | Myself |

main areas of interest concern the effects (if any) of the service-learning experience on their development as scientists, their choice of careers, their understanding of third world issues involving social justice (especially the role that scientists can play in addressing these problems), and the effects of the experience on their personal lives and/or their attitudes about community service and volunteerism.

Over the years, some of the students who traveled to Tanzania as part of the DNA-HIT, Tanzania, service-learning program have put their comments in writing, and I have provided the following excerpts from their letters:

> My choice to become a Family Nurse Practitioner was influenced by our work abroad. When I was in Africa, I saw first-hand the devastation of hunger, disease, and lack of adequate health care. The Masaai inundated us with ailments and complaints. I wished that I had the knowledge and skills to help them with their medical problems. When I returned to the United States, I became aware of the immediate need for qualified nurses. After I finish my education, I plan to work either with an underserved population here in California or to become a traveling nurse so that I can help those abroad. (Eileen Andrae)

> First and foremost, my experiences rewarded me with an increased awareness of the depth and breadth of humanity and the common threads that

so beautifully interconnect us all. Through my experiences, my respect for community was not only reaffirmed and deepened, but most significantly, it was fostered into reaching beyond the local level to the global level, which today is undeniably more important to me than ever. Although philanthropy and altruism are not always easy, thanks to my experiences I have witnessed what can be achieved with nothing more than courage, compassion, and conviction. (Kraig Brustad)

This awareness of community service that Dr. Ballard has impressed upon me has influenced me to work for, as I consider it, the community itself. Employed as a Biomedical Scientist for Lawrence Livermore National Laboratory, I find providing national security a direct service to the community. The positive feelings of providing that service were only experienced because Dr. Ballard introduced me to it in so many ways. (Lauren Baughman)

My most memorable experiences about the trip were not collecting the samples, but giving antibiotic ointment to children surrounded by flies and covered with filth and disease. I learned about how women would walk miles to bring back water just to do the same thing the next day and how men 13 or 14 years of age could be responsible for tending goats while watching over a 3 year old sibling. Survival no longer meant spell-checking a term paper at 7 AM in the morning on my laptop in a café at school when it was due at 8 AM the same morning. Survival meant making sure that the goats did not get attacked that night so there was a means of barter and food for the family. I learned how naïve I really was. (Bryan Forward)

These comments are typical of those I have heard from other students who have participated in the program as well as those recorded by the assessment volunteers in their formal posttrip interviews. Interestingly, the overwhelming majority of the comments have to do with a change in career path or attitude toward community service as a result of the program, not with the development of the students as scientists. Clearly, the students perceive the value of the program in these terms, with the benefit to their scientific education as secondary and of decidedly lesser impact.

## Social Justice

DNA-HIT, Tanzania, was born out of a combination of scientific curiosity and the desire to address problems of social injustice within a desperately poor third world nation. However, the scientific problems have proved far more tractable than the social ones. In 2005, the students in my laboratory finished the human DNA identification marker frequency database for the intermixing Tanzanian population as well as for the reproductively isolated Masai, and the Meru database was finished in 2006. Completion of these databases marks a major scientific accomplishment for the DNA-HIT project but is just the beginning of what will undoubtedly prove to be the longer and far more difficult task of achieving the community impact goals of the program.

Tanzania's judicial system has five levels and combines tribal, Islamic, and British common law. The role of men in the society is firmly established as primary, and a father is allowed to remove his children from their mother at the age of seven for any reason. For the most part, these laws are administered locally because of the large number of administrative regions (26) and the concentration of power in nine district councils that are referred to as "local government authorities." Thus, the DNA-HIT project faces an uphill battle to establish DNA-based paternity testing in the country. Even though the project has received strong support at the national level, local authorities are unlikely to unilaterally adopt a new approach to designating the rights and responsibilities of parents within their jurisdictions.

Even if the test is adopted at the local level, it is difficult to predict how many Tanzanian fathers are actually capable of supporting the families they have abandoned. Jobs, even urban ones, can be difficult to obtain, particularly if the applicant is uneducated and cannot speak English. While some, like Nuruana's husband, appear to simply be "deadbeat dads," others are undoubtedly struggling to feed themselves and find adequate nightly shelter. In a country as poor as Tanzania, the distribution of wealth can only be equalized if there is wealth to be had. Thus, it is imperative that the DNA-HIT project support the efforts of other projects and agencies that provide rural Tanzanian women with information on birth control and family planning. Fortunately, such programs are already in place (largely church based) because of the growing need to prevent the spread of HIV, and the problem is thus being attacked from both ends. Ultimately, success will undoubtedly involve a multifaceted, integrated approach between DNA-HIT and the organizations that provide such services.

In the meantime, Nuruana's situation remains largely unchanged since we first visited her in 2002. She still has not received a Tanzanian shilling of support from her husband, and she and her children continue to live hand-to-mouth and day to day. When I last saw her in September 2005, I explained to her that it will probably be many years before the single mothers of Orkesumet receive any benefits from our work there. But I think I gave her reason to hope as well. Social change often follows on the heels of technological innovation, and nations are quite capable of rooting out social injustice when the benefits outweigh the costs. South Africa has ended apartheid, and Uganda has made dramatic progress in reducing the AIDS epidemic within its borders by loosening deeply entrenched social and sexual practices through a massive educational campaign. Thus, Nuruana's story is not just her own, but belongs to oppressed groups everywhere, and history has shown that the stories of one generation do not have to be the same as the stories of those that follow.

Appendix

## CALIFORNIA STATE UNIVERSITY, SACRAMENTO
Department of Biological Sciences

# BIO 199–SPECIAL PROBLEMS

Summer Sessions 1–3, 2005:

## *"GENETICS RESEARCH AND SERVICE LEARNING IN TANZANIA, AFRICA"*

| | |
|---|---|
| **INSTRUCTOR:** | Dr. Ruth Ballard |
| **OFFICE HOURS:** | TBA, on site |
| **LABORATORY:** | 108 Sequoia Hall; **http://www.ballardlab.org** |
| **RESEARCH AREA:** | DNA Forensics |
| **PHONE/E-MAIL:** | 278-6244; e-mail: **ballardr@csus.edu** |
| **WEB SITE:** | **http://www.csus.edu/indiv/b/ballardr** |

## COURSE POLICIES

### ABOUT MENTORED RESEARCH

**BIO 199** is designed to give students the opportunity to complete a semester or more of mentored research prior to earning an undergraduate degree in Biological Sciences at C.S.U.S. In the context of this course, **mentored research** can be defined as student research conducted under the formal guidance of a professor and under the direct supervision of the professor and/or an experienced graduate student.

**BIO 199** differs from other courses in that **students are asked to take a greater level of responsibility for their own learning experience**. Although students are evaluated by a letter grade on the basis of a variety of criteria (see Evaluation, page 2), the absence of lectures, graded homework, and examinations makes it more difficult for the instructor to gauge the intellectual progress of each student during the course. In addition, since it would be unreasonable and unfair to evaluate undergraduate researchers purely on the basis of their experimental results, it is difficult to objectively compare the progress students have made in mastering laboratory techniques and protocols. As a result, students who achieve the same grade in the course may differ greatly in the extent to which they have maximized their learning potential in the mentored research environment. **Thus, internal, rather than external, motivating factors, will, to a large extent, determine how much you take away from this course.** This course provides you with a terrific opportunity—and you are strongly urged to take full advantage of it!

## ABOUT SERVICE LEARNING

**This section of BIO 199 is unusual in that it has a service-learning component.** Hands-on community-based projects that involve students *and* are closely tied to the academic content of a course are called "Service-Learning" projects. (See 2003–04 Class Schedule, pg. 47.) Opportunities to participate in Service-Learning projects are becoming increasingly common on college campuses but are still rare in the natural and physical sciences. Yet, pedagogical literature is rich with evidence that Service-Learning can greatly enhance a student's ability to learn and retain information across a wide variety of disciplines.

The teaching philosophy behind Service-Learning is grounded in the work of Dewey, Kolb, Piaget, and other educators who strongly advocated experiential ("hands-on") learning. Kolb, in particular, was responsible for developing a model called the "Learning Wheel" that places concrete experience at the foundation of all learning. In this model, four learning strategies are used in succession to achieve the ultimate goal of "integrated learning," a state characterized by a person's "ownership" of knowledge and by his or her ability to apply that knowledge in new situations (an acquired ability that might also be called "wisdom").

The model can be diagrammed as shown in figure 13A.1.

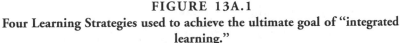

**FIGURE 13A.1**
**Four Learning Strategies used to achieve the ultimate goal of "integrated learning."**

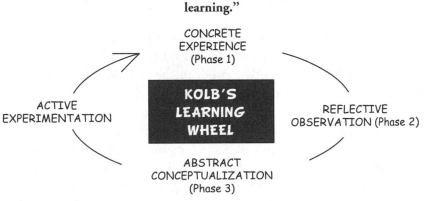

In Phase 1, learning is initiated by "hands-on" experiences or concrete observations. The learner then reflects on the experience (Phase 2), and organizes the information to form theories (abstract conceptualization, Phase 3), which are then tested in the real world through active, natural experimentation (Phase 4). This completes the cycle, which then begins anew. Over time, this wheel actually takes on the form of a spiral, where higher and higher levels of understanding and integration are achieved.

For example, if a young child touches an oven door and gets burned (Concrete Experience), the child will probably immediately think about what has just happened (Reflective Observation) and come to the conclusion (Abstract Conceptualization) that all oven doors are hot and should not be touched. (This process happens very rapidly and is not necessarily conscious.) However, if the child later on sees his mother cleaning the oven door without getting burned, he might now tentatively touch the oven door again (Active Experimentation) and find that it is cool (Concrete Experience). Now the wheel begins to spiral upward because, when he thinks about this new, contradictory evidence (Reflective Observation), he will come to a more accurate and sophisticated conclusion (Abstract Conceptualization): Oven doors are sometimes hot and sometimes cool. Again, this process happens naturally and largely unconsciously, as it does with all human beings. The child knows nothing about Kolb's Learning Wheel or pedagogical theory. The child is simply following the inborn pattern of acquiring information that was critical for human survival during evolution and thus became instinctual over time.

Traditional classroom approaches to education largely circumvent this natural process by providing students with abstract concepts *only after they have been developed and tested by others*. Students then take examinations and/or write papers that essentially "spit back" or regurgitate what they've been told. While this allows a tremendous amount of knowledge to be passed on to students in a short period of time (and therefore has its place and value, particularly in lower-division classes), it does not tend to promote student "ownership" of the knowledge, challenge students to work on the skills they need to move efficiently through the Learning Wheel on their own (to generate new knowledge), or help students *integrate* and *retain* what they have learned so they can apply it to future problems or in different situations. See figure 13A.2.

## FIGURE 13A.2.
**Traditional classroom approaches to education largely circumvent the natural process by providing students with abstract concepts *only after they have been developed and tested by others*.**

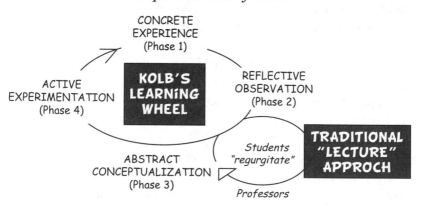

As a result, our traditional lecture format largely fails to help students make the critical transition from being a knowledge *consumer* to becoming a knowledge *producer*—a transition that must be made before students can be successful in graduate school, in the professional working world, or effect meaningful change in their communities, where the production of *new* knowledge is what is valued. **New knowledge is not produced by regurgitating the ideas of others, but involves taking a fresh look at a changing world.**

For these reasons, as students near graduation, it is especially important that they be provided with opportunities to move beyond the traditional limits of the classroom to engage in hands-on learning. This can take the form of inquiry-based laboratories (as in Cellular Physiology, BIO 121) or community-based projects, as in this course. In the latter strategy, the community becomes a place where students are encouraged to navigate the Learning Wheel from start to finish. Moreover, the traditional lines between student and teacher become blurred as students both learn from and teach the community at the same time that the community learns from and teaches them.

## LOGISTICS OF THE COURSE

In this course, you will be traveling to Tanzania, East Africa and living and working there for two months. About 2 weeks of your time will be spent on a "saliva safari" gathering saliva samples from Tanzanian residents in rural areas of the country, with a focus on the Masaai and Meru tribes. The remainder of your time (about 6 weeks) will be spent in the Biochemistry Laboratory of Dr. Thomas Nyambo at Muhimbili University College of Health Sciences (MUCHS) in the coastal city of Dar es Salaam. In his lab, you will be extracting the DNA from the saliva samples you collected in the field, quantifying the amount of human DNA present in each sample, and training MUCHS scientists, technicians, and students in how to perform these techniques.

Your work in Tanzania will take place in the context of a much larger, multi-year research and service-learning collaboration between MUCHS and my research laboratory at CSUS. The goal of this collaboration, DNA-HIT, Tanzania, is to bring DNA human identification testing technology and expertise to Tanzania, enabling Tanzanian scientists to perform DNA-based forensic and paternity analyses.

## EVALUATION

Students may earn a total of **500 points** in the course. Points will be assigned on the basis of the following criteria:

| | |
|---|---|
| Completion of Field Work Assignment | 100 |
| Completion of Bench Work Assignment | 100 |
| Service Learning Journals | 150 |
| Weekly Reflective Discussions | 150 |
| | 500 |

The specific tasks and the guidelines for keeping your reflective journals and participating in discussions will be provided on a separate handout after we reach Tanzania.

At the end of the summer, points from all assignments will be totaled and grades will be assigned on a straight percentage basis. Plus and minus grades will be assigned in the categories below as appropriate.

$$90.0–100\% = A \qquad 60.0\text{-}69.9\% = D$$
$$80.0–89.9\% = B \qquad \text{less than } 60\% = F$$
$$70.0–79.9\% = C$$

## LEARNING GOALS

*Learning Goals* are broad statements that identify the general educational outcomes students should be able to display upon completing a course. *Learning Objectives* are concrete measures by which these goals will be realized, and *Assessment Tools* link the learning objectives to specific course assignments (usually graded) that enable instructors to objectively assess what students have learned. It is very helpful for instructors to develop learning goals, learning objectives, and assessment tools for their courses and to tie them together in a way that makes sense to students. Assignments are more meaningful to students when they can see how they are linked to the overall goals of the course.

Although I develop learning goals for most of the courses I teach, I have found that international service-learning in a Third World country like Tanzania tends to create many surprising and unpredictable learning experiences for students that cannot be anticipated beforehand. Therefore, I like to leave the learning goals for the course open and fluid and to have the students take part in defining them. A few examples of possible learning goals you may achieve during the trip are given in the first three rows of the table below. We will fill in additional learning goals, objectives, and assessment tools during our weekly meetings in Tanzania.

| LEARNING GOAL | LEARNING OBJECTIVES | ASSESSMENT TOOLS |
|---|---|---|
| 1. To become familiar with some of the social, political, and economic problems in Tanzania | • Students will demonstrate the ability to write about and critically discuss issues of social, political, and economic import in Tanzania | • Reflective journals<br>• Weekly discussions |
| 2. To gain competence in gathering, storing, and transporting saliva samples under field conditions in rural Tanzania | • Students will demonstrate the proper techniques for collecting, storing, and transporting saliva samples in the Masaai Steppe | • Successful completion of bench work assignment |
| 3. To understand the potential role of DNA as a tool for social reform in Tanzania | • Students will be able to critically write about and discuss the goals of the DNA-HIT program | • Reflective journals<br>• Weekly discussions |

## IMPORTANT DATES (Please mark on your calendar)

| | |
|---|---|
| First pre-trip meeting: | February 19, 2005, 9–11 AM, Sequoia 108 |
| Pre-trip assessment interview | April 22, 2005, 1–3 PM, Humboldt 220 |
| Second pre-trip meeting: | May 7, 2005, 9–11 AM, Sequoia 108 |

| | |
|---|---|
| Departure for Tanzania: | June 6, 2005 |
| Return from Tanzania: | August 2, 2005 |
| First post-trip assessment interview: | August 13, 2005, 1–3 PM, Humboldt 220 |
| Second post-trip assessment interview | TBA |

## Notes

1. See 2002 Population and Housing Census, http://www.tanzania,go.tz/census/
2. See http://www.un.org/esa/population/publications/WUP2005WUP_urban_ruralchart.pdf

## References

Ballard, R. E. (2005). Learning goals and service learning: Lessons from saliva safaris. *CSU Impact, 2*(5). Retrieved from http://www.calstate.edu/csl/news_pubs/csu_impact/0205_files/Ballard-Assessment_Method.shtml

Wooten, J. (2004). *We are all the same: A story of a boy's courage and a mother's love.* New York: Penguin.

# INDEX

dress: gendered meaning of, 45–60; term, 45
Durkheim, Émile, 84
Dwyer, J., 137

East Los Angeles Women's Center, 17
ecological perspective: on etiology of rape, 161–72; on rape, 159–80
Eisman, Gerald, xv–xvii
empowerment, 1–2; Amazonian feminism and, 109; Black women and, 105; of older women, 217–36; social justice education and, 146–49; versus volunteerism, 117; YWSC and, 130–31
engagement, 19–21
environment, ecological perspective and, 159
epistemological pedagogy, 32–33; lesson plans in, 37–40
ethnic backgrounds, of older women, in research studies, 218
ethnic studies, and service learning, 26–27
evaluation. *See* assessment
Eviota, Elizabeth Uy, 30
exercise interventions, for older women, 222

faculty: in feminist pedagogy, 16; interaction patterns with students, 69–70; role of, recommendations for, 212; and YWSC, 133
family: conflict in, and sexual aggression, 163; and etiology of rape, 165–66
Family Violence Prevention Fund, 191
fashion studies: methodology in, 47–48; service learning in, 45–60

feminist pedagogy, 1; Amazonian, 103–20; and civic learning, 2; classroom practices in, 104–6, 124; goal of, 83; professor role in, 16; in psychology, 202; tenets of, 104
field experience, and gender equity, 73–75
films, review worksheet for, 77–78
Final Project Runway, 25–44; Spring 2005 Show, 35–36
Forward, Bryan, 250
fraternities, and etiology of rape, 165–66
Freire, Paolo, 47, 54, 122
friendship enrichment, for older women, 221–22
FTM, term, 23n2
FTM-LA Alliance, 16

Gelmon, Sherril, 55
gender: and classroom teaching practices, 63–82; concept of, 84–85; expectations on, learning activity on, 57–58; issues, in primary school classroom, 83–100; and office behavior evaluation, 143, 153; role plays on, 149–51; socialization and, 140, 143–44
gender competence, service learning and, 121–38
gender differentiation: assessment on observation of, 92; definition of, 85
gender-equitable pedagogy, 63–82
gender equity: in classroom, 69–72; and field experience, 73–75; teaching practices for, 72–73
gender inequality: in classroom, 63; and etiology of rape, 186
gender-neutral language, 143, 145
gender roles: assessment on observation of, 93–94; factors affecting, 85–86; YWSC and, 130–32

older women: demographics of, 218; service-learning research and, 217–36
oppression, social justice education on,
139–55
Oragene, 243
oral herstory project, in Asian American
studies, 33
organizational level, and etiology of
rape, 167–68
Orkesumet, 237–38, 239*f*

papers: in philosophy service learning,
18–21; in social justice education,
173–74; in sociology service learning, 90; in teacher preparation service learning, 74–75; in violence
prevention program, 183–84; in
women's studies service learning,
113–15, 118, 126–29
passive learners, service learning and, 110
paternity testing, 237–59; affordability
of, 247–48, 247*t*; inclusion in project, 241–42; mechanism of, 240–41
pedagogy: critical, 31, 122; epistemological, 32–33, 37–40; Freireian, 47, 54;
gender-equitable, 63–82; performance, 33, 40–41; visual art, 34, 41–
43. *See also* feminist pedagogy
peer groups, and etiology of rape, 165
pensionadas, 29, 43n2
performance: lesson plans in, 40–41;
pedagogy, 33; poetry, 33–34
philosophy, service learning in, 11–24
physical activity interventions, for older
women, 222
Pickeral, Terry, 134
poetry: lesson plans in, 40; performance,
33–34
politics: engagement with, evaluation of,
21; theory and, 12; women in, 108

polysemy, 48
pornography, and etiology of rape, 170
prejudice, social justice education on,
139–55
privilege: and service learning, 146–47;
study of, 142–46
problem-posing education, 47, 54
productive work, 30
professional demeanor, in service learning settings, 89–90, 97
protected groups, 154n1
psychology, service learning in, 159–213,
217–36
public sociology: characteristics of, 84;
service learning in, 83–100

questions, reflection: in philosophy service learning, 18–19; in social justice education, 172–73

race, in primary school classroom, 86–88
rape: ecological perspective on, 159–80;
etiology of, 161–72, 186; legal definition of, 160; prevalence of,
160–61; prevention of, 181–200;
YWSC and, 132. *See also* violence
rape crisis centers, 164, 171
rape myths, 164, 167, 170, 186, 203, 206
reflection: in Asian American studies
service learning, 36–37; in DNA research project, 246–48; in fashion
studies service learning, 51–55; in
philosophy service learning, 18–19,
21–22; in social justice education,
172–74; in teacher preparation service learning, 73–74; in women's
studies service learning, 126–29,
135–36
reports. *See* papers